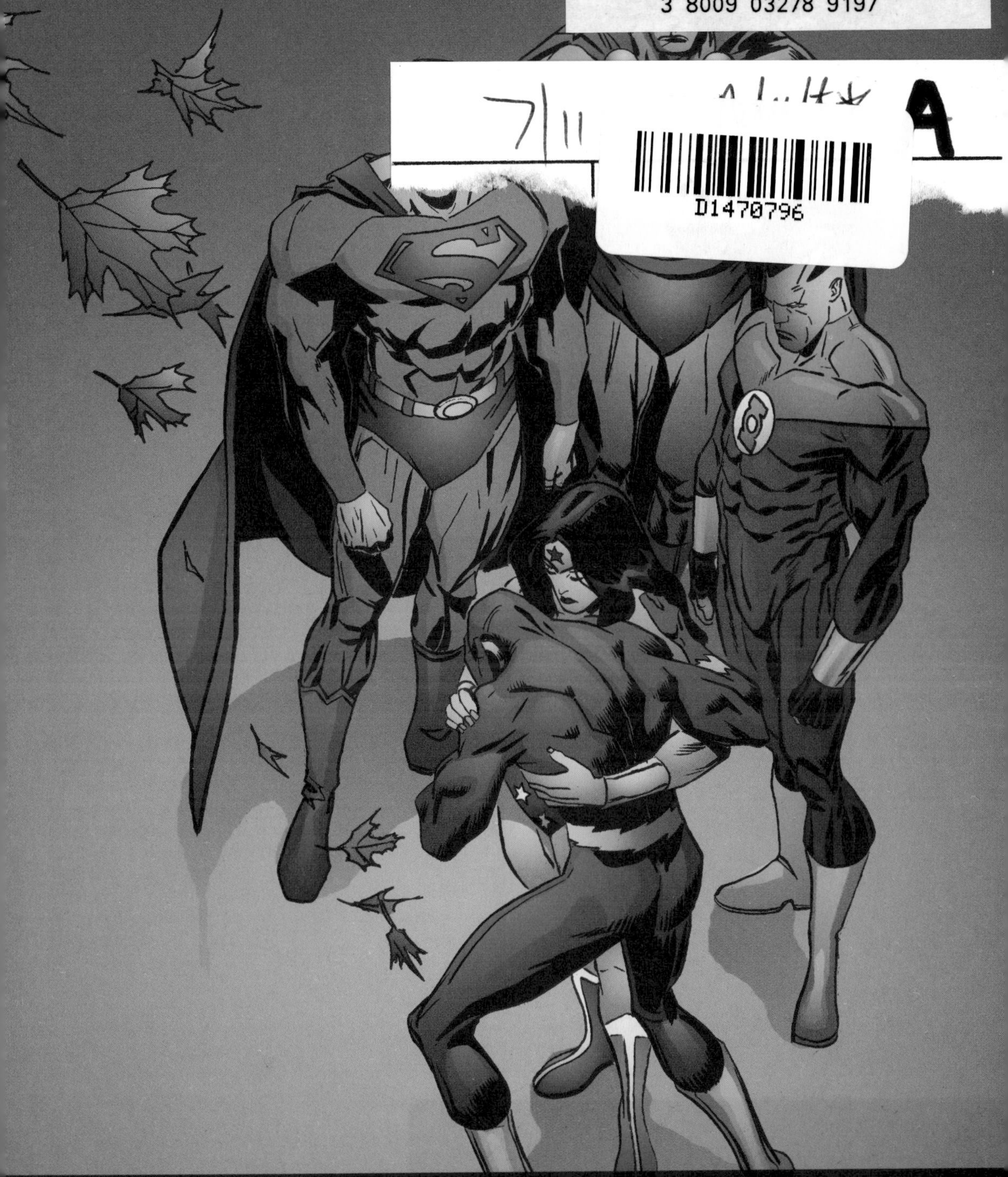

JLA PAIN OF THE GODS

Chuck Austen Writer **Ron Garney** Artist and original series covers **David Baron** Colorist **Ken Lopez** Letterer **Superman** created by **Jerry Siegel** and **Joe Shuster** **Batman** created by **Bob Kane** **Wonder Woman** created by **William Moulton Marston**

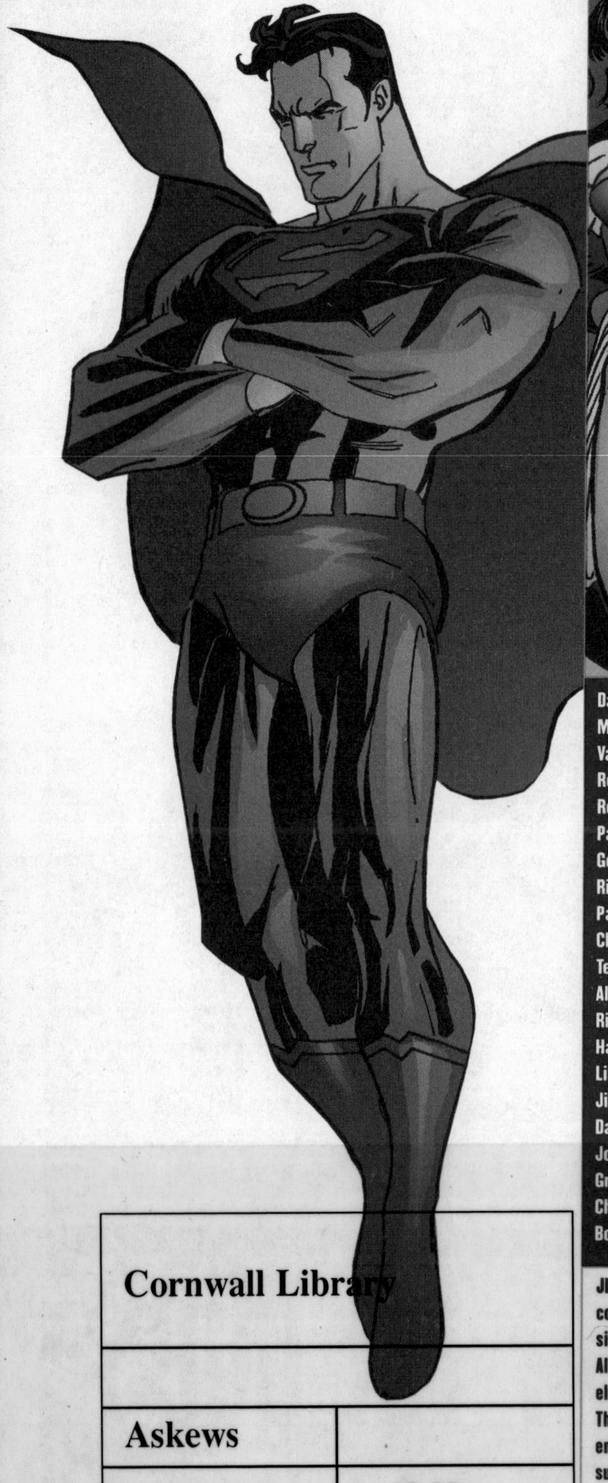

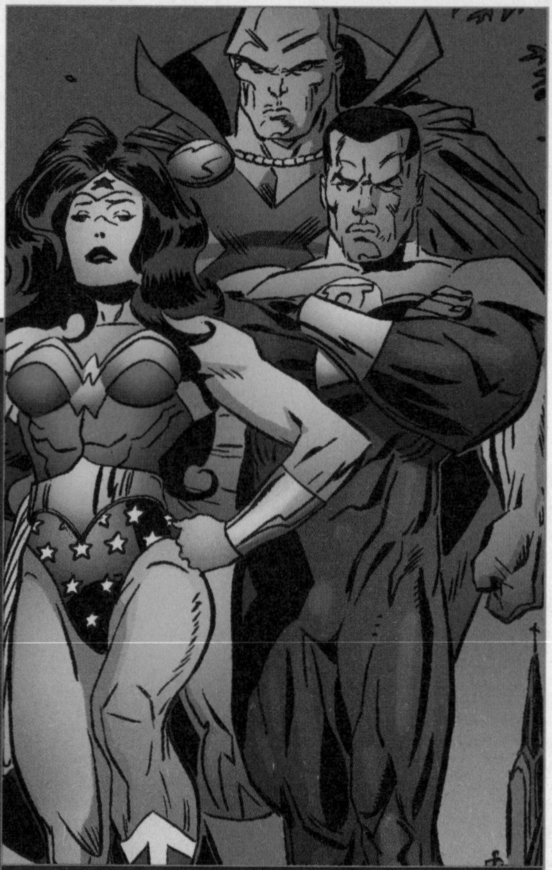

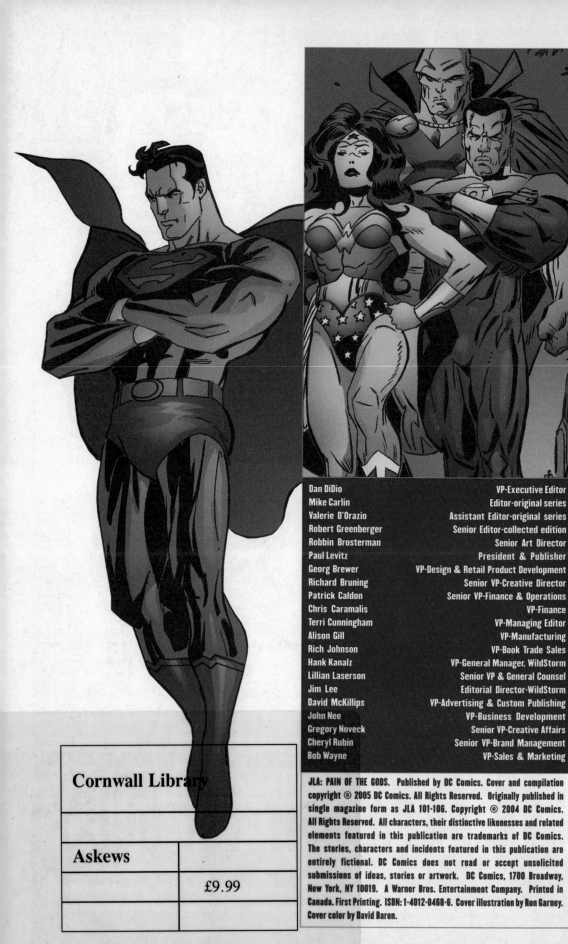

Dan DiDio	VP-Executive Editor
Mike Carlin	Editor-original series
Valerie D'Orazio	Assistant Editor-original series
Robert Greenberger	Senior Editor-collected edition
Robbin Brosterman	Senior Art Director
Paul Levitz	President & Publisher
Georg Brewer	VP-Design & Retail Product Development
Richard Bruning	Senior VP-Creative Director
Patrick Caldon	Senior VP-Finance & Operations
Chris Caramalis	VP-Finance
Terri Cunningham	VP-Managing Editor
Alison Gill	VP-Manufacturing
Rich Johnson	VP-Book Trade Sales
Hank Kanalz	VP-General Manager, WildStorm
Lillian Laserson	Senior VP & General Counsel
Jim Lee	Editorial Director-WildStorm
David McKillips	VP-Advertising & Custom Publishing
John Nee	VP-Business Development
Gregory Noveck	Senior VP-Creative Affairs
Cheryl Rubin	Senior VP-Brand Management
Bob Wayne	VP-Sales & Marketing

DC Comics, 1700 Broadway, New York, NY 10019. A Warner Bros. Entertainment Company. Printed in Canada. First Printing. ISBN: 1-4012-0468-6. Cover illustration by Ron Garney. Cover color by David Baron.

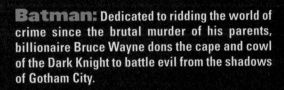

JLA

JLA: The Justice League of America is Earth's first and last line of defense, a pantheon of super-powered protectors watching over the Earth from a fortress on the Moon.

Superman: The last son of the doomed planet Krypton, Kal-El uses his incredible powers of flight, super-strength, and invulnerability to fight for truth and justice on his adopted planet, Earth. When not protecting the planet, he is *Daily Planet* reporter Clark Kent, married to fellow journalist Lois Lane.

Batman: Dedicated to ridding the world of crime since the brutal murder of his parents, billionaire Bruce Wayne dons the cape and cowl of the Dark Knight to battle evil from the shadows of Gotham City.

Wonder Woman: Born an Amazonian princess, Diana was chosen to serve as her people's ambassador of peace in the World of Man. Armed with the Lasso of Truth and indestructible bracelets, she directs her gods-given abilities of strength and speed toward the betterment of mankind.

The Flash: A member of the Teen Titans when he was known as Kid Flash, Wally West now takes the place of the fallen Flash, Barry Allen, as the speedster of the Justice League.

Green Lantern: John Stewart has worn the power ring, symbol of the intergalactic Green Lantern Corps, during several tours of duty. Controlled by his will power, the ring makes his imagination manifest, and being an architect, he conceives some pretty cool objects.

Martian Manhunter: J'onn J'onzz has been a member of the JLA for every one of the team's many incarnations. His strength rivals that of Earth's mightiest heroes, and his shape-shifting abilities allow him to pass anonymously among our planet's populace. His awesome mental powers serve to link the entire League in thought.

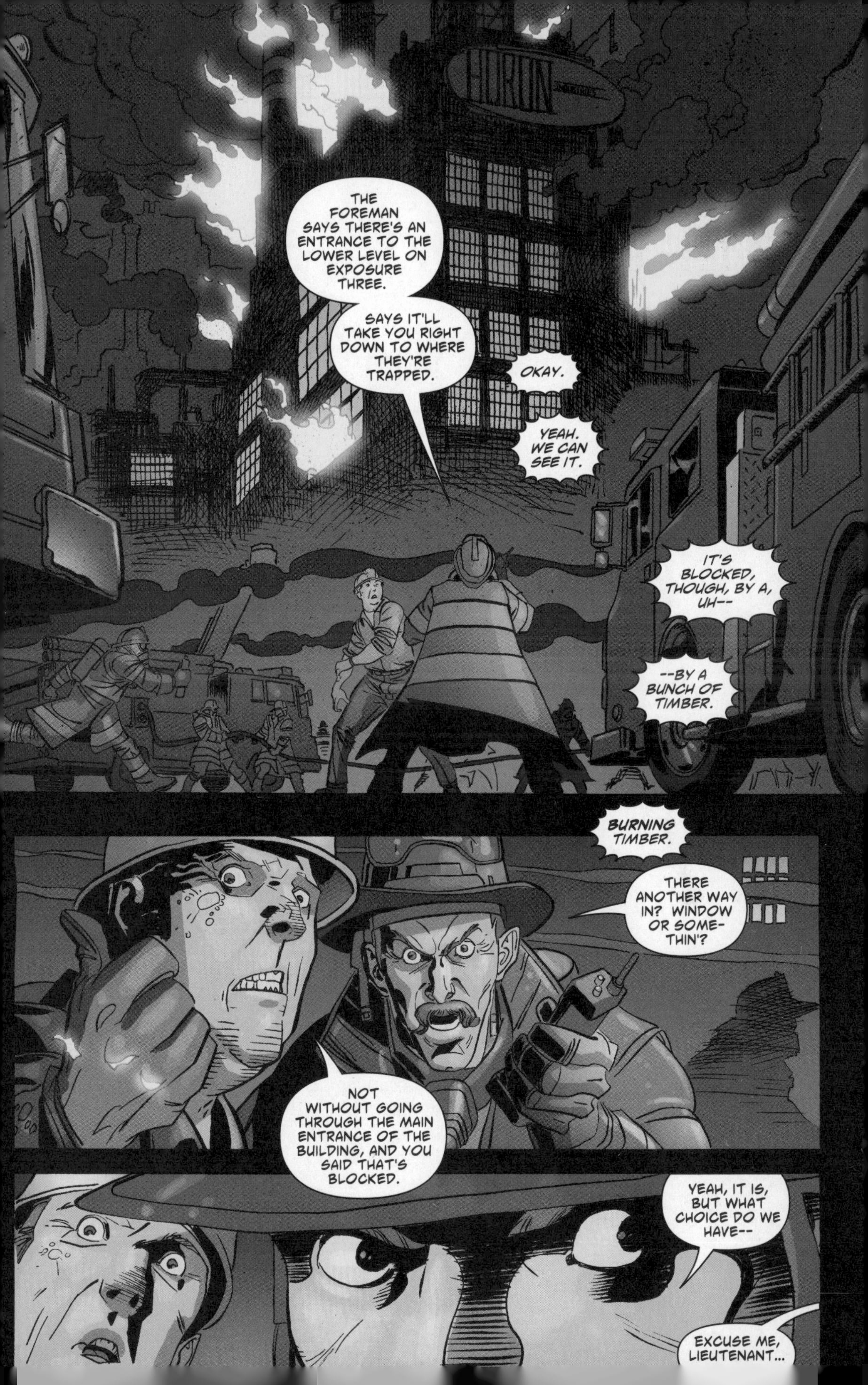
HORON
THE FOREMAN SAYS THERE'S AN ENTRANCE TO THE LOWER LEVEL ON EXPOSURE THREE.
SAYS IT'LL TAKE YOU RIGHT DOWN TO WHERE THEY'RE TRAPPED.
OKAY.
YEAH. WE CAN SEE IT.
IT'S BLOCKED, THOUGH, BY A, UH--
--BY A BUNCH OF TIMBER.
BURNING TIMBER.
THERE ANOTHER WAY IN? WINDOW OR SOME-THIN'?
NOT WITHOUT GOING THROUGH THE MAIN ENTRANCE OF THE BUILDING, AND YOU SAID THAT'S BLOCKED.
YEAH, IT IS, BUT WHAT CHOICE DO WE HAVE--
EXCUSE ME, LIEUTENANT...

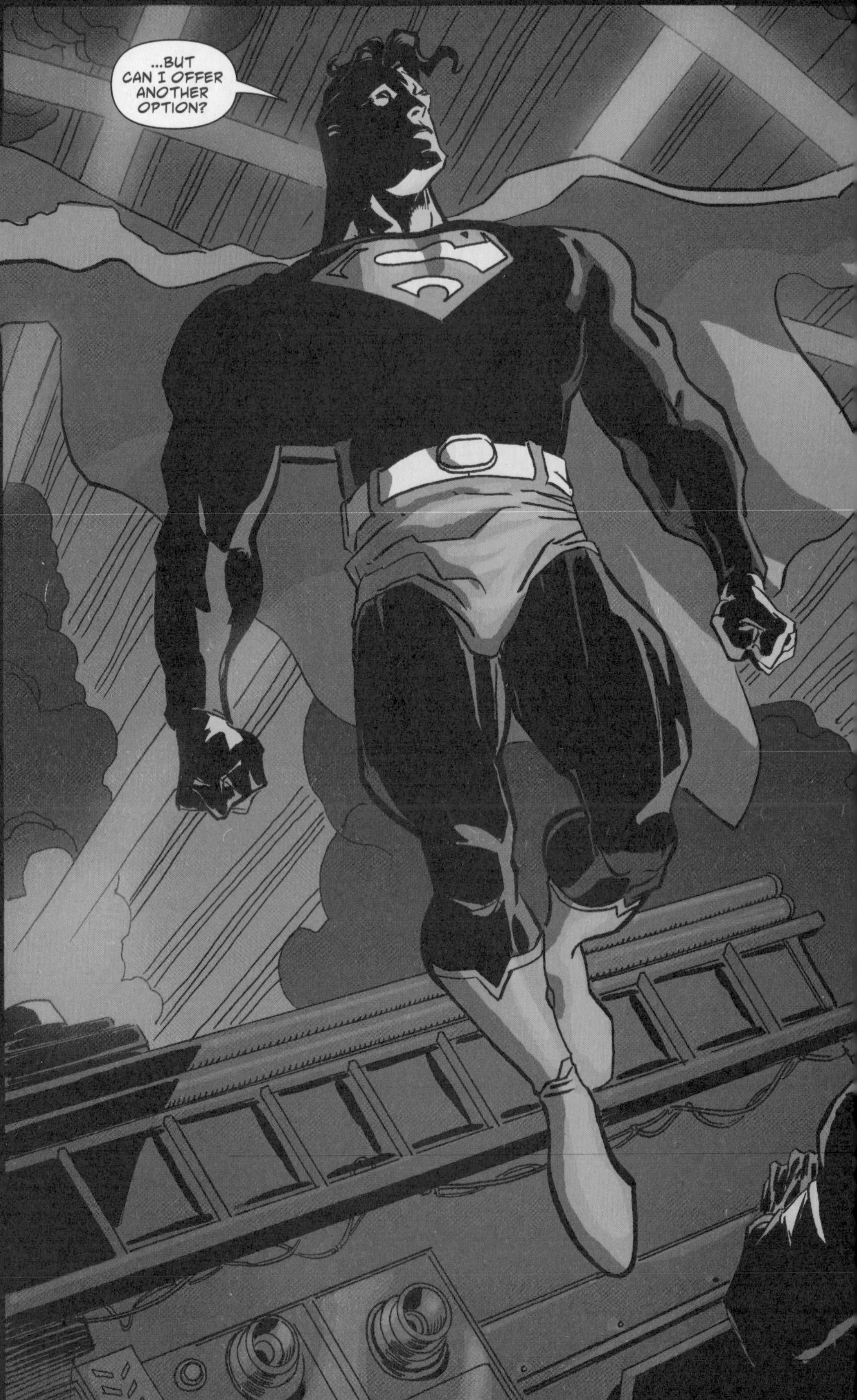
...BUT CAN I OFFER ANOTHER OPTION?

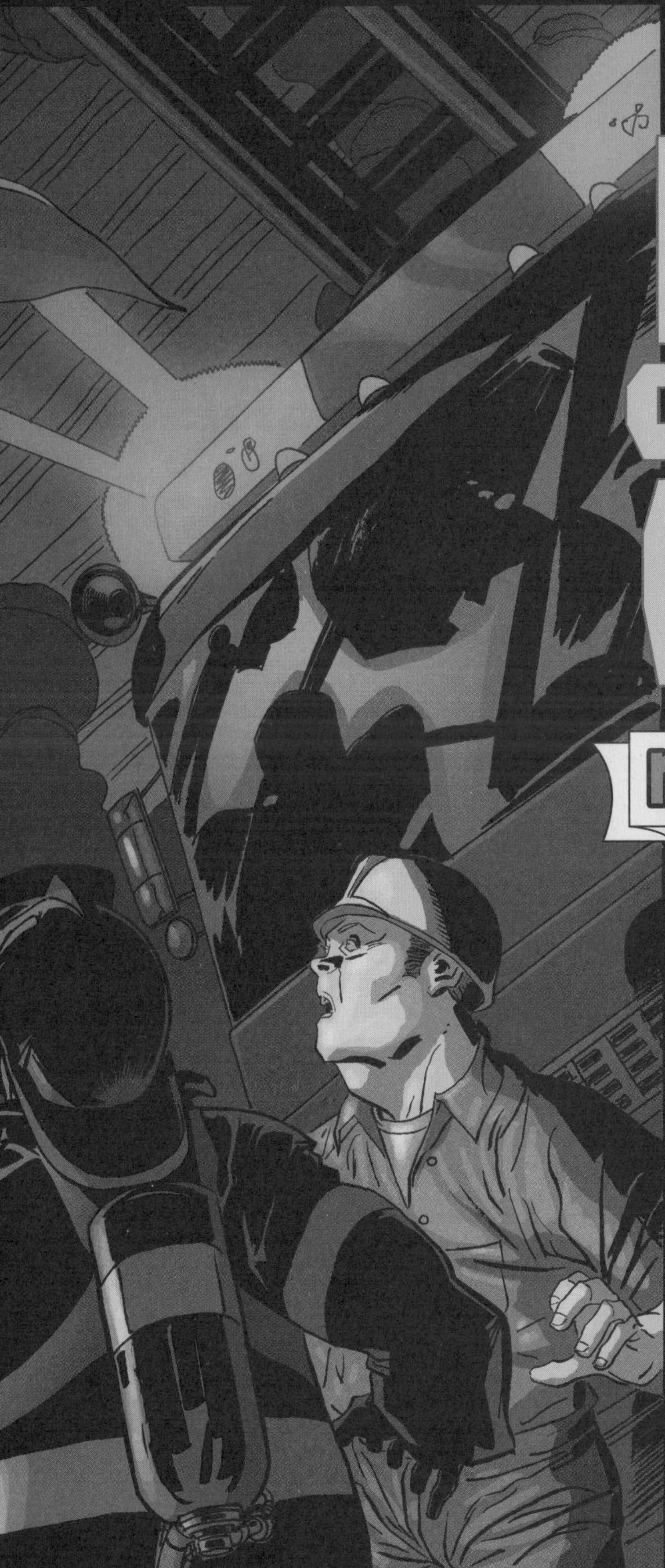

THE PAIN OF THE GODS

MAN OF STEEL

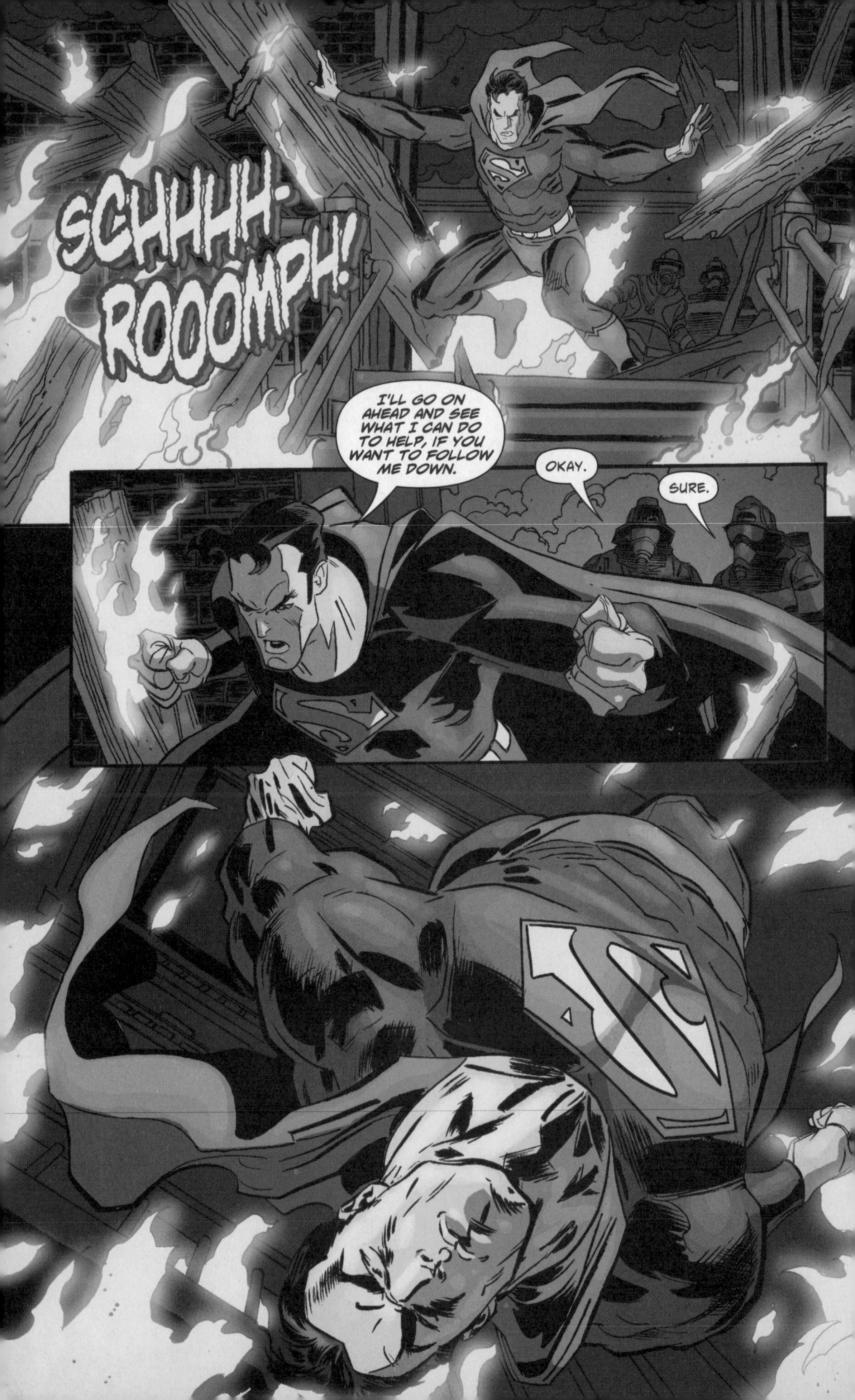
SCHHHH-ROOOMPH!
I'LL GO ON AHEAD AND SEE WHAT I CAN DO TO HELP, IF YOU WANT TO FOLLOW ME DOWN.
OKAY.
SURE.

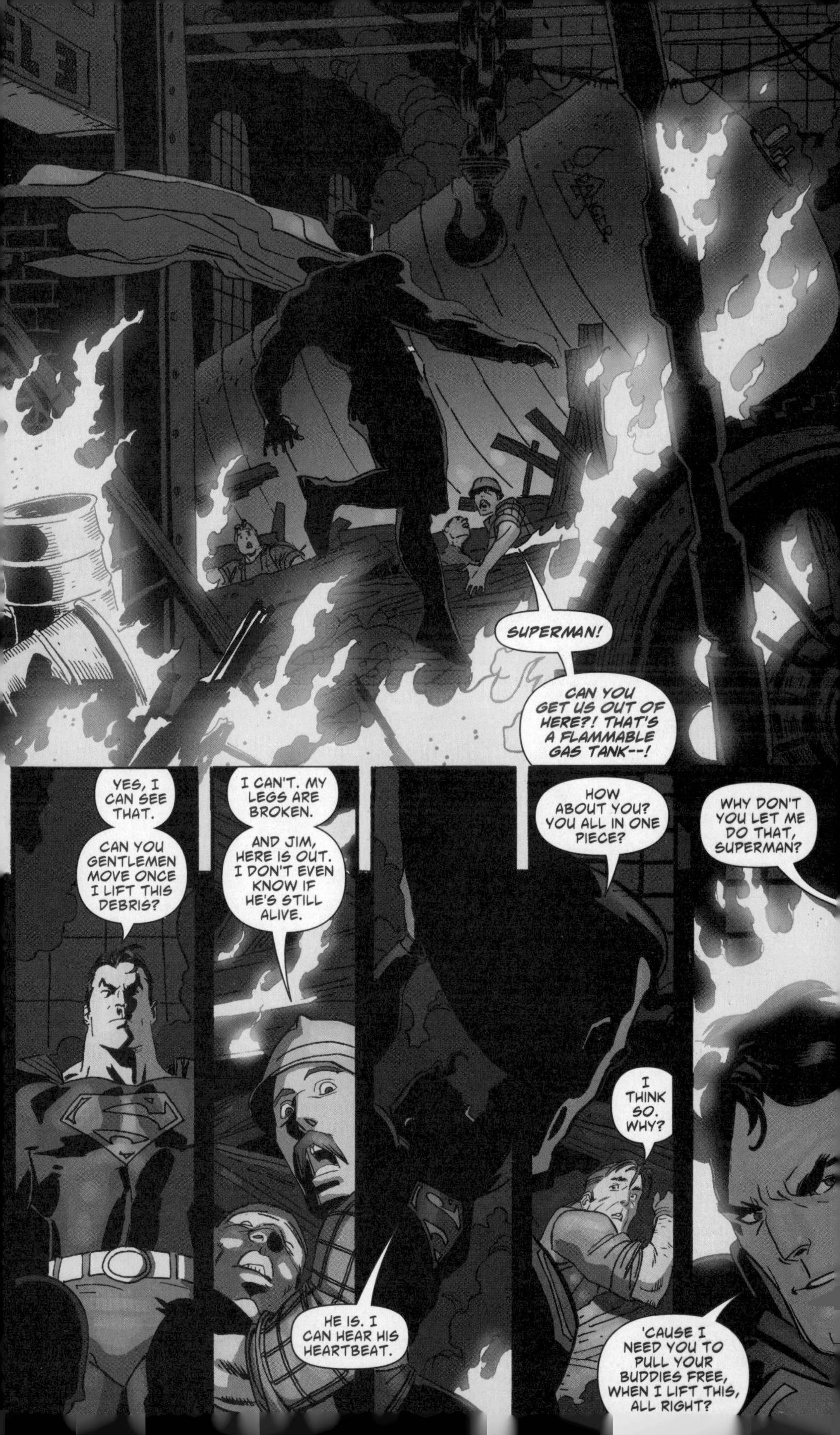
SUPERMAN!
CAN YOU GET US OUT OF HERE?! THAT'S A FLAMMABLE GAS TANK--!
YES, I CAN SEE THAT.
CAN YOU GENTLEMEN MOVE ONCE I LIFT THIS DEBRIS?
I CAN'T. MY LEGS ARE BROKEN.
AND JIM, HERE IS OUT. I DON'T EVEN KNOW IF HE'S STILL ALIVE.
HE IS. I CAN HEAR HIS HEARTBEAT.
HOW ABOUT YOU? YOU ALL IN ONE PIECE?
I THINK SO. WHY?
WHY DON'T YOU LET ME DO THAT, SUPERMAN?
'CAUSE I NEED YOU TO PULL YOUR BUDDIES FREE, WHEN I LIFT THIS, ALL RIGHT?

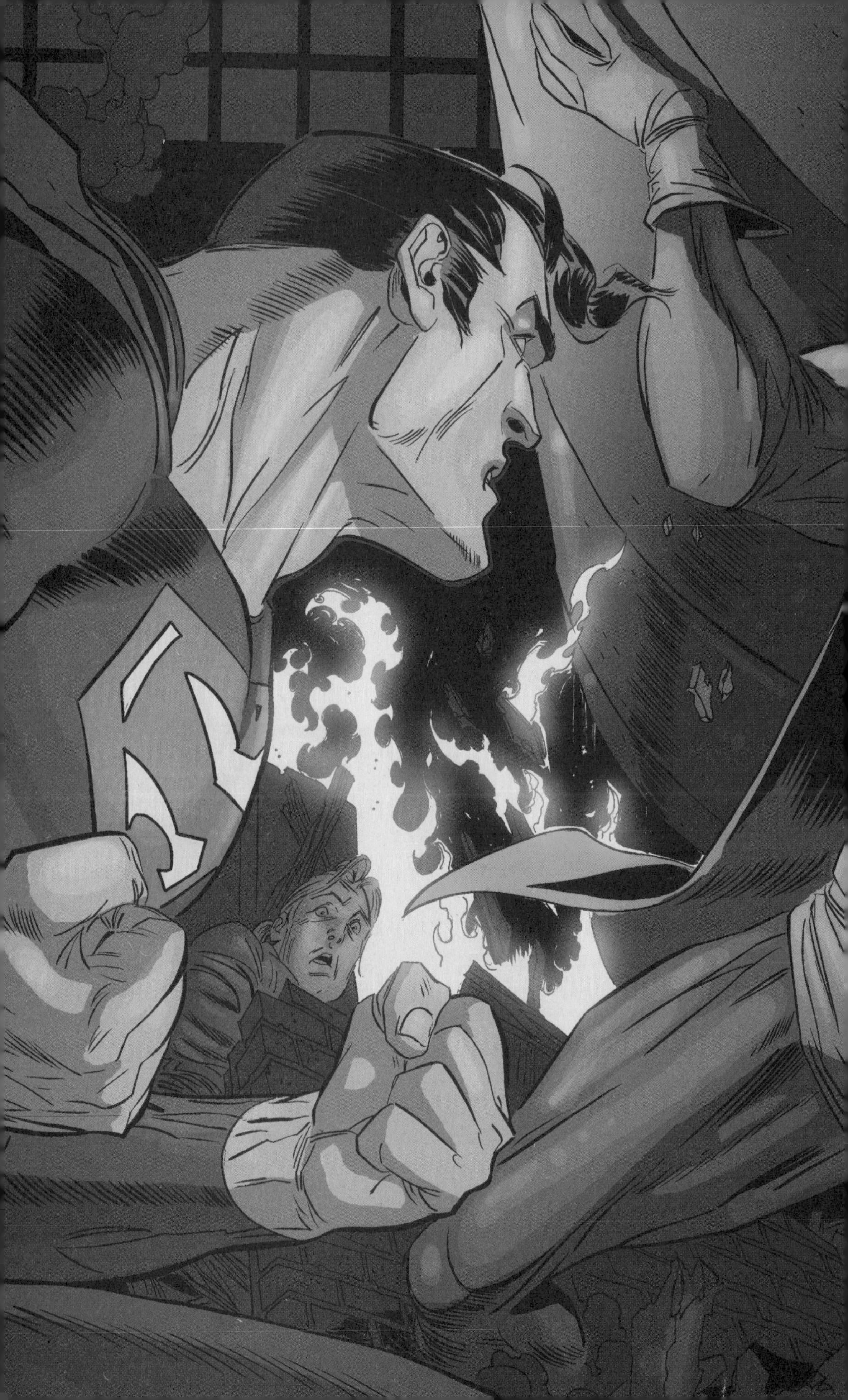

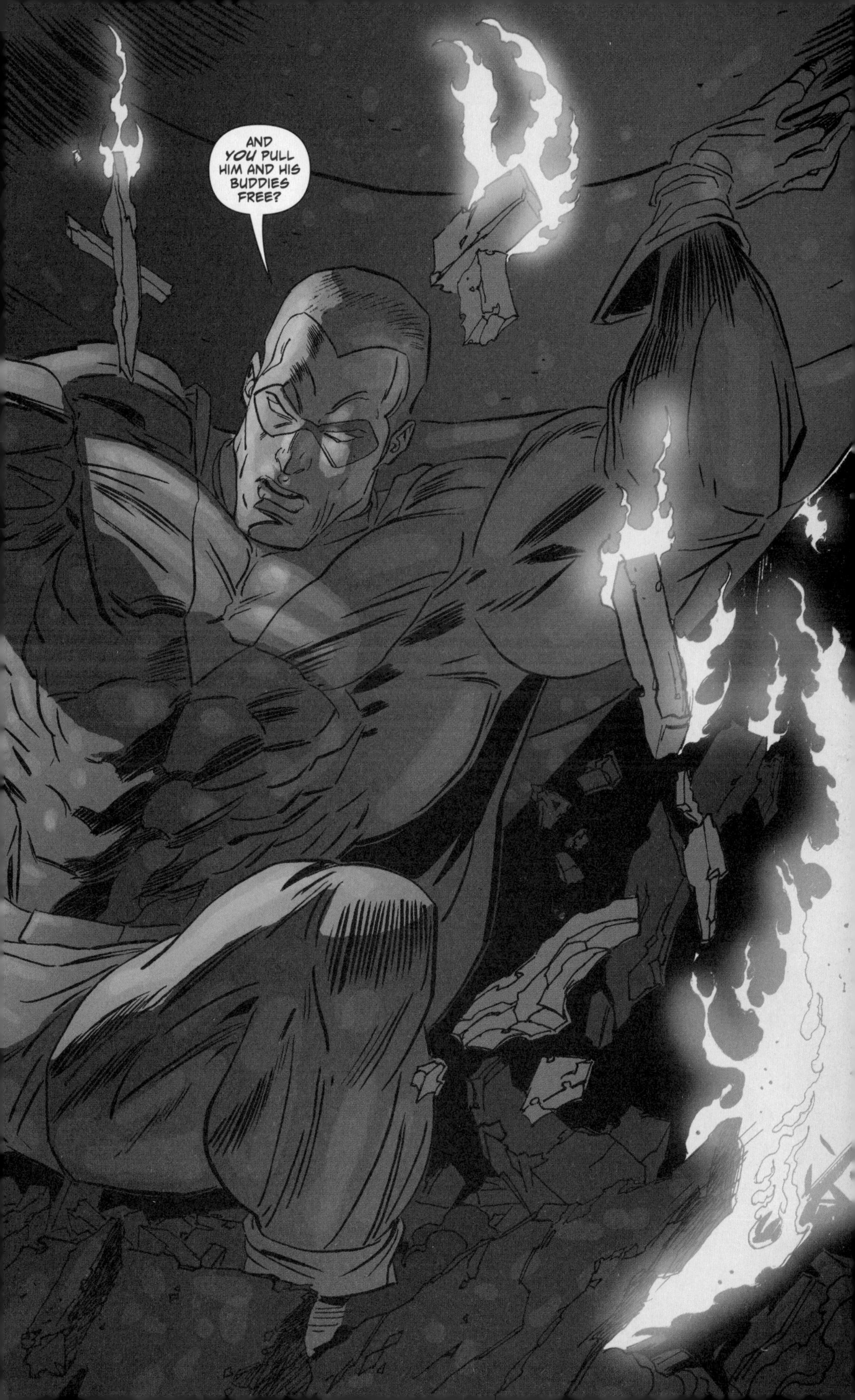
AND *YOU* PULL HIM AND HIS BUDDIES FREE?

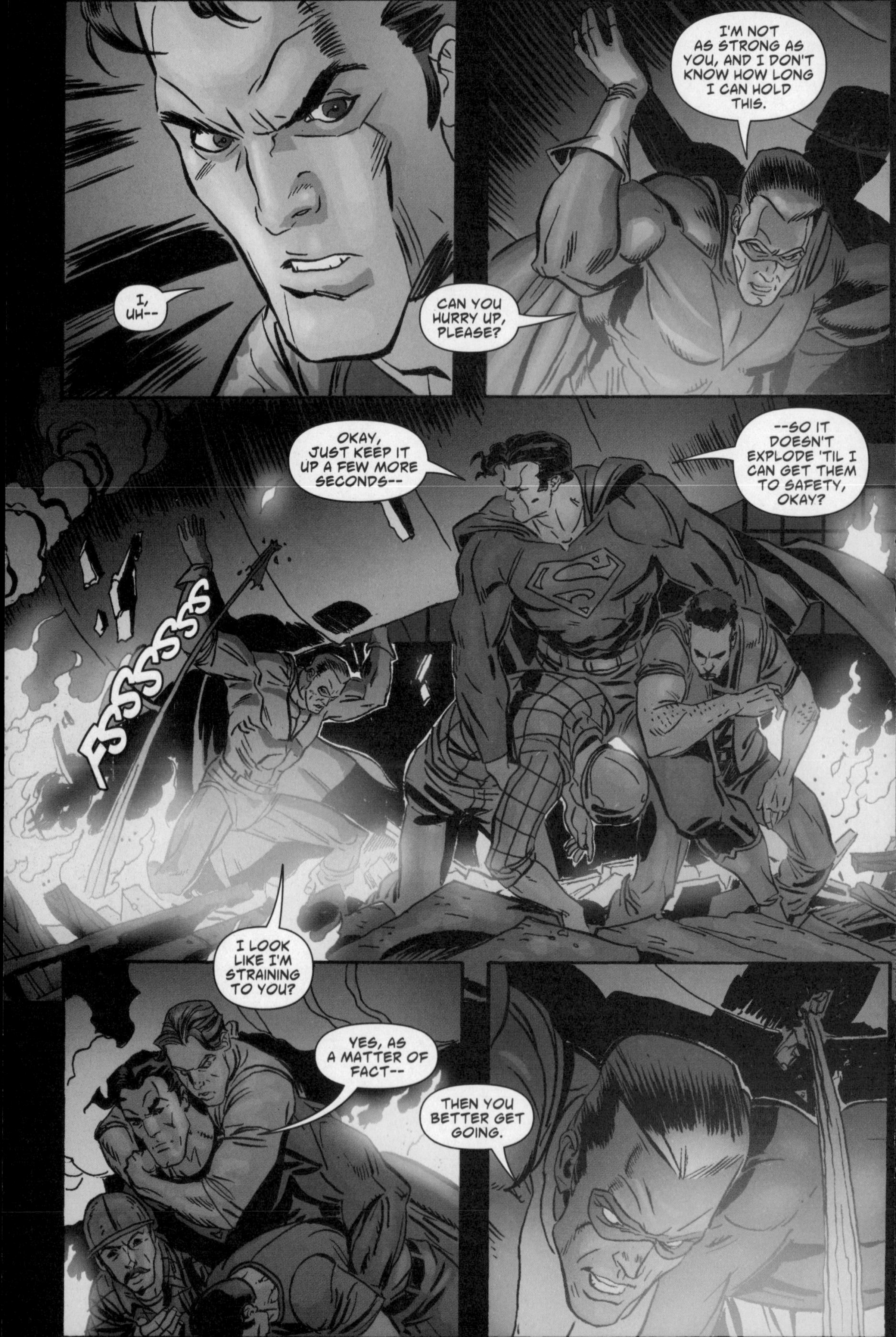
I, UH--
I'M NOT AS STRONG AS YOU, AND I DON'T KNOW HOW LONG I CAN HOLD THIS.
CAN YOU HURRY UP, PLEASE?
OKAY, JUST KEEP IT UP A FEW MORE SECONDS--
--SO IT DOESN'T EXPLODE 'TIL I CAN GET THEM TO SAFETY, OKAY?
FSSSSSS
I LOOK LIKE I'M STRAINING TO YOU?
YES, AS A MATTER OF FACT--
THEN YOU BETTER GET GOING.

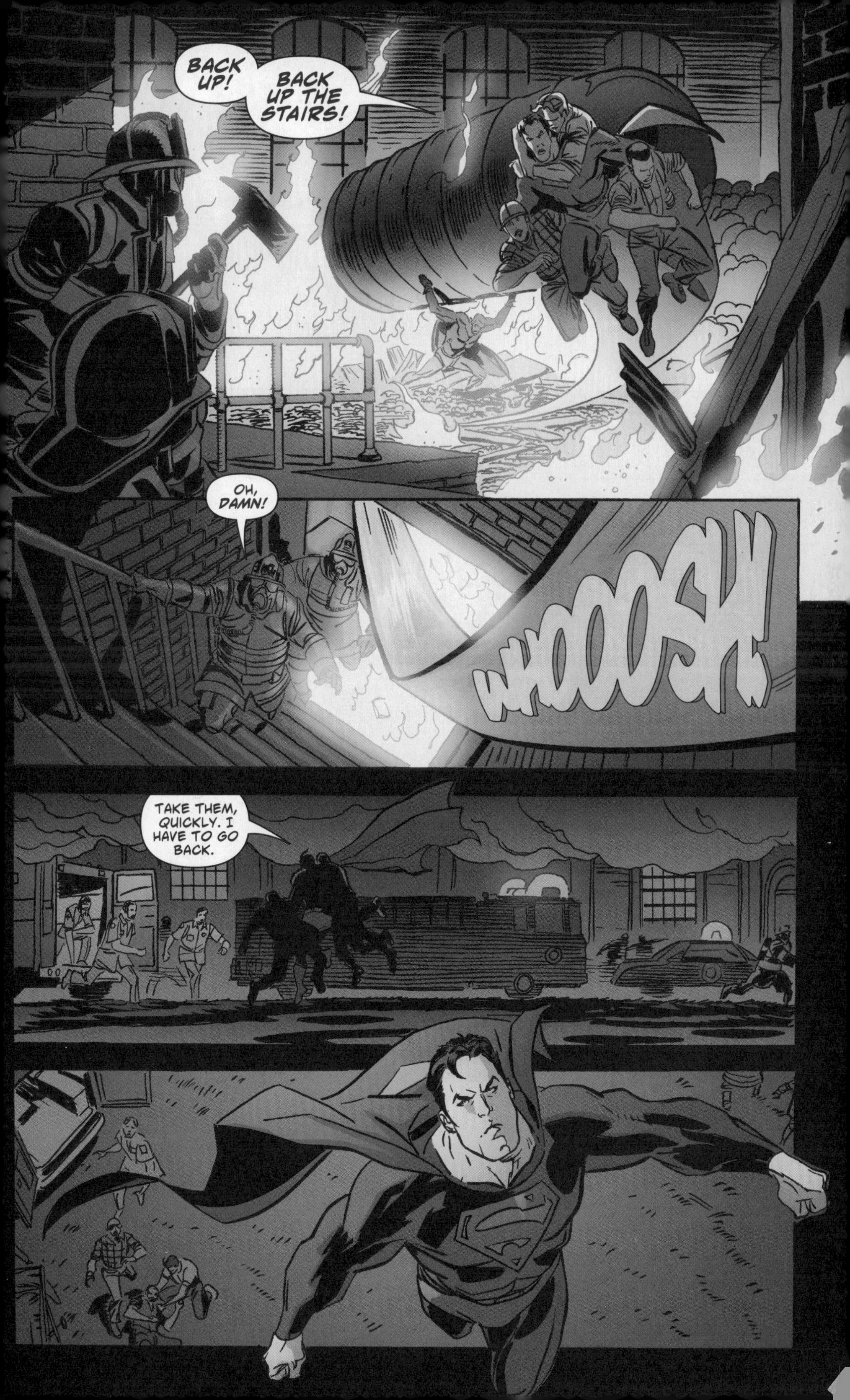
BACK UP!
BACK UP THE STAIRS!
OH, DAMN!
WHOOOSH
TAKE THEM, QUICKLY. I HAVE TO GO BACK.

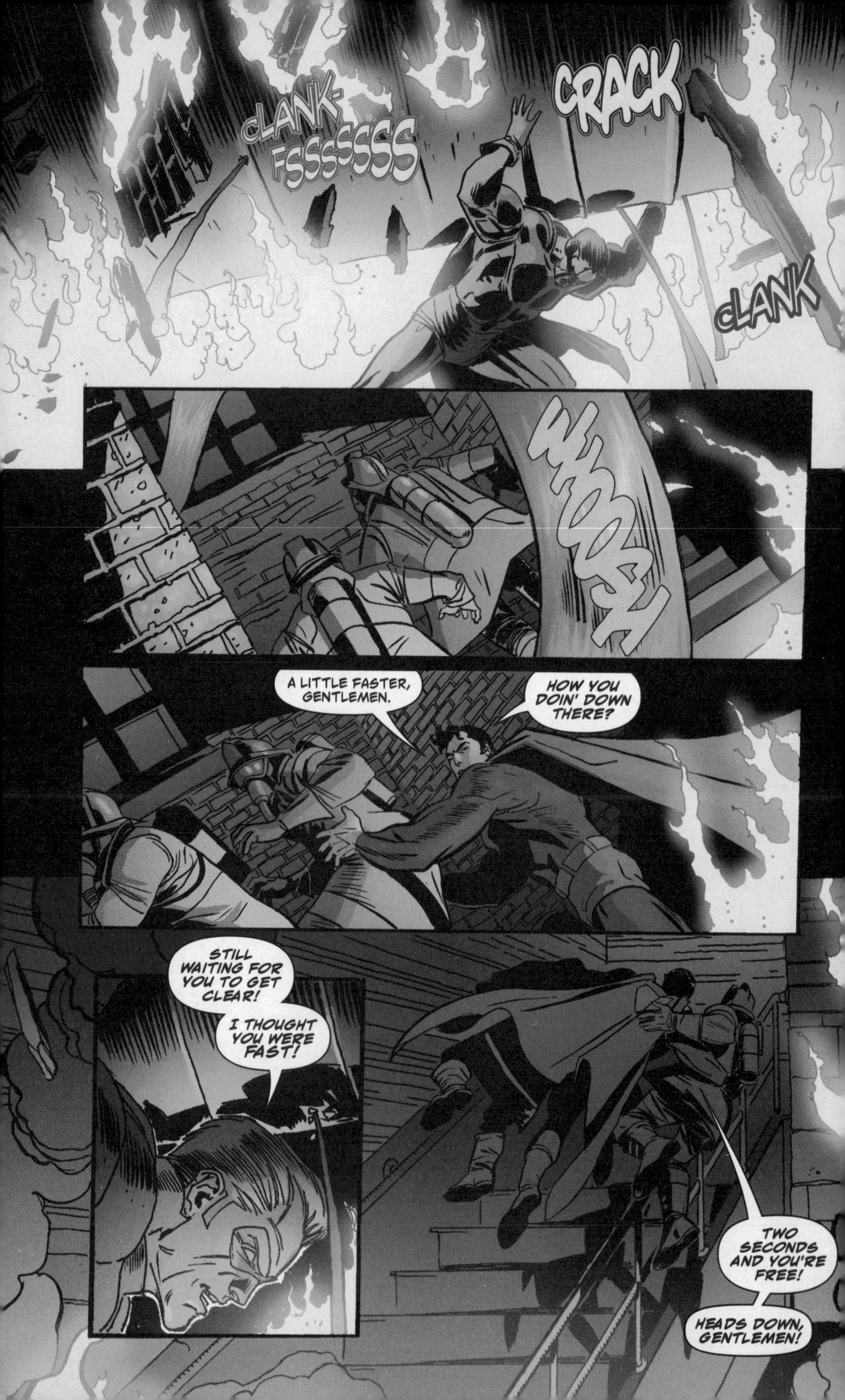
CLANK-
FSSSSSSS
CRACK
CLANK
WHOOSH
A LITTLE FASTER, GENTLEMEN.
HOW YOU DOIN' DOWN THERE?
STILL WAITING FOR YOU TO GET CLEAR!
I THOUGHT YOU WERE FAST!
TWO SECONDS AND YOU'RE FREE!
HEADS DOWN, GENTLEMEN!

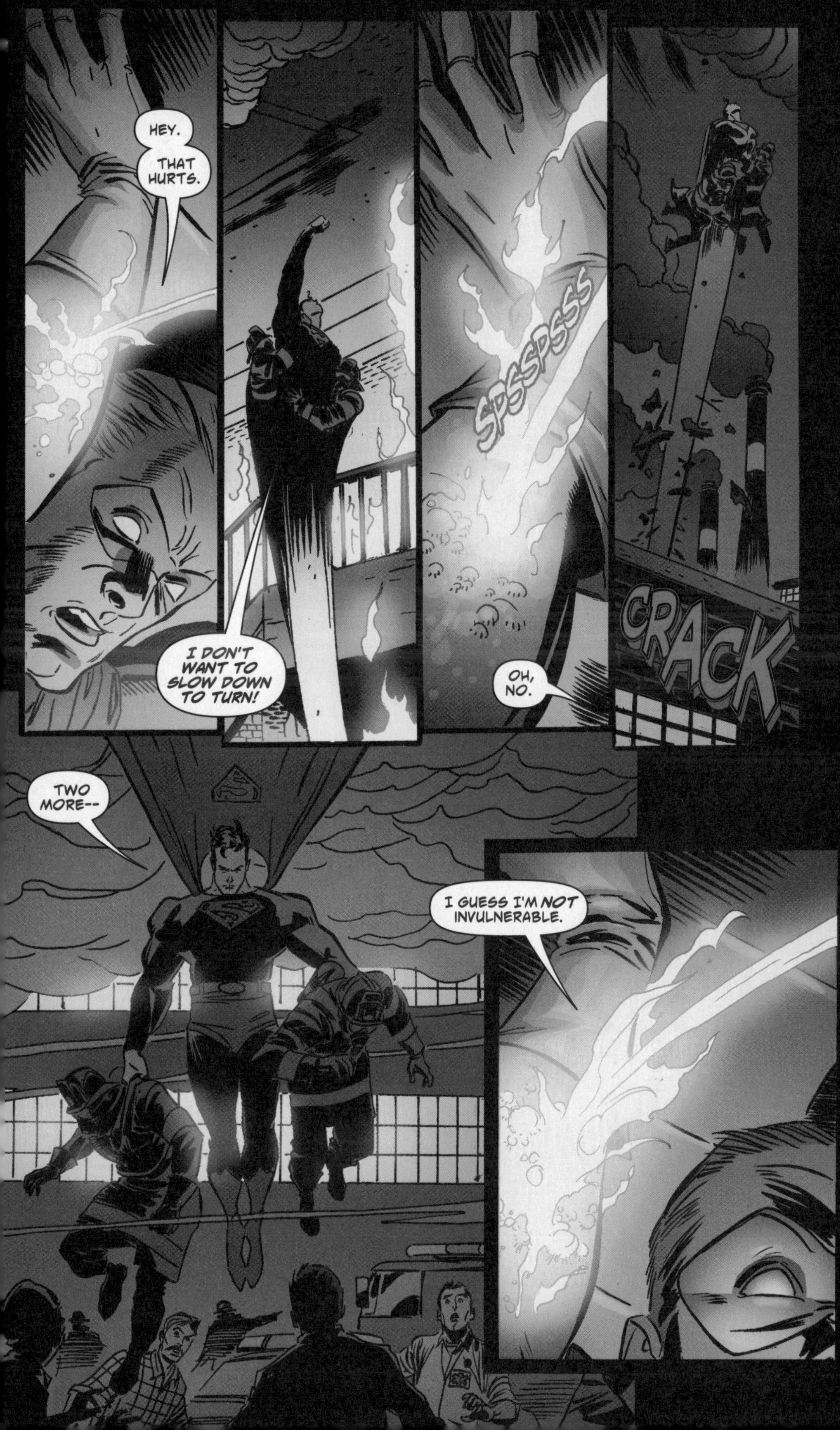
HEY.
THAT HURTS.
I DON'T WANT TO SLOW DOWN TO TURN!
SPSSPSSS
OH, NO.
CRACK
TWO MORE--
I GUESS I'M NOT INVULNERABLE.

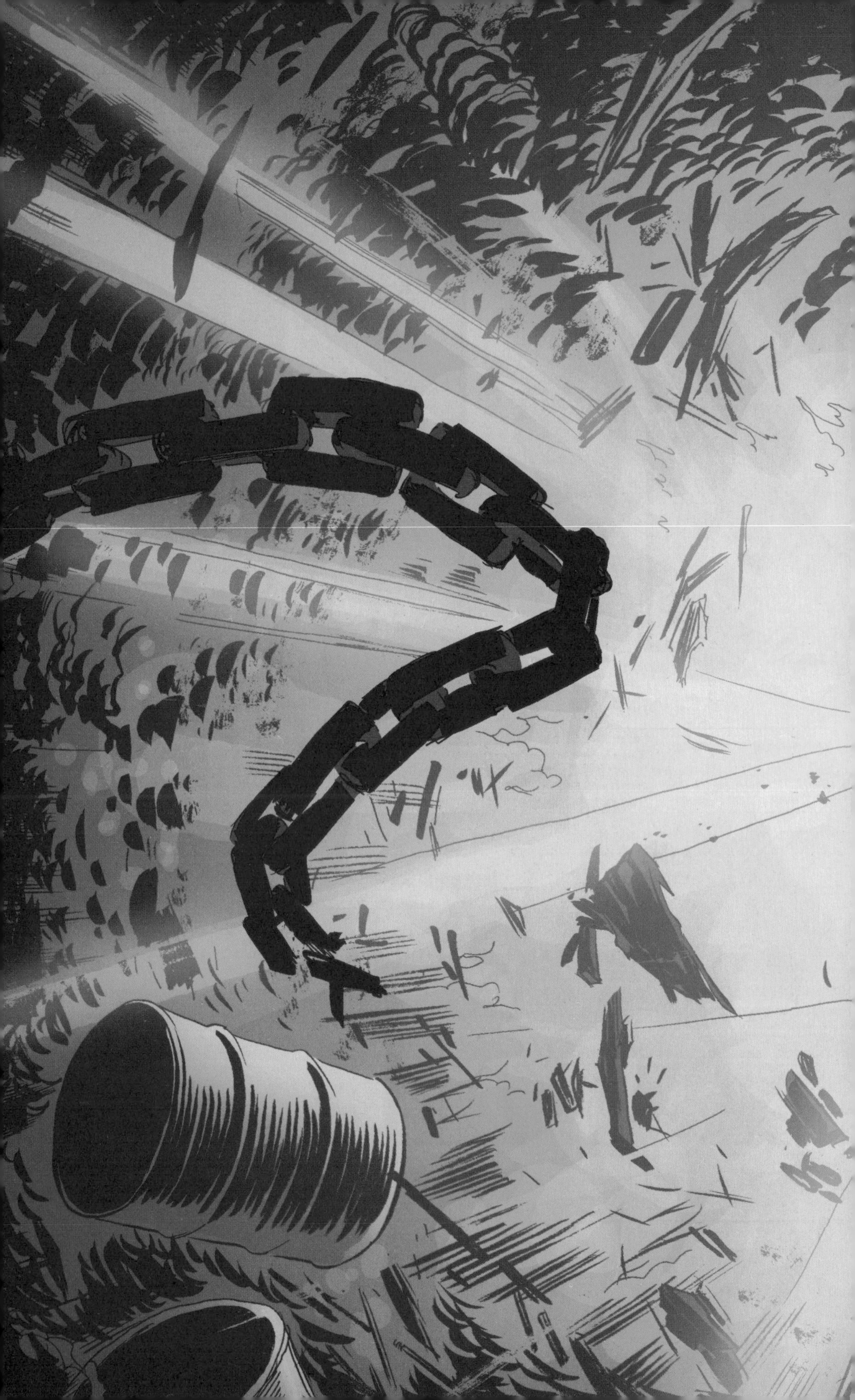

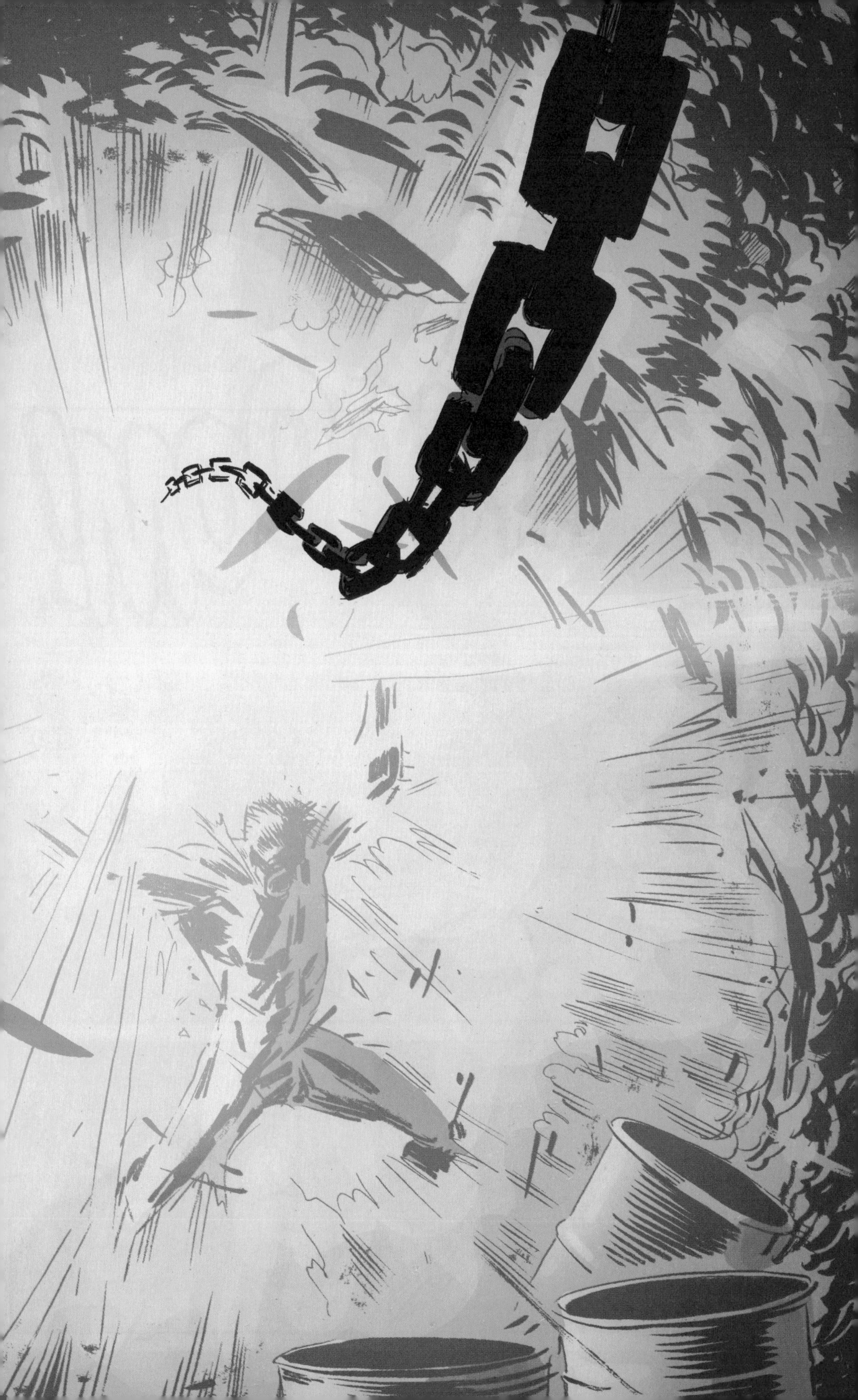

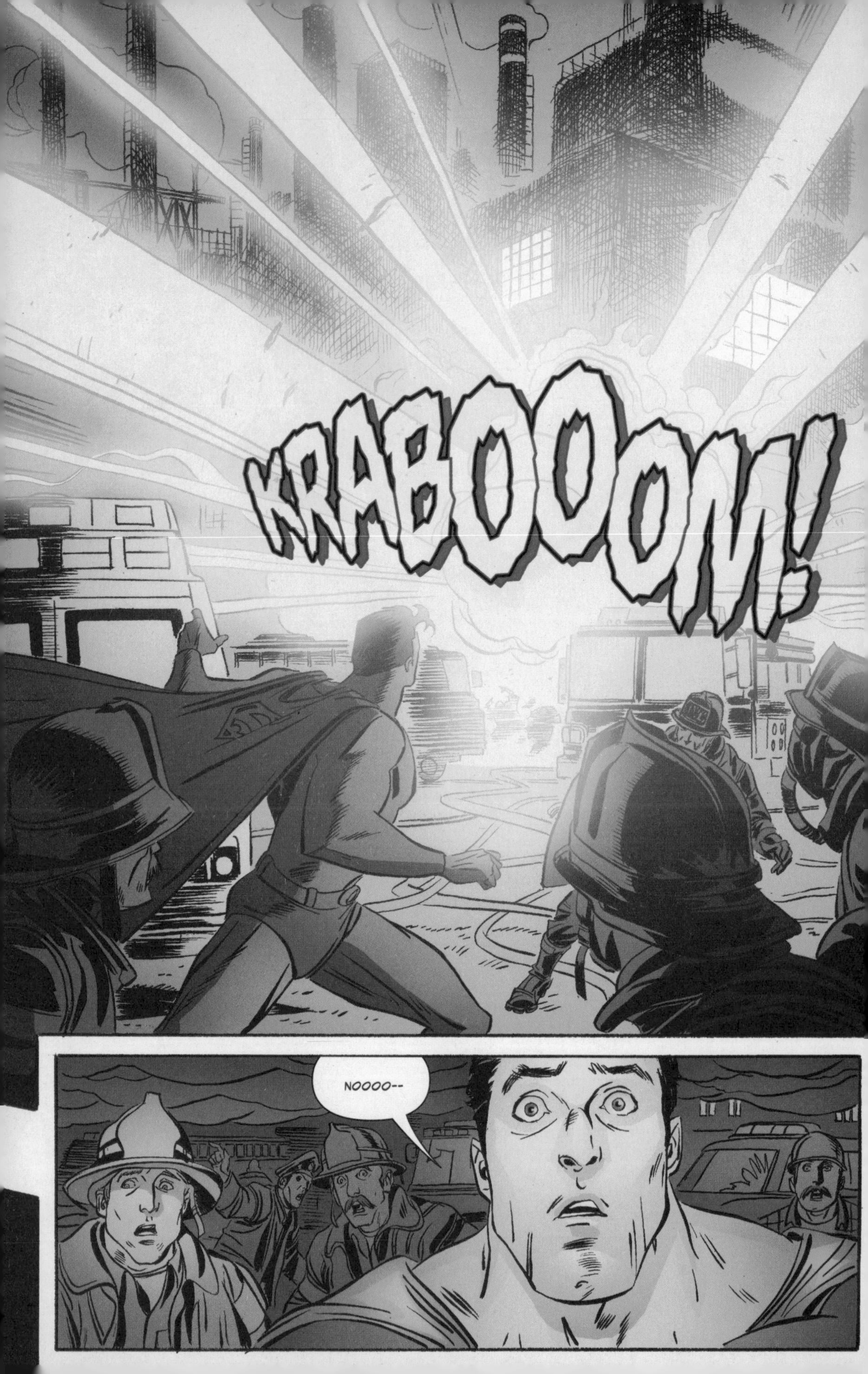
KRABOOOM!
NOOOO--

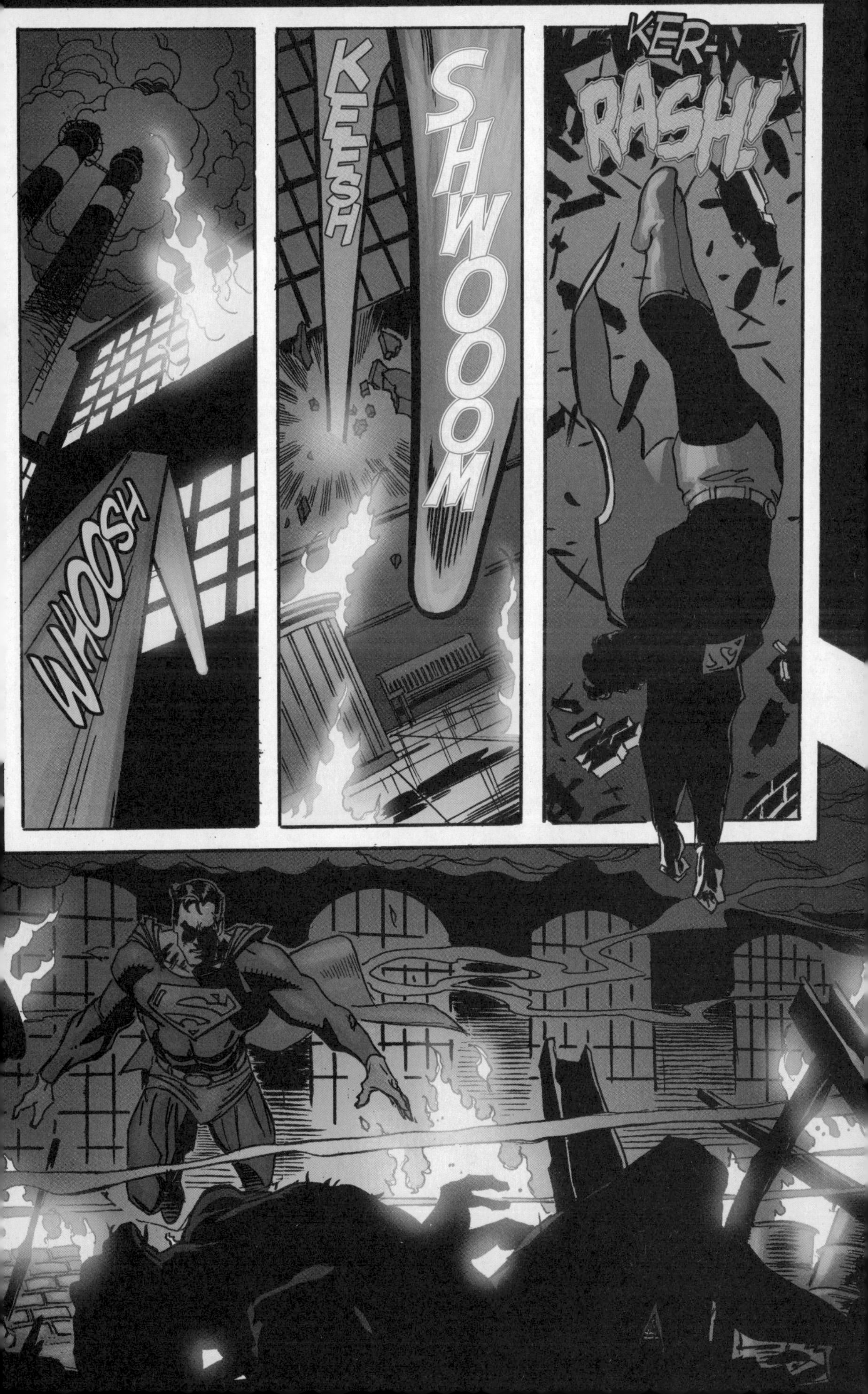
WHOOSH
KEESH
SHWOOOM
KER-
RASH!

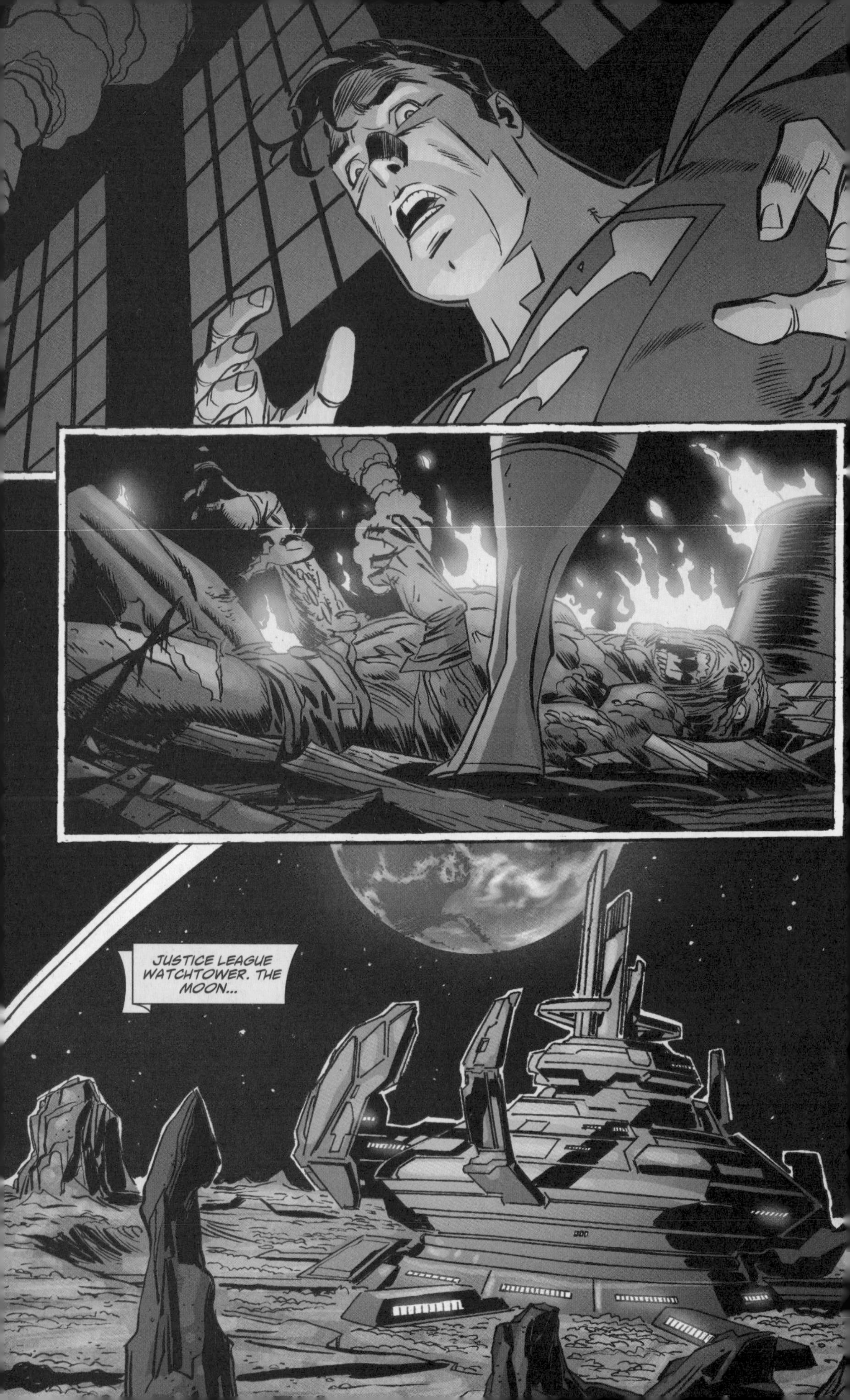
JUSTICE LEAGUE WATCHTOWER. THE MOON...

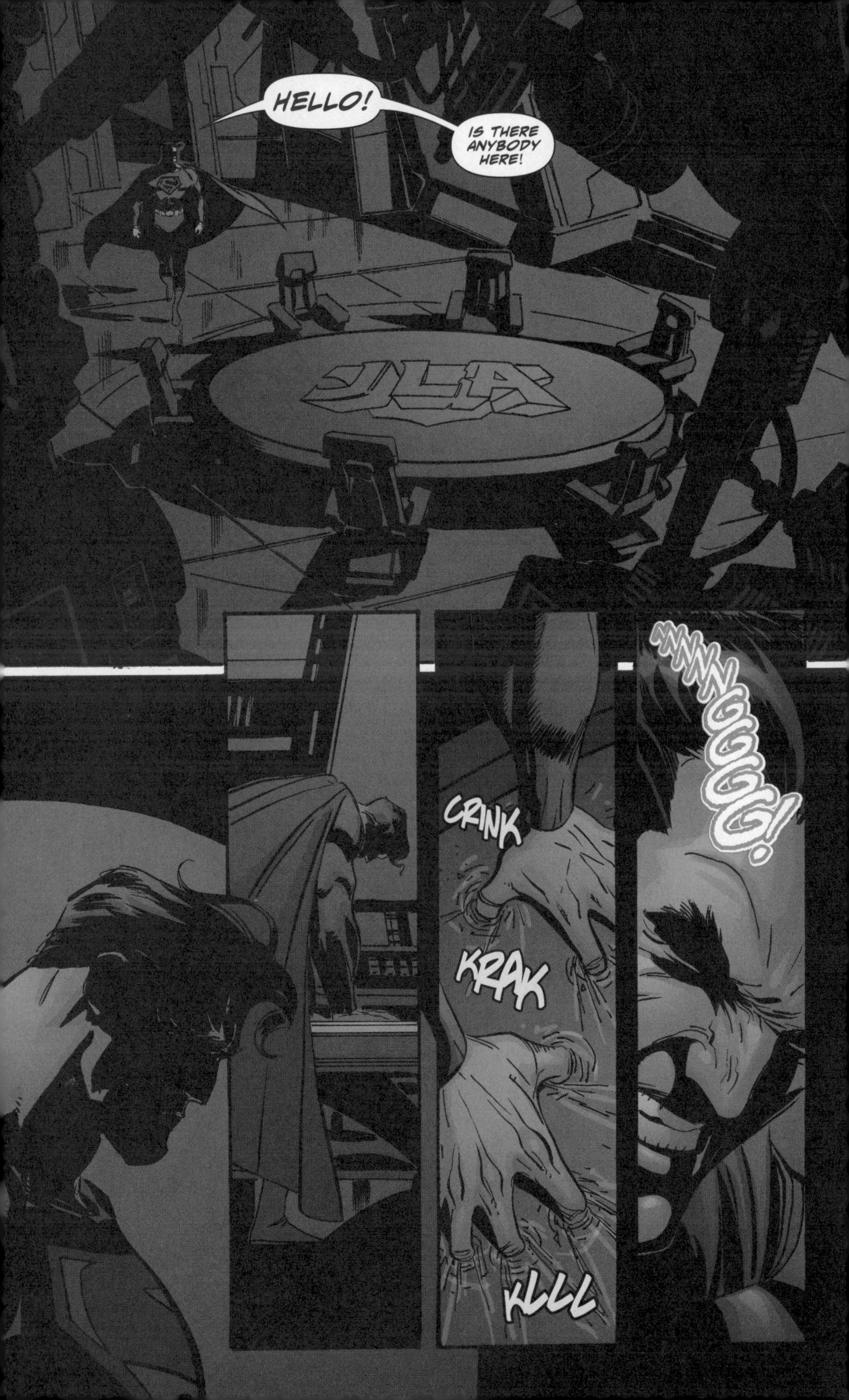
HELLO!
IS THERE ANYBODY HERE!
JLA
CRINK
KRAK
KLLL
NNNNGGGGG!

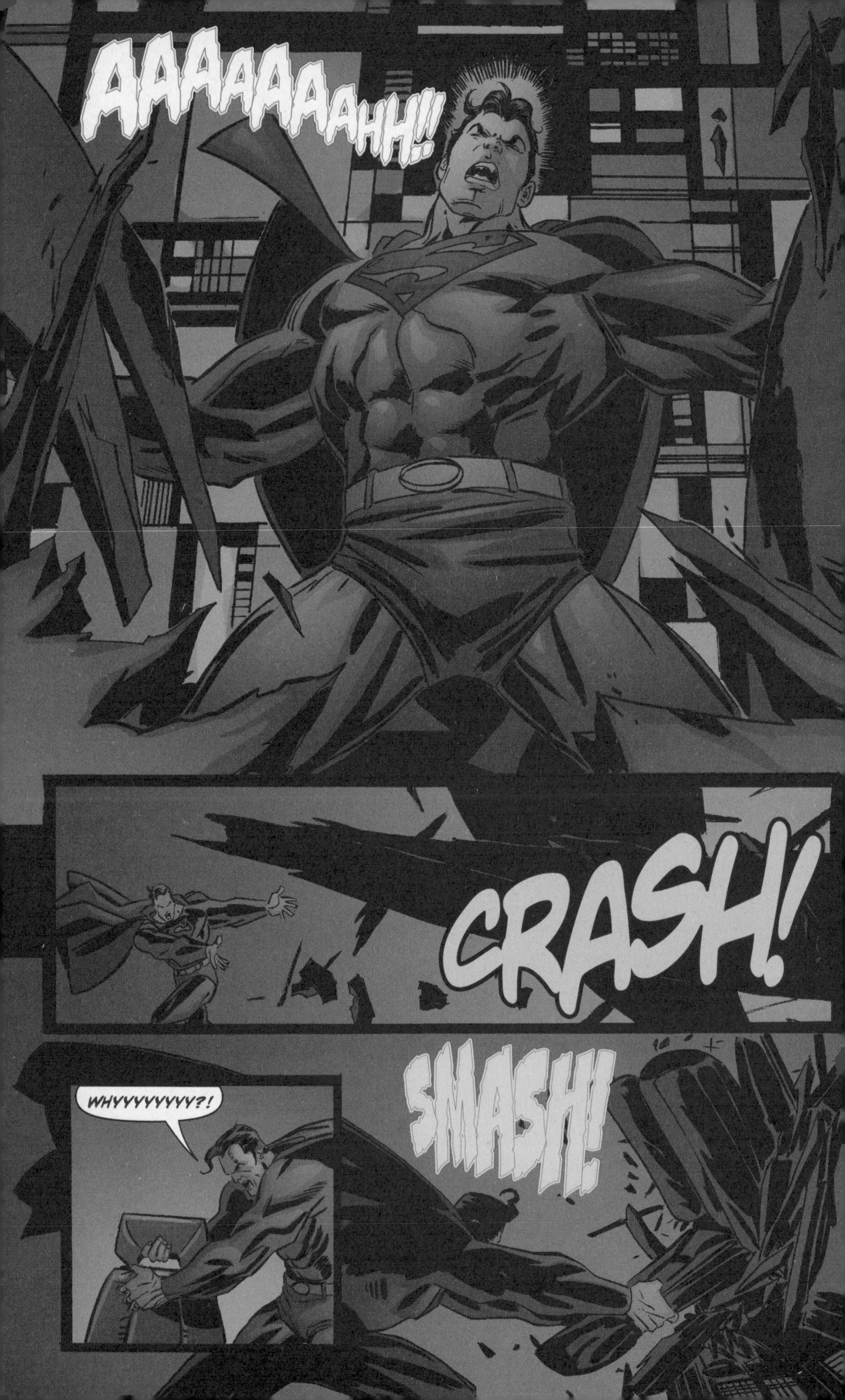
AAAAAAAHH!!
CRASH!
WHYYYYYYYY?!
SMASH!

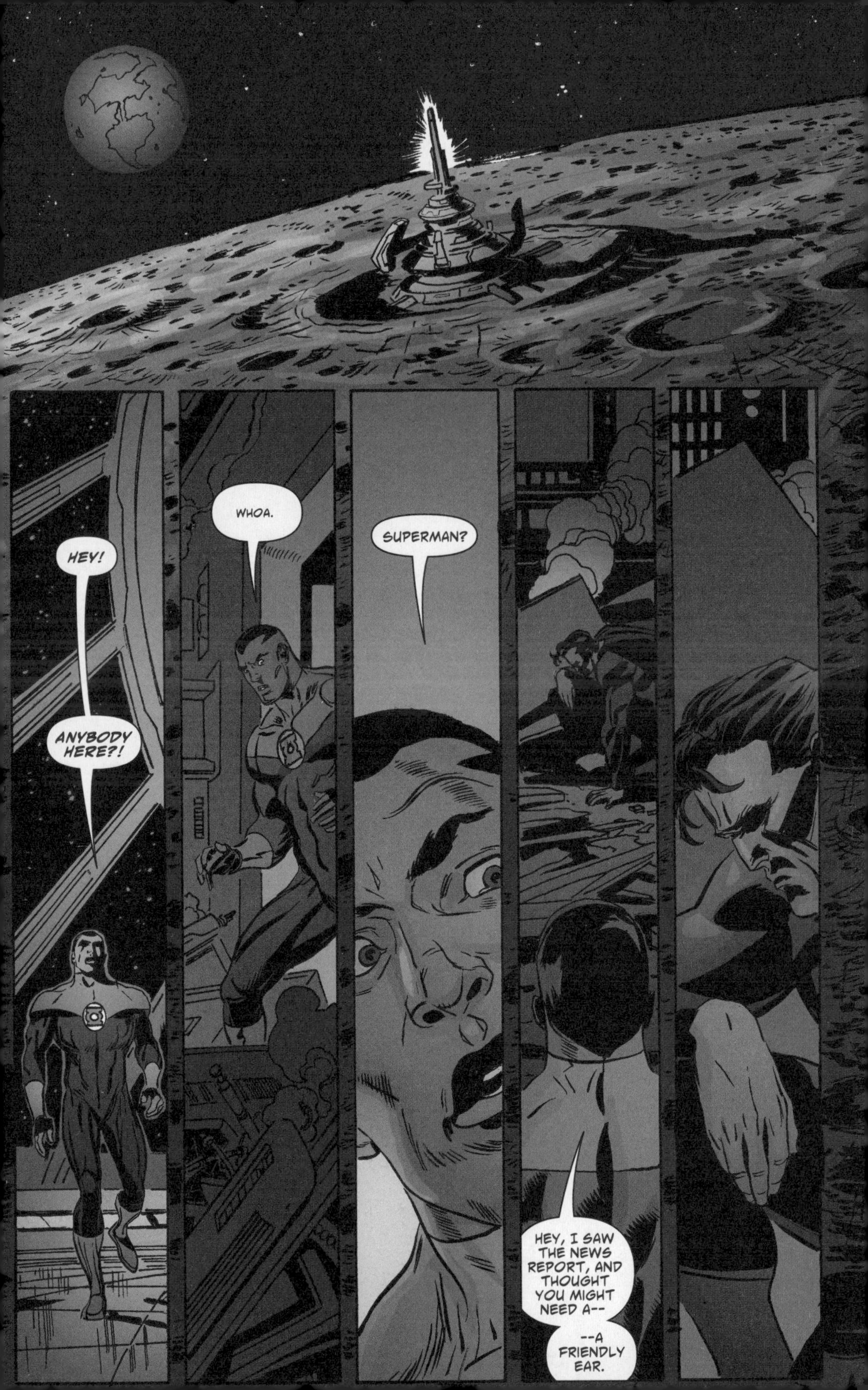

HEY!
ANYBODY HERE?!
WHOA.
SUPERMAN?
HEY, I SAW THE NEWS REPORT, AND THOUGHT YOU MIGHT NEED A--
--A FRIENDLY EAR.

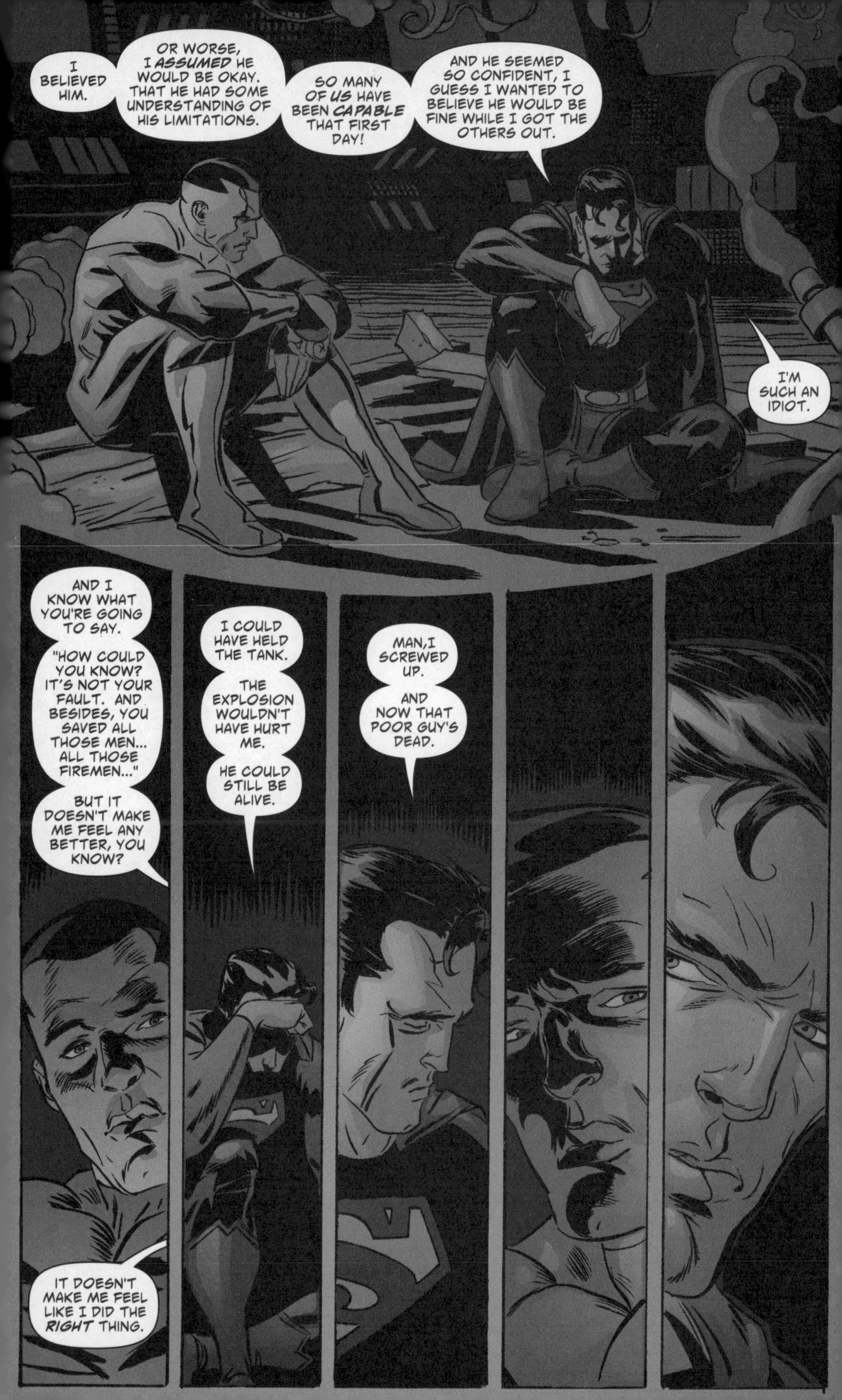
I BELIEVED HIM.
OR WORSE, I ASSUMED HE WOULD BE OKAY. THAT HE HAD SOME UNDERSTANDING OF HIS LIMITATIONS.
SO MANY OF US HAVE BEEN CAPABLE THAT FIRST DAY!
AND HE SEEMED SO CONFIDENT, I GUESS I WANTED TO BELIEVE HE WOULD BE FINE WHILE I GOT THE OTHERS OUT.
I'M SUCH AN IDIOT.
AND I KNOW WHAT YOU'RE GOING TO SAY.
"HOW COULD YOU KNOW? IT'S NOT YOUR FAULT. AND BESIDES, YOU SAVED ALL THOSE MEN... ALL THOSE FIREMEN..."
BUT IT DOESN'T MAKE ME FEEL ANY BETTER, YOU KNOW?
IT DOESN'T MAKE ME FEEL LIKE I DID THE RIGHT THING.
I COULD HAVE HELD THE TANK.
THE EXPLOSION WOULDN'T HAVE HURT ME.
HE COULD STILL BE ALIVE.
MAN, I SCREWED UP.
AND NOW THAT POOR GUY'S DEAD.

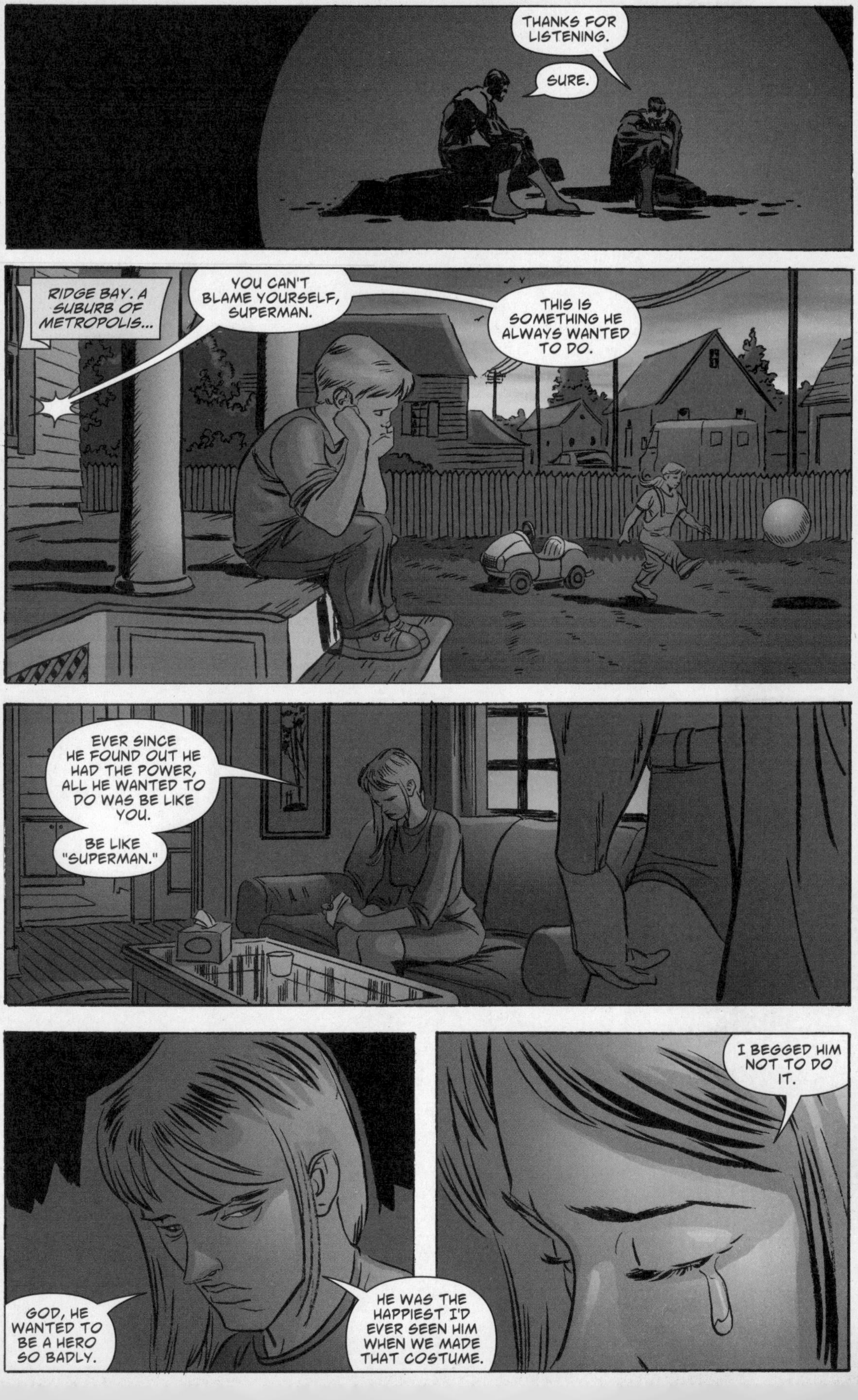
THANKS FOR LISTENING.
SURE.
RIDGE BAY. A SUBURB OF METROPOLIS...
YOU CAN'T BLAME YOURSELF, SUPERMAN.
THIS IS SOMETHING HE ALWAYS WANTED TO DO.
EVER SINCE HE FOUND OUT HE HAD THE POWER, ALL HE WANTED TO DO WAS BE LIKE YOU.
BE LIKE "SUPERMAN."
GOD, HE WANTED TO BE A HERO SO BADLY.
HE WAS THE HAPPIEST I'D EVER SEEN HIM WHEN WE MADE THAT COSTUME.
I BEGGED HIM NOT TO DO IT.

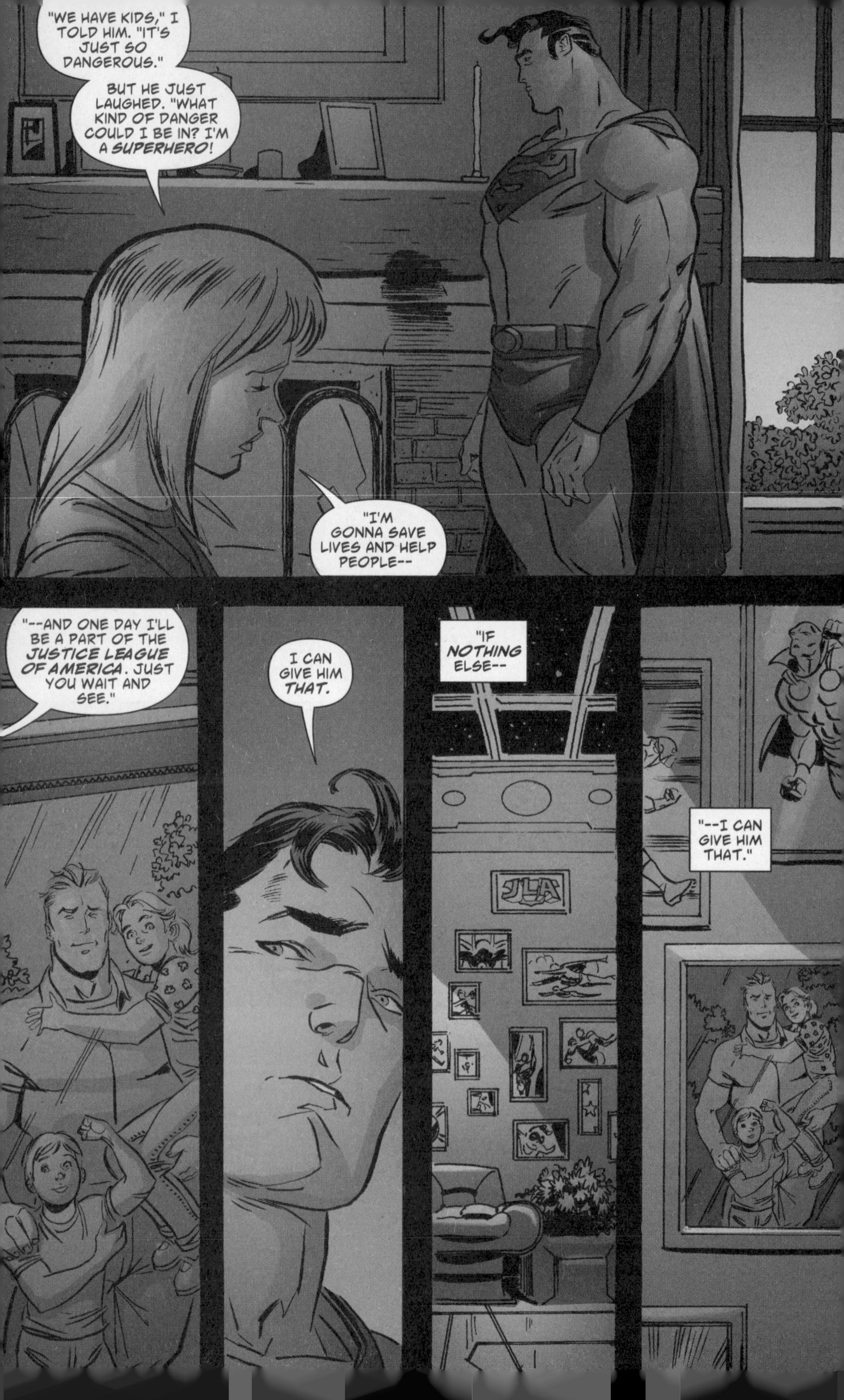
"WE HAVE KIDS," I TOLD HIM. "IT'S JUST SO DANGEROUS."
BUT HE JUST LAUGHED. "WHAT KIND OF DANGER COULD I BE IN? I'M A *SUPERHERO*!
"I'M GONNA SAVE LIVES AND HELP PEOPLE--
"--AND ONE DAY I'LL BE A PART OF THE ***JUSTICE LEAGUE OF AMERICA***. JUST YOU WAIT AND SEE."
I CAN GIVE HIM ***THAT.***
"IF ***NOTHING*** ELSE--
JLA
"--I CAN GIVE HIM THAT."

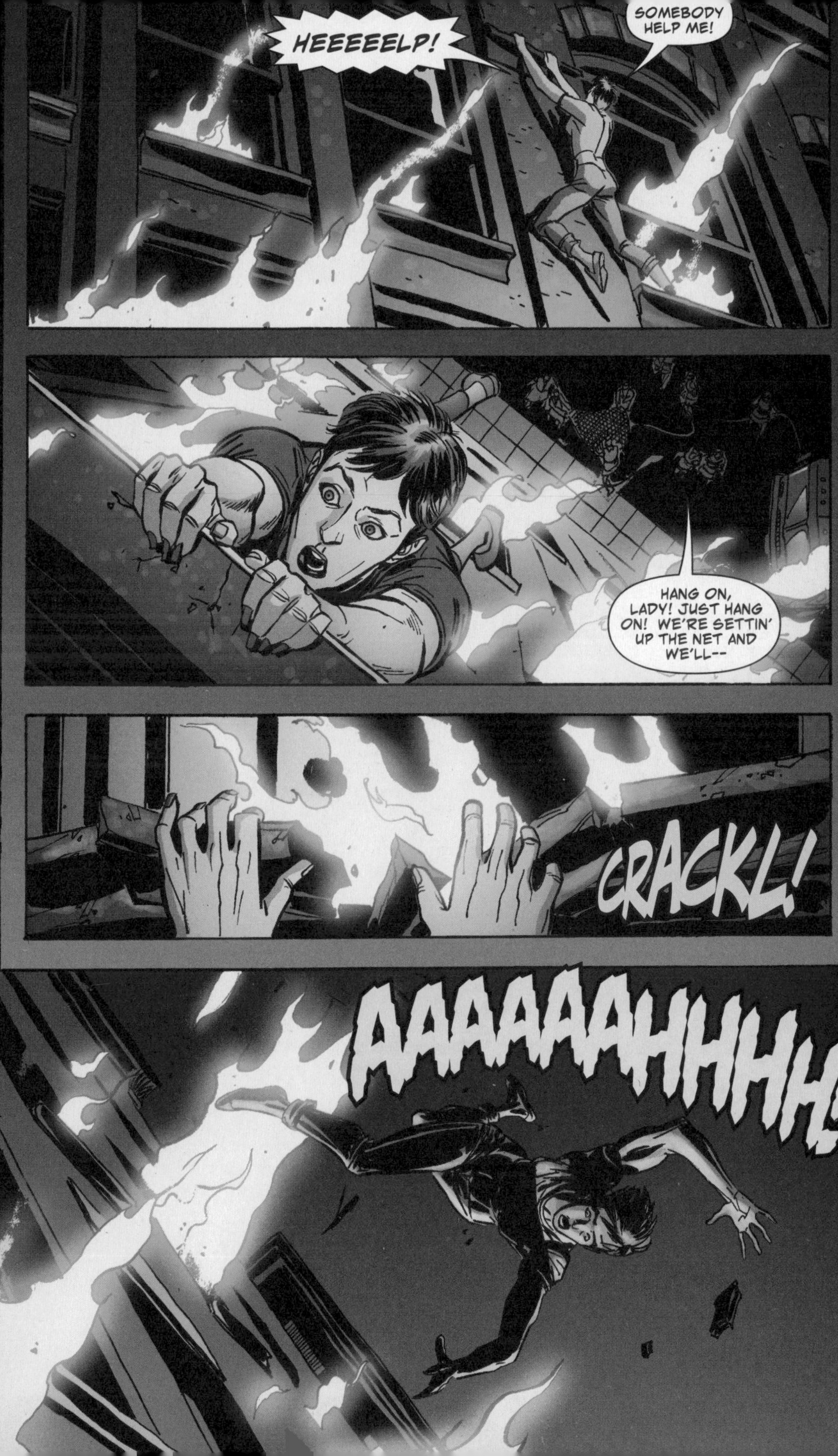
HEEEEELP!
SOMEBODY HELP ME!
HANG ON, LADY! JUST HANG ON! WE'RE SETTIN' UP THE NET AND WE'LL--
CRACKL!
AAAAAHHHH!

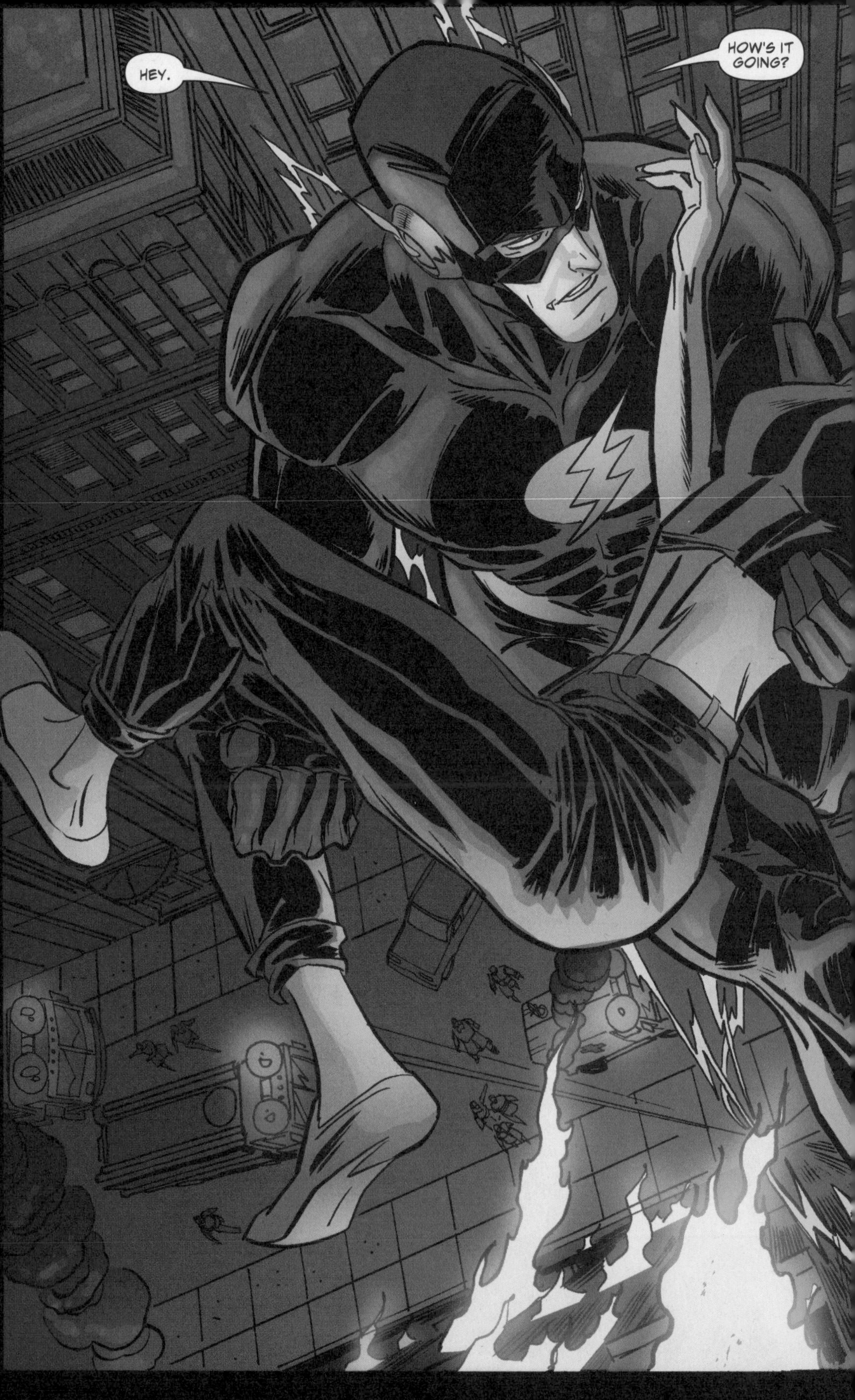
HEY.
HOW'S IT GOING?

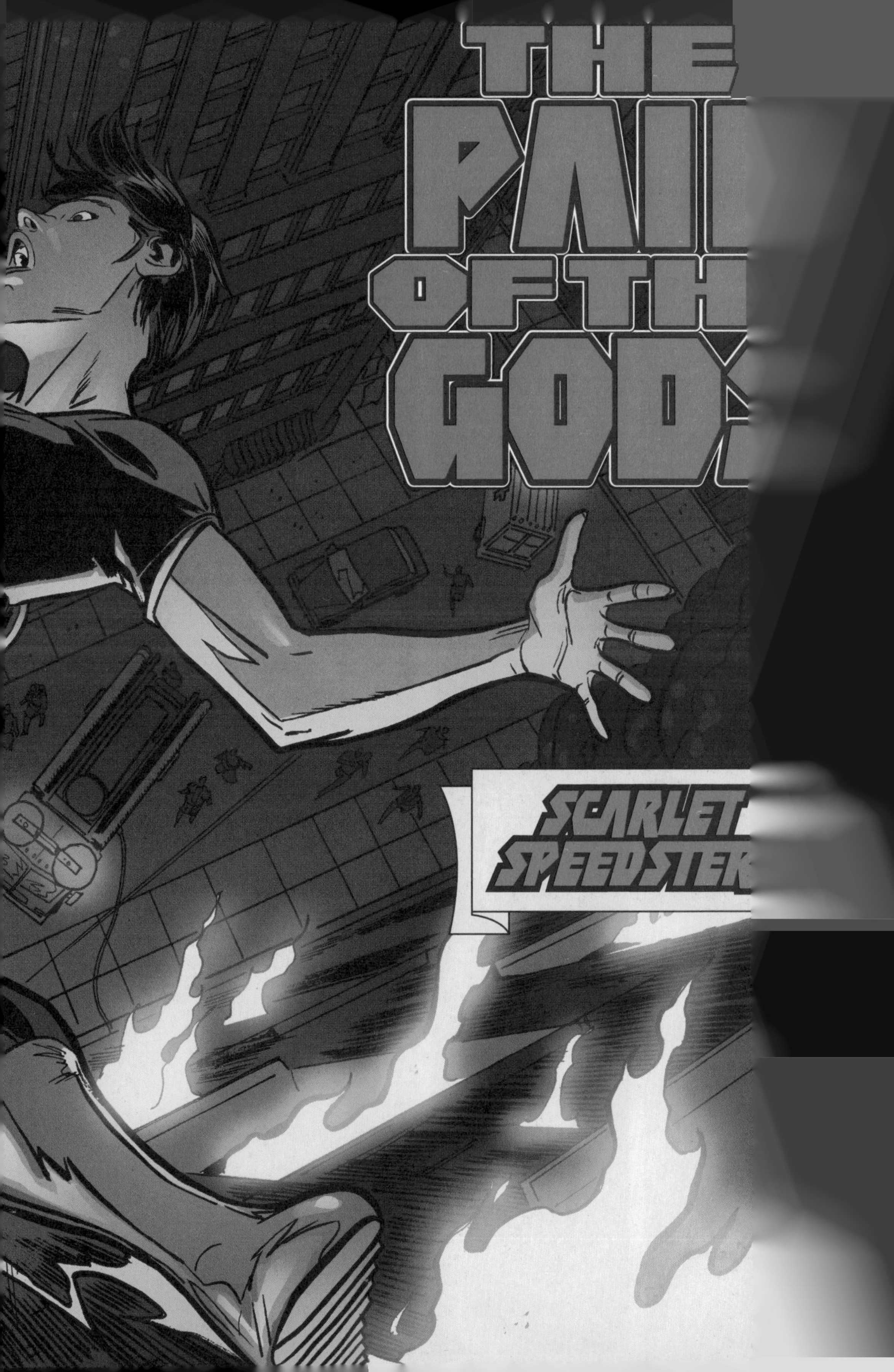
THE
SCARLET
SPEEDSTER

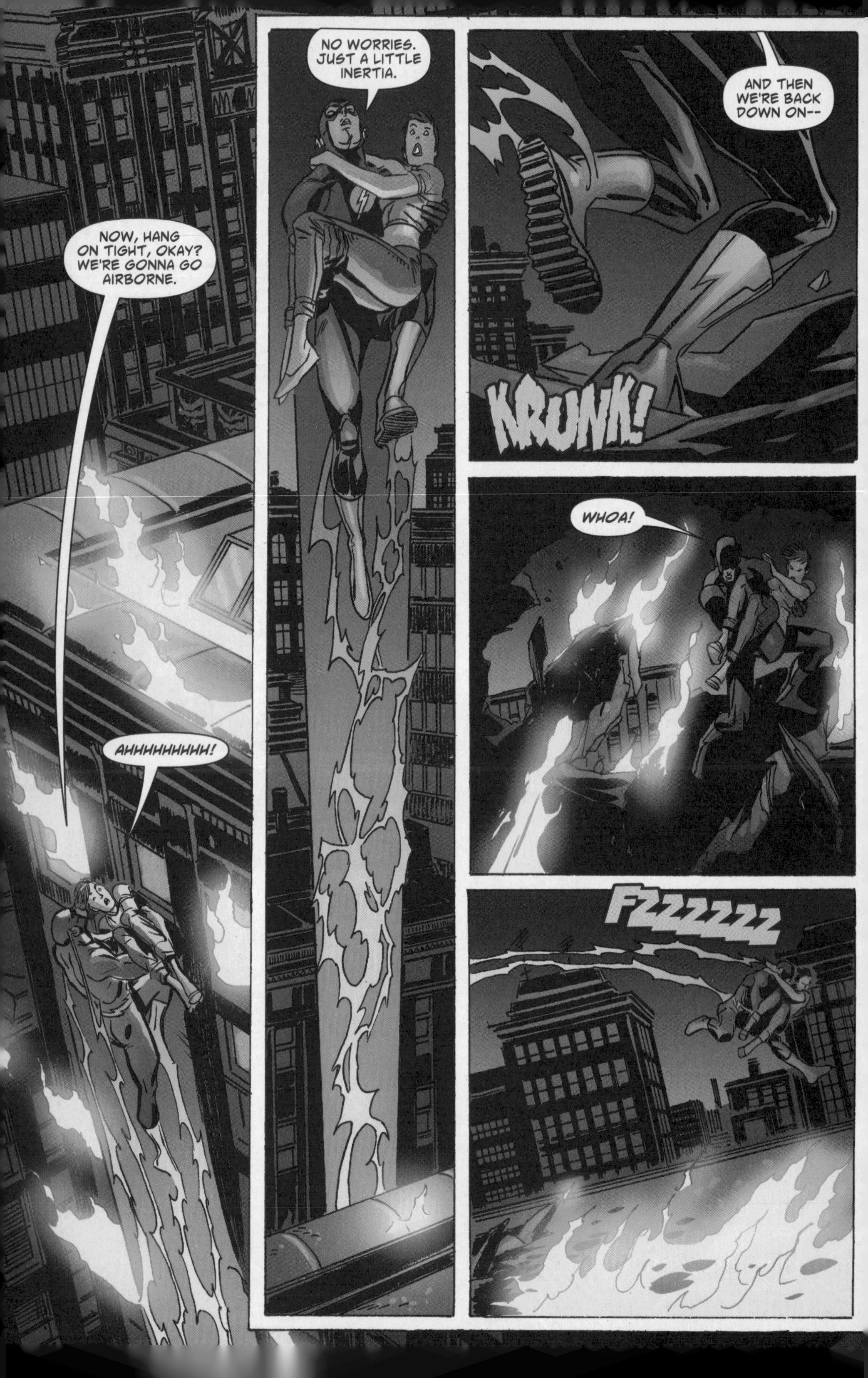
NOW, HANG ON TIGHT, OKAY? WE'RE GONNA GO AIRBORNE.
AHHHHHHHHH!
NO WORRIES. JUST A LITTLE INERTIA.
AND THEN WE'RE BACK DOWN ON--
KRUNK!
WHOA!
FZZZZZZ

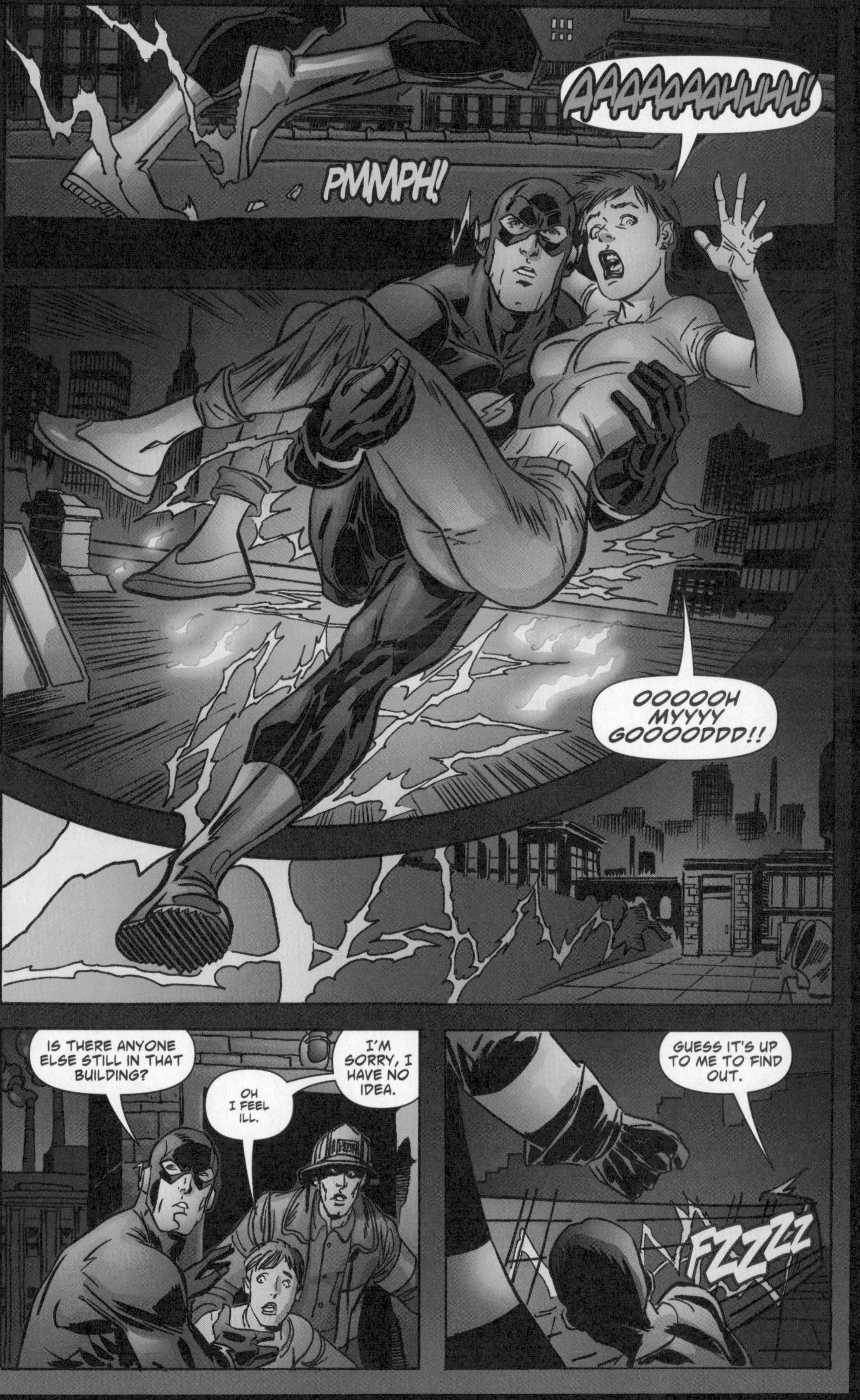
PMMPH!
AAAAAAAHHHH!
OOOOOH MYYYY GOOOODDD!!
IS THERE ANYONE ELSE STILL IN THAT BUILDING?
OH I FEEL ILL.
I'M SORRY, I HAVE NO IDEA.
GUESS IT'S UP TO ME TO FIND OUT.
FZZZZ

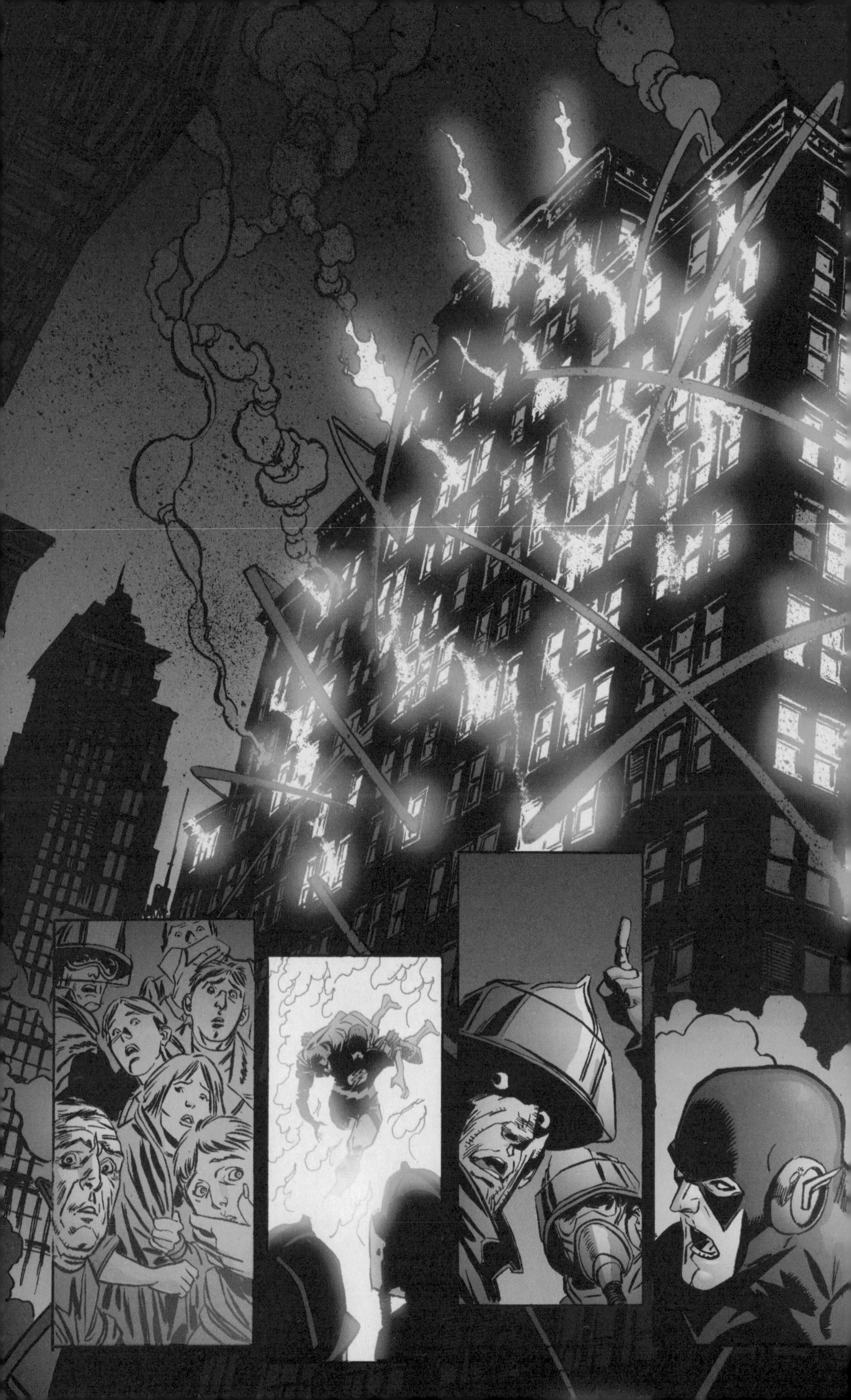

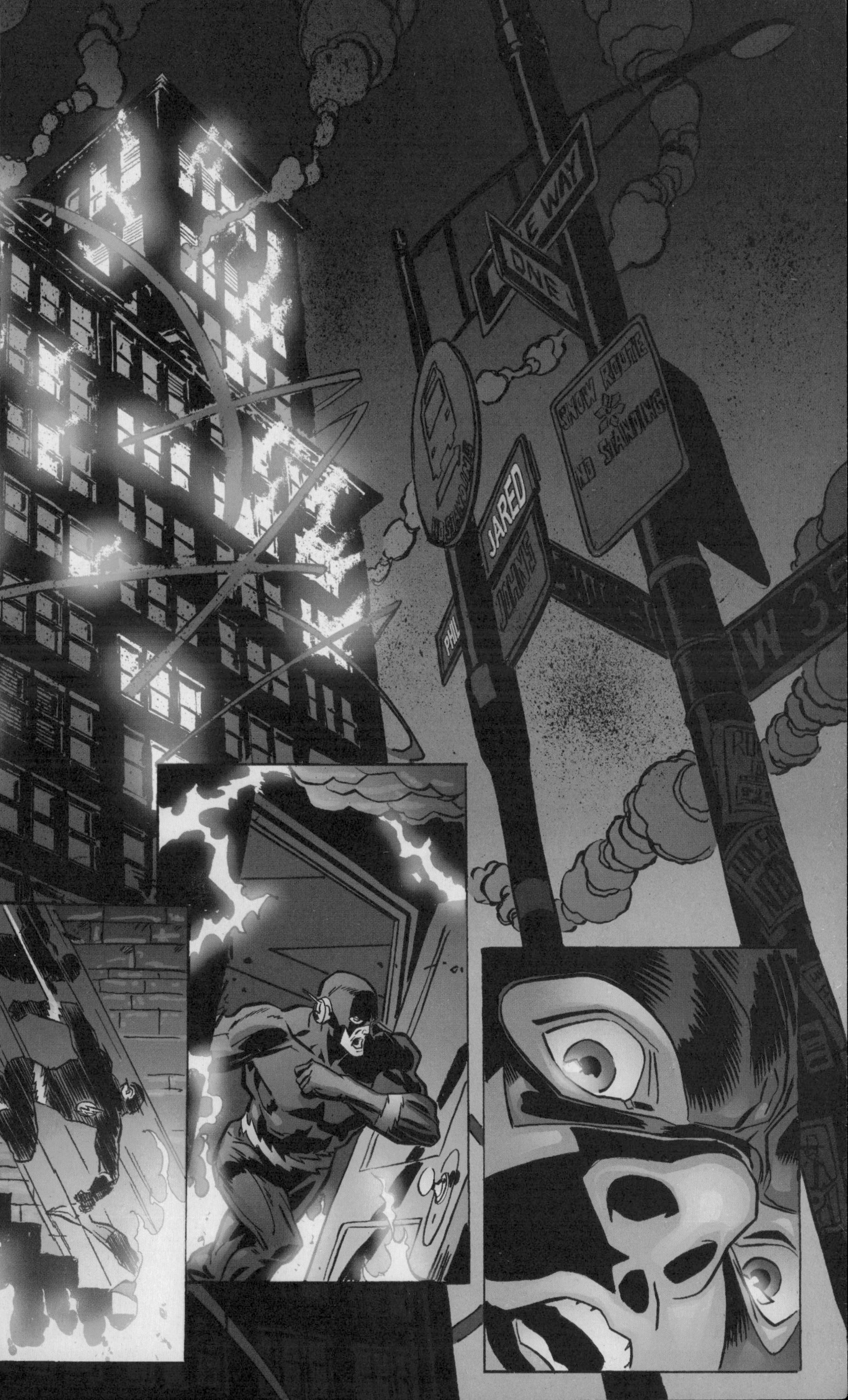
ONE
JARED
SNOW ROUTE
NO STANDING

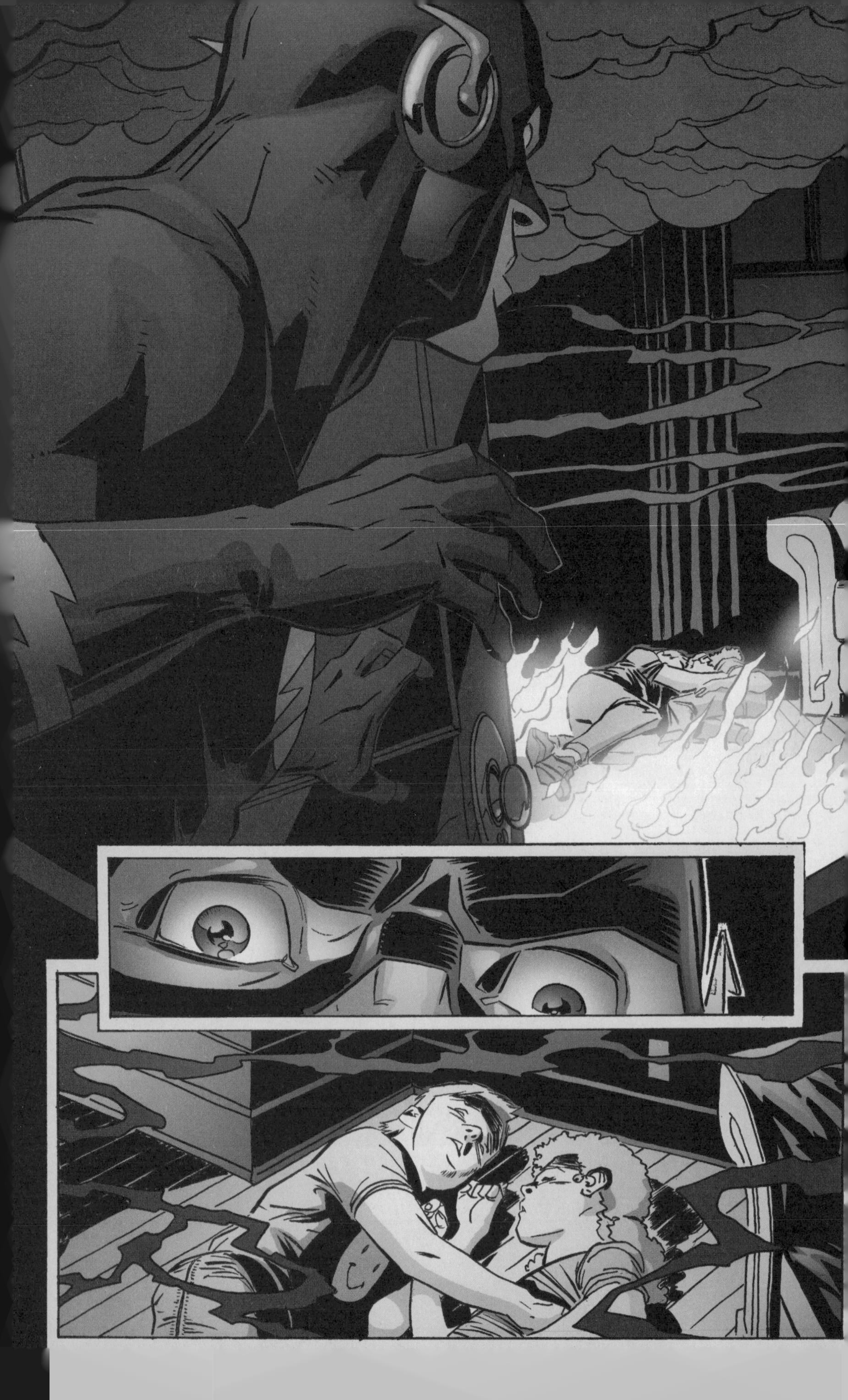

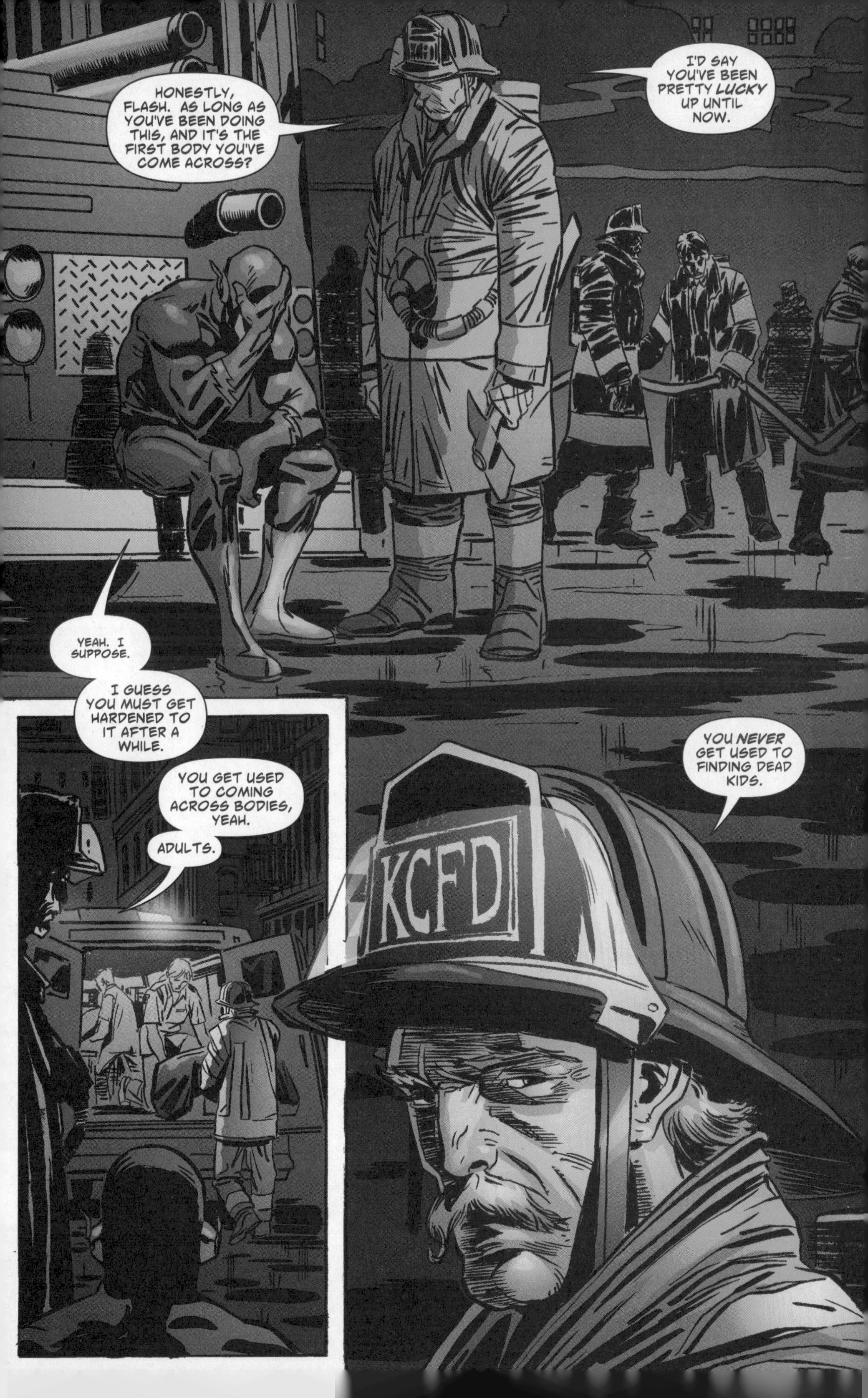
HONESTLY, FLASH. AS LONG AS YOU'VE BEEN DOING THIS, AND IT'S THE FIRST BODY YOU'VE COME ACROSS?
I'D SAY YOU'VE BEEN PRETTY LUCKY UP UNTIL NOW.
YEAH. I SUPPOSE.
I GUESS YOU MUST GET HARDENED TO IT AFTER A WHILE.
YOU GET USED TO COMING ACROSS BODIES, YEAH.
ADULTS.
YOU NEVER GET USED TO FINDING DEAD KIDS.
KCFD

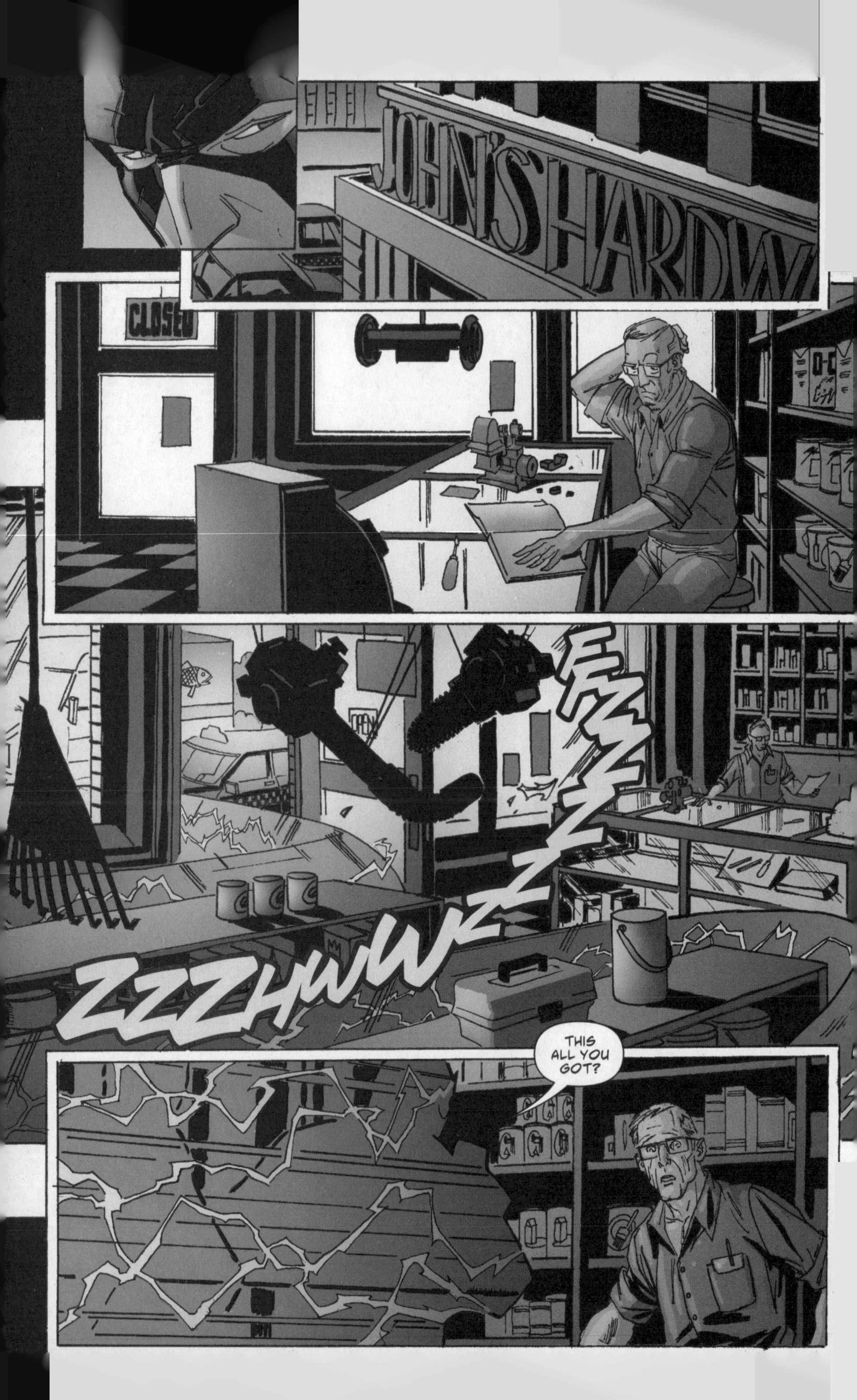

JOHN'S HARDW
CLOSED
OPEN
FZZZZZZHWWW
ZZZHWW
THIS ALL YOU GOT?

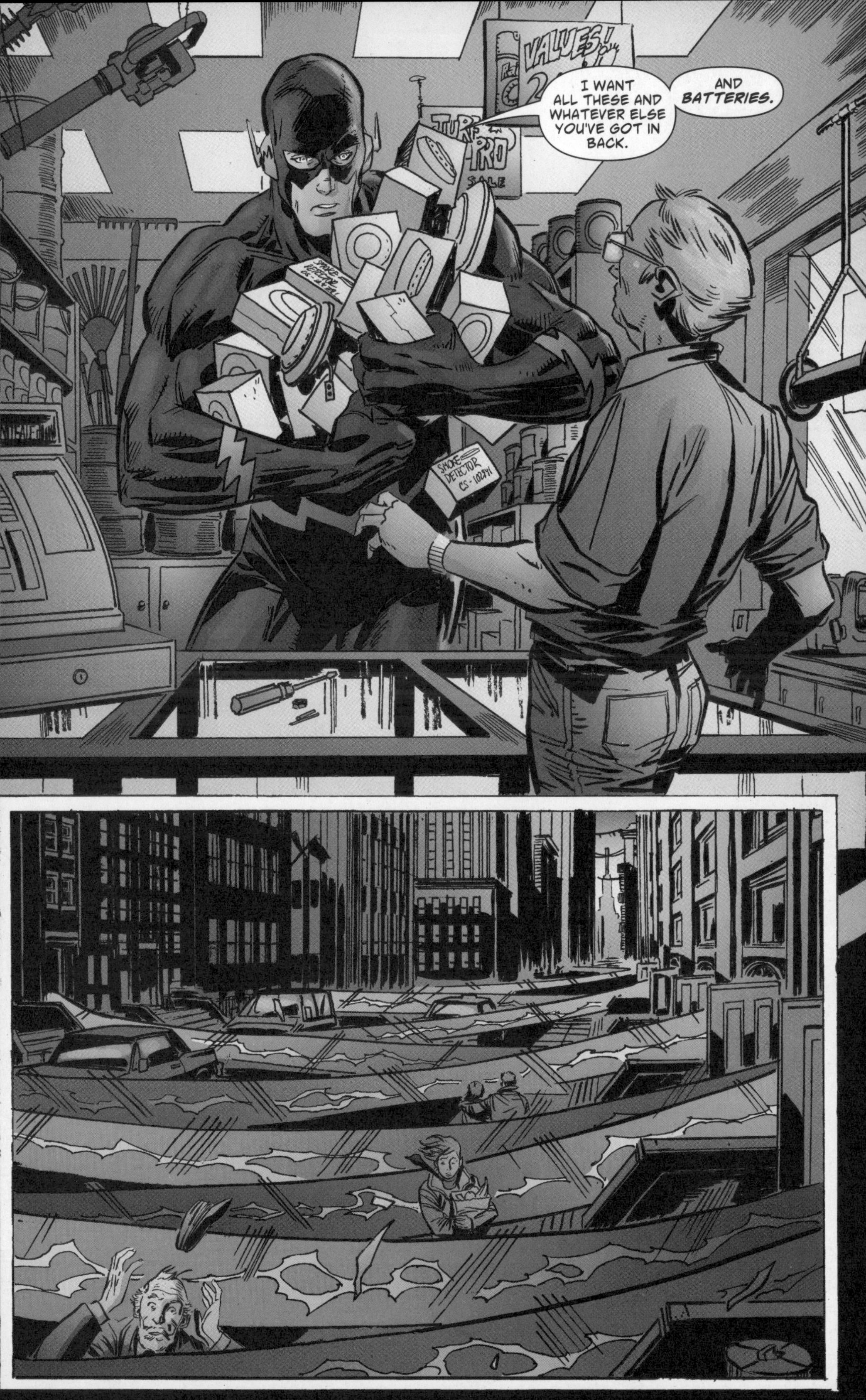
VALUES!
SALE
I WANT ALL THESE AND WHATEVER ELSE YOU'VE GOT IN BACK.
AND BATTERIES.
SMOKE DETECTOR

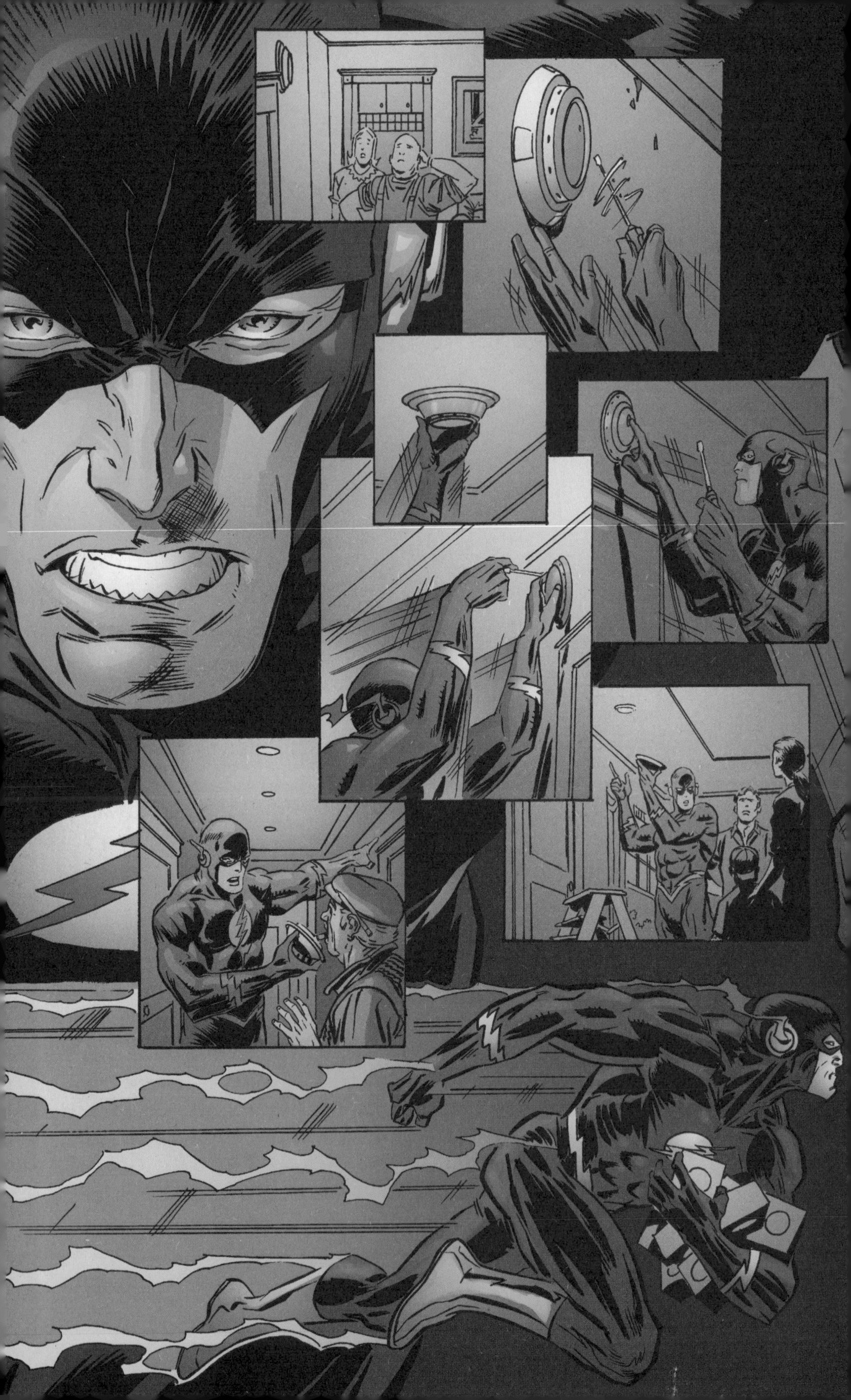

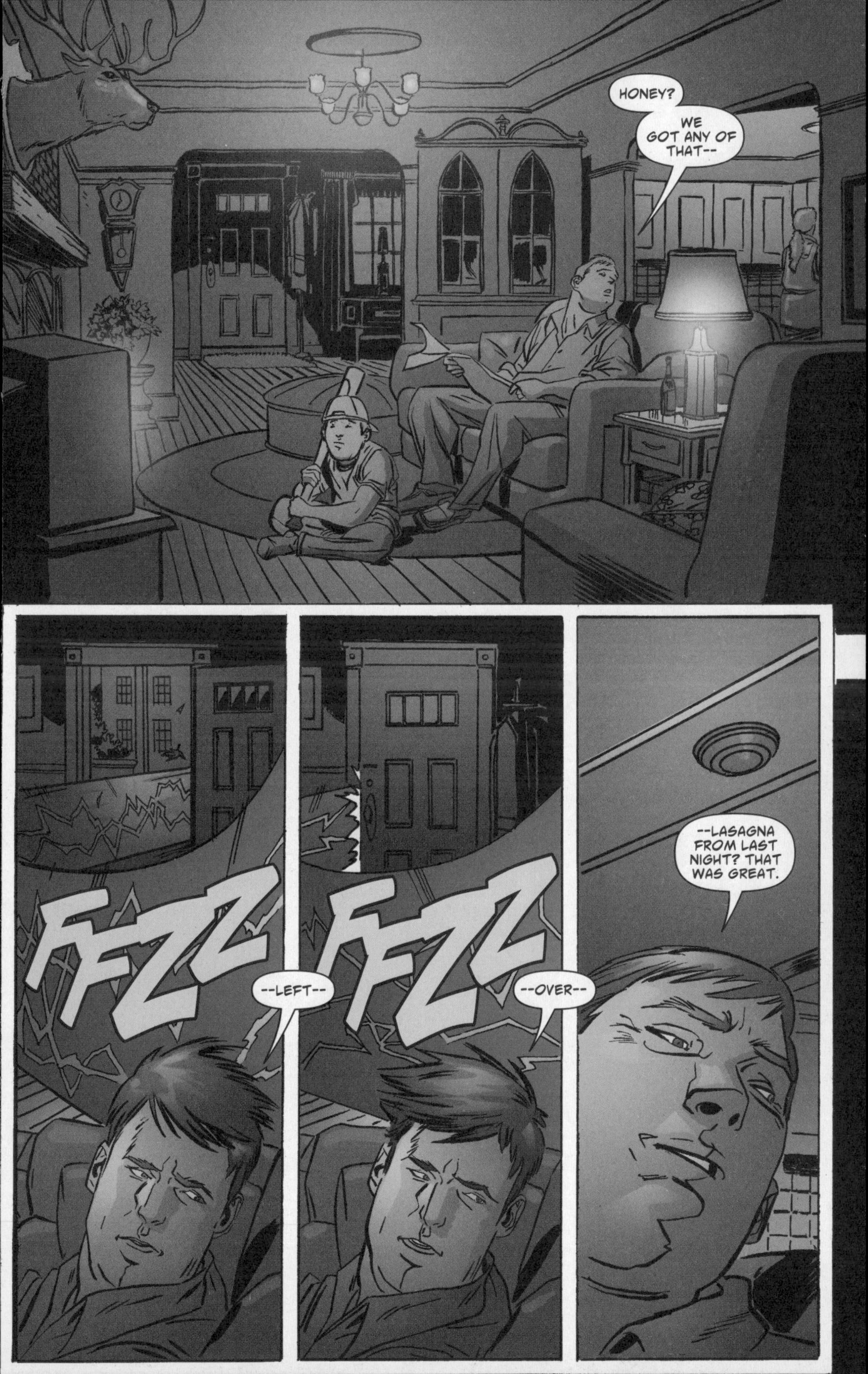
HONEY?
WE GOT ANY OF THAT--
FFZZ
--LEFT--
FFZZ
--OVER--
--LASAGNA FROM LAST NIGHT? THAT WAS GREAT.

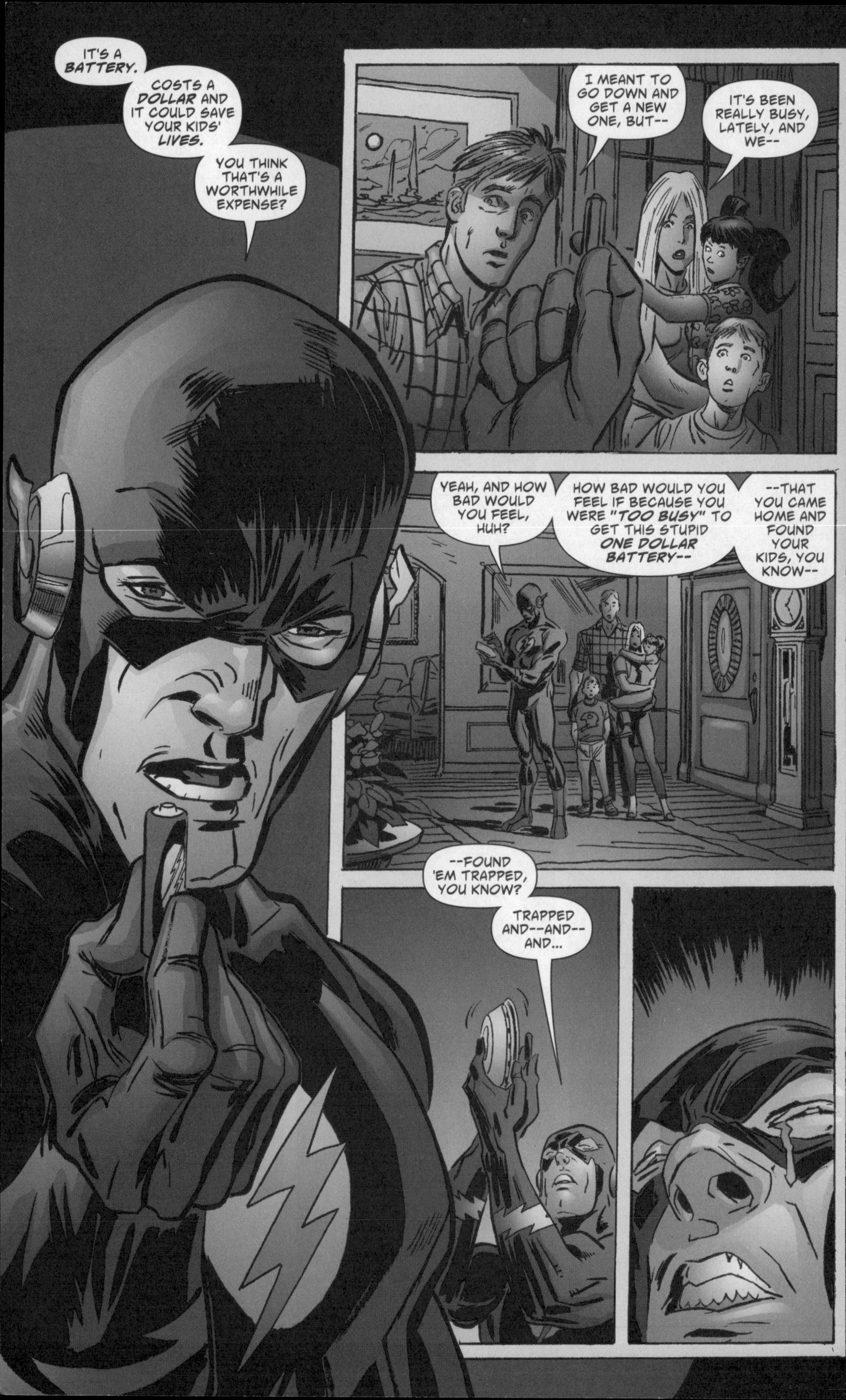
IT'S A BATTERY.
COSTS A DOLLAR AND IT COULD SAVE YOUR KIDS' LIVES.
YOU THINK THAT'S A WORTHWHILE EXPENSE?
I MEANT TO GO DOWN AND GET A NEW ONE, BUT--
IT'S BEEN REALLY BUSY, LATELY, AND WE--
YEAH, AND HOW BAD WOULD YOU FEEL, HUH?
HOW BAD WOULD YOU FEEL IF BECAUSE YOU WERE "TOO BUSY" TO GET THIS STUPID ONE DOLLAR BATTERY--
--THAT YOU CAME HOME AND FOUND YOUR KIDS, YOU KNOW--
--FOUND 'EM TRAPPED, YOU KNOW?
TRAPPED AND--AND--AND...

JUST MAKE THE TIME!

PUT IT UP!

EEEEWWWWWWWWW

FZZZZZZ

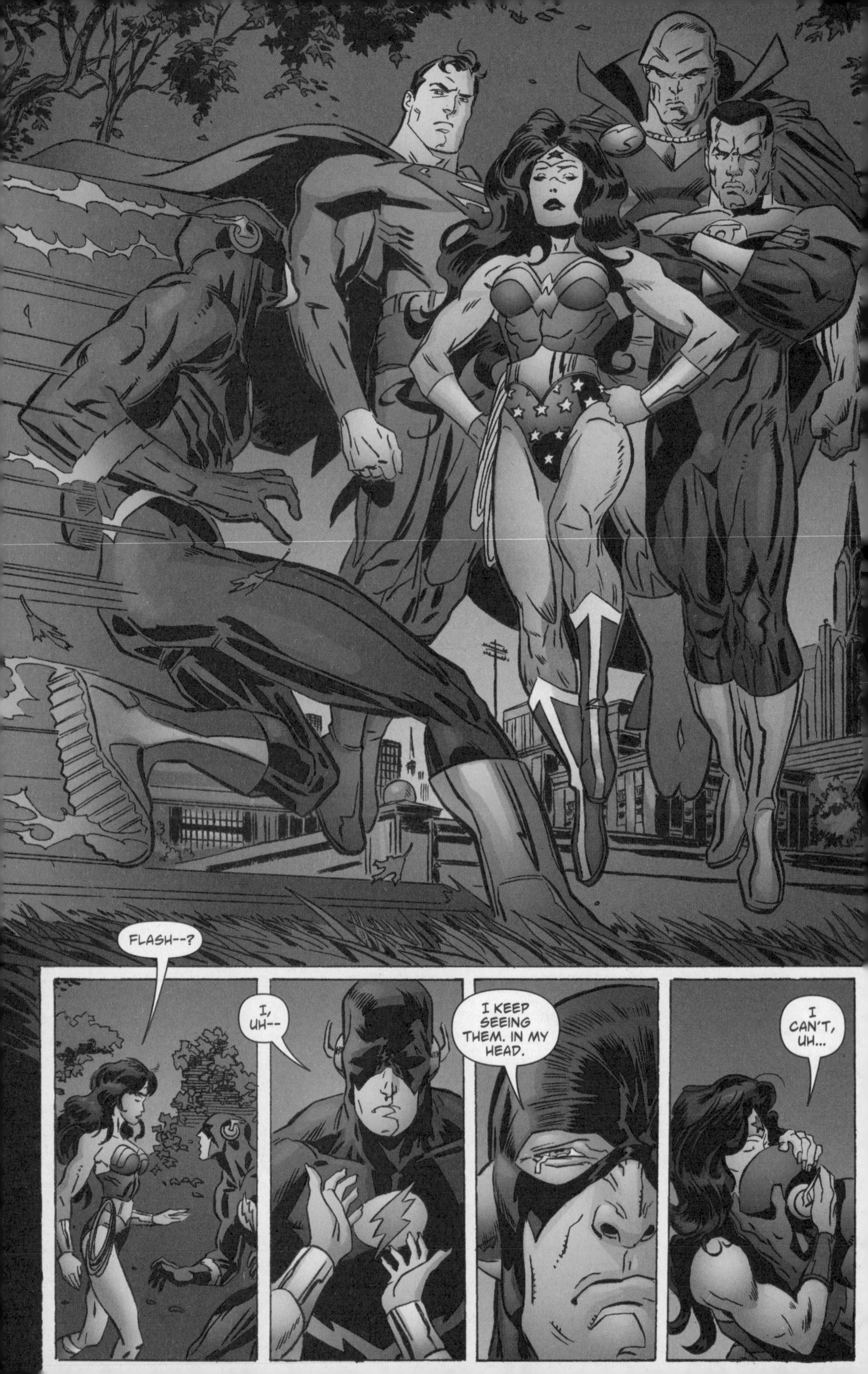
FLASH--?
I, UH--
I KEEP SEEING THEM. IN MY HEAD.
I CAN'T, UH...

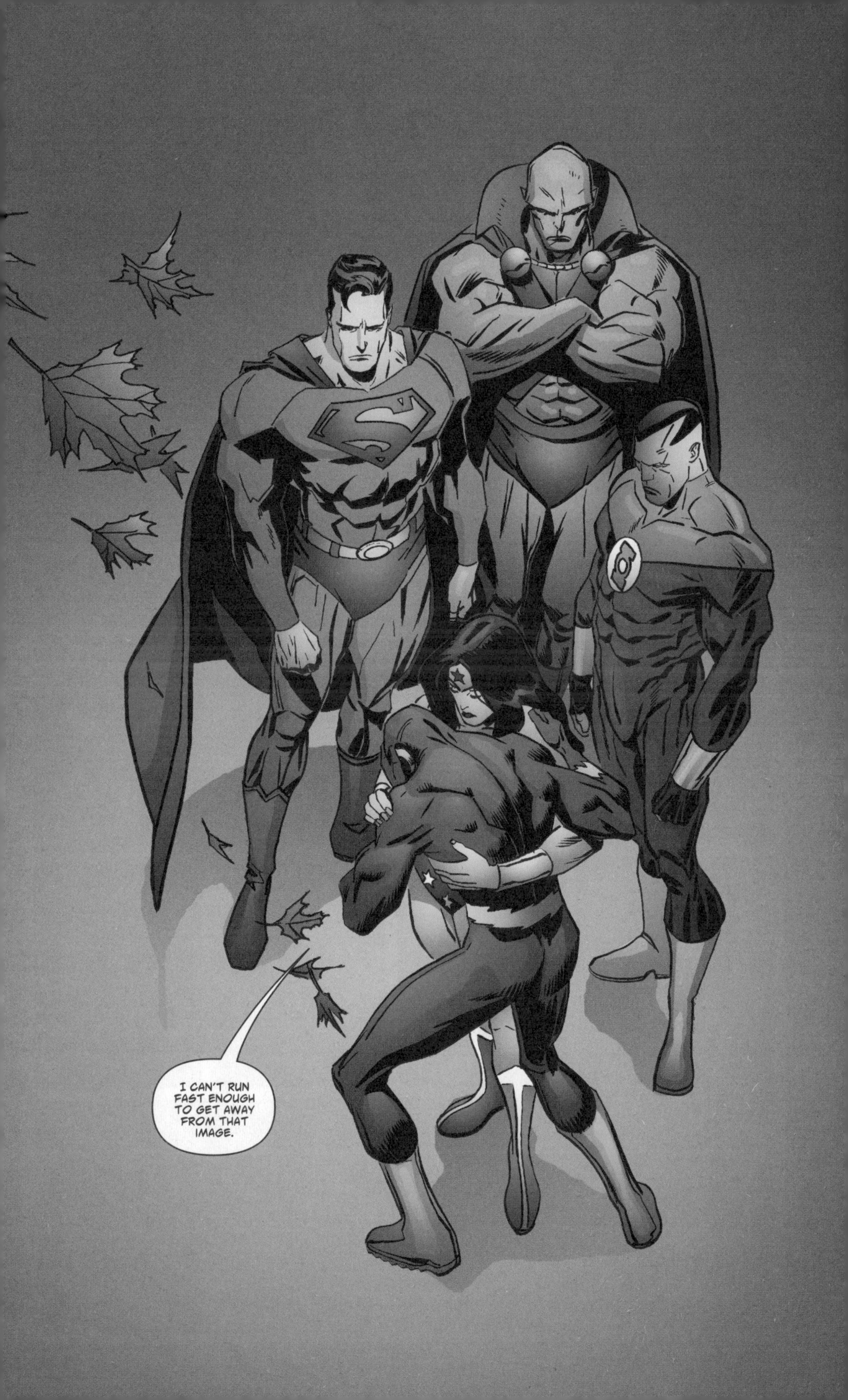
I CAN'T RUN FAST ENOUGH TO GET AWAY FROM THAT IMAGE.

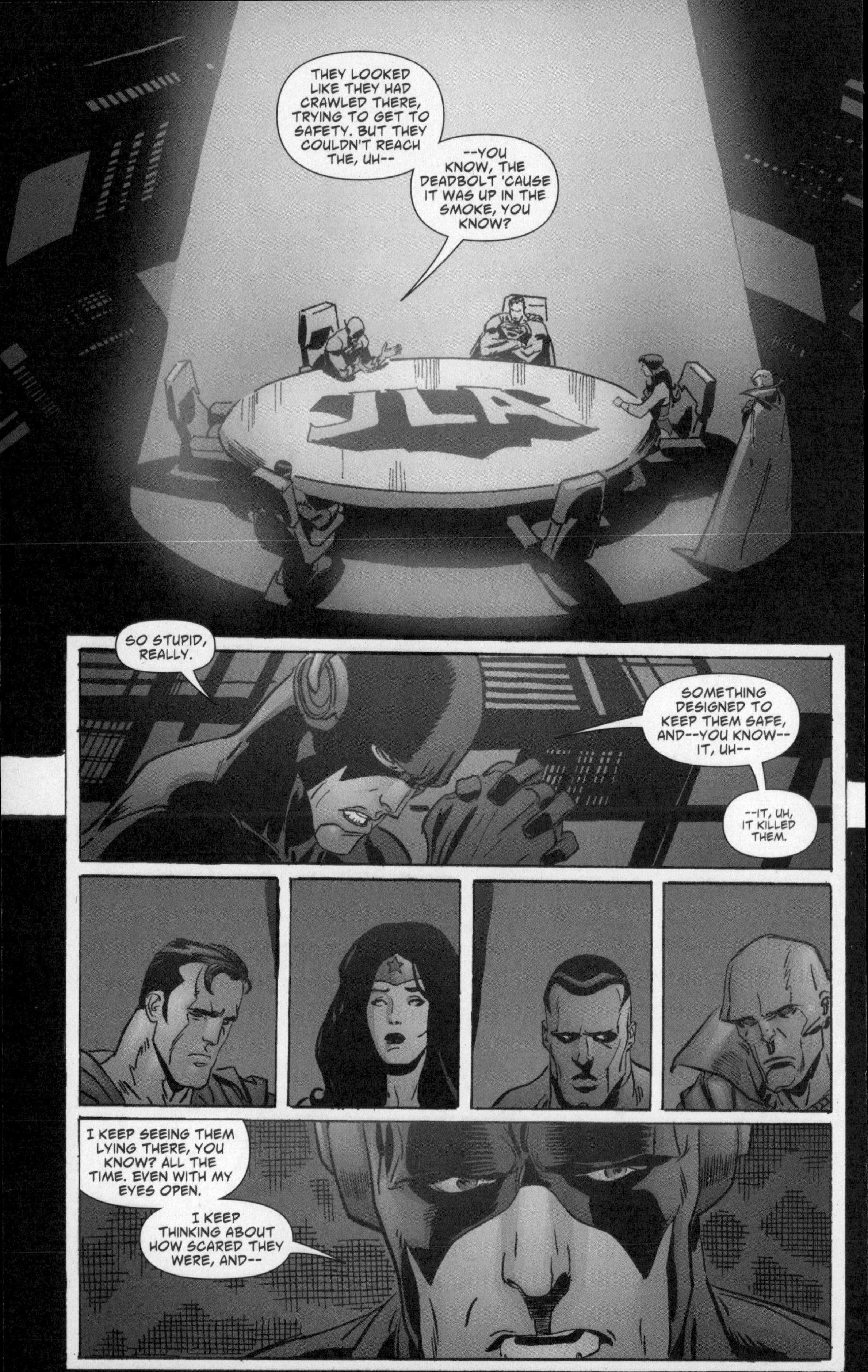
THEY LOOKED LIKE THEY HAD CRAWLED THERE, TRYING TO GET TO SAFETY. BUT THEY COULDN'T REACH THE, UH--
--YOU KNOW, THE DEADBOLT 'CAUSE IT WAS UP IN THE SMOKE, YOU KNOW?
SO STUPID, REALLY.
SOMETHING DESIGNED TO KEEP THEM SAFE, AND--YOU KNOW--IT, UH--
--IT, UH, IT KILLED THEM.
I KEEP SEEING THEM LYING THERE, YOU KNOW? ALL THE TIME. EVEN WITH MY EYES OPEN.
I KEEP THINKING ABOUT HOW SCARED THEY WERE, AND--

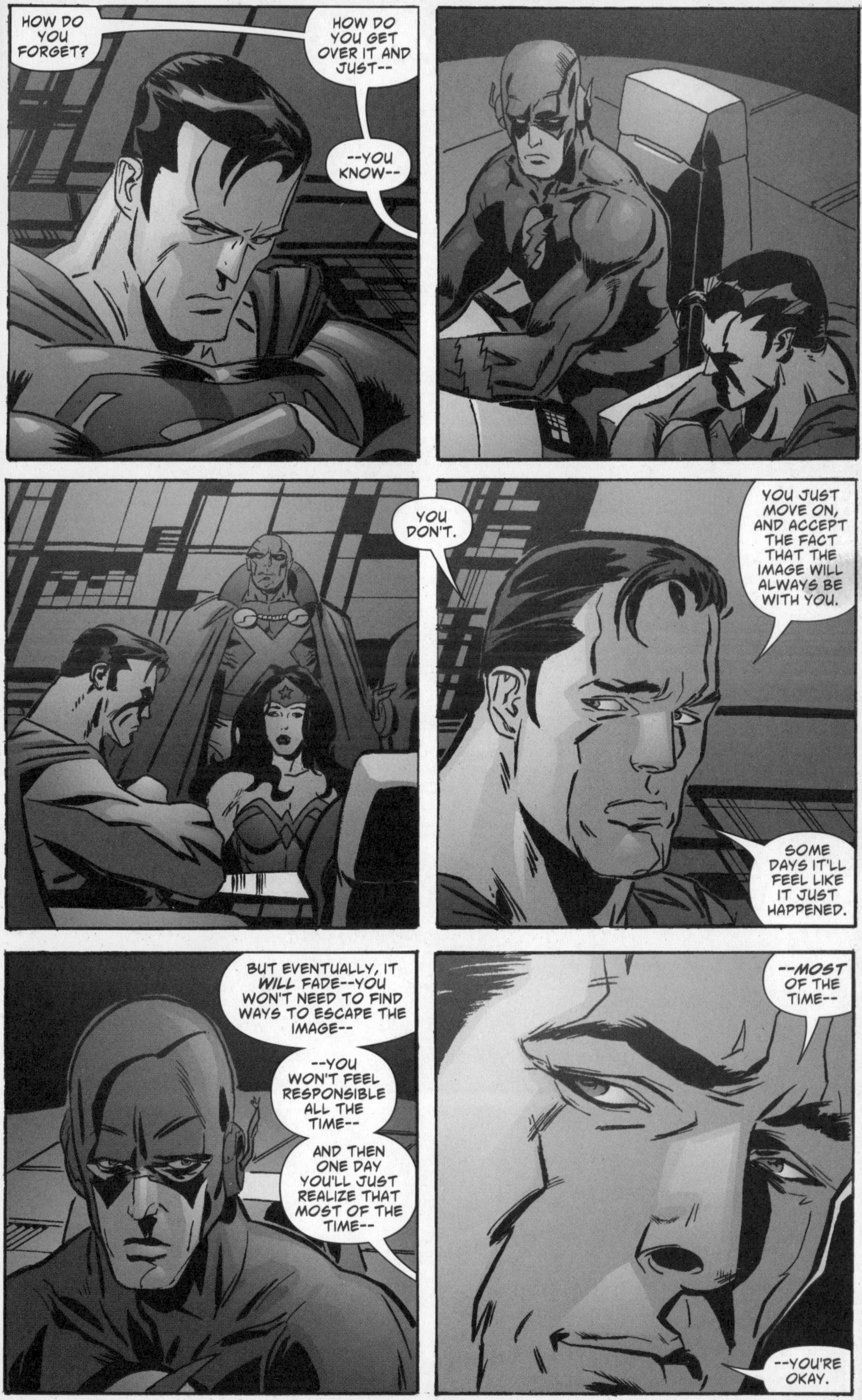
HOW DO YOU FORGET?
HOW DO YOU GET OVER IT AND JUST--
--YOU KNOW--
YOU DON'T.
YOU JUST MOVE ON, AND ACCEPT THE FACT THAT THE IMAGE WILL ALWAYS BE WITH YOU.
SOME DAYS IT'LL FEEL LIKE IT JUST HAPPENED.
BUT EVENTUALLY, IT *WILL* FADE--YOU WON'T NEED TO FIND WAYS TO ESCAPE THE IMAGE--
--YOU WON'T FEEL RESPONSIBLE ALL THE TIME--
AND THEN ONE DAY YOU'LL JUST REALIZE THAT MOST OF THE TIME--
--*MOST* OF THE TIME--
--YOU'RE OKAY.

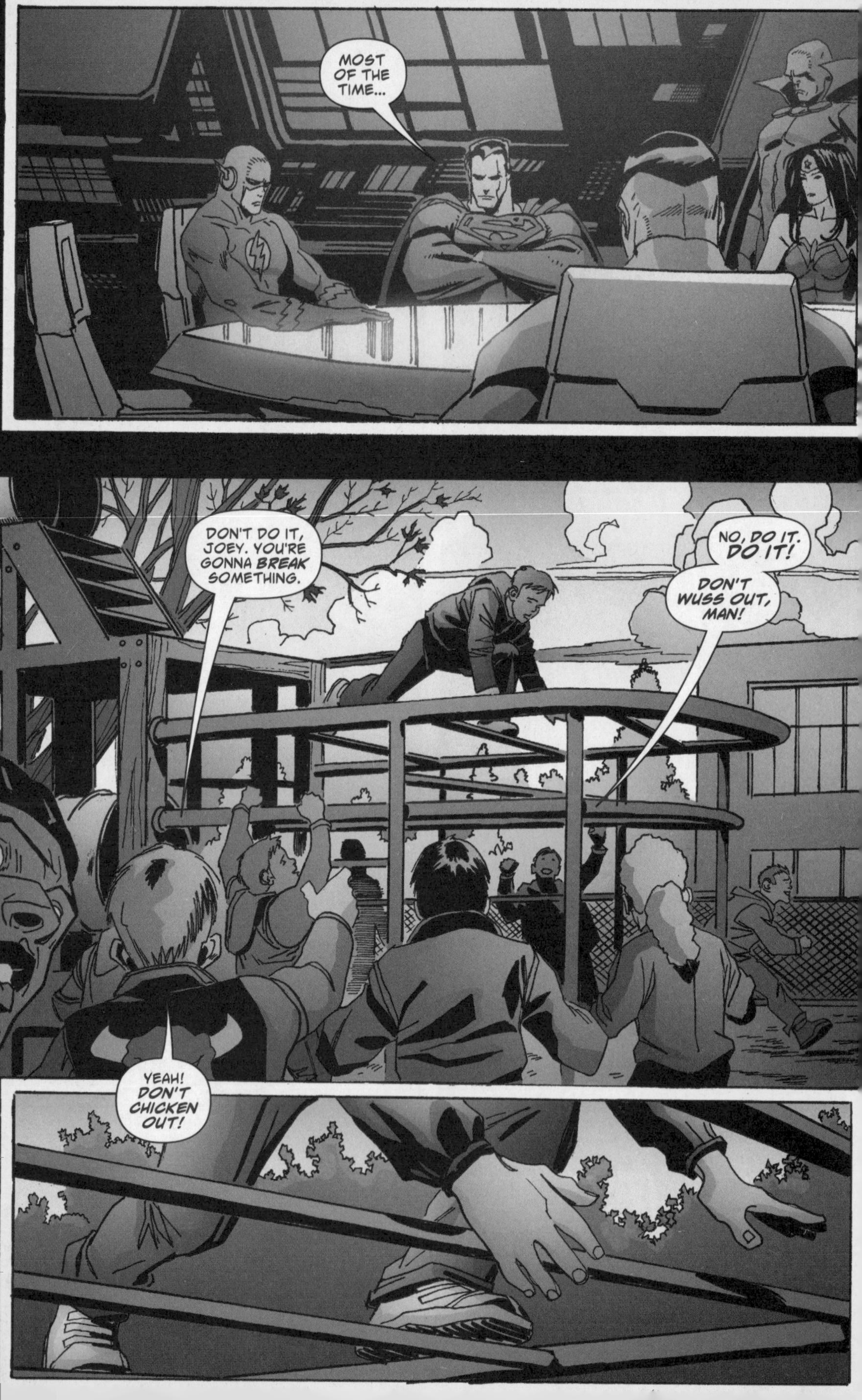
MOST OF THE TIME...
DON'T DO IT, JOEY. YOU'RE GONNA BREAK SOMETHING.
NO, DO IT. DO IT!
DON'T WUSS OUT, MAN!
YEAH! DON'T CHICKEN OUT!

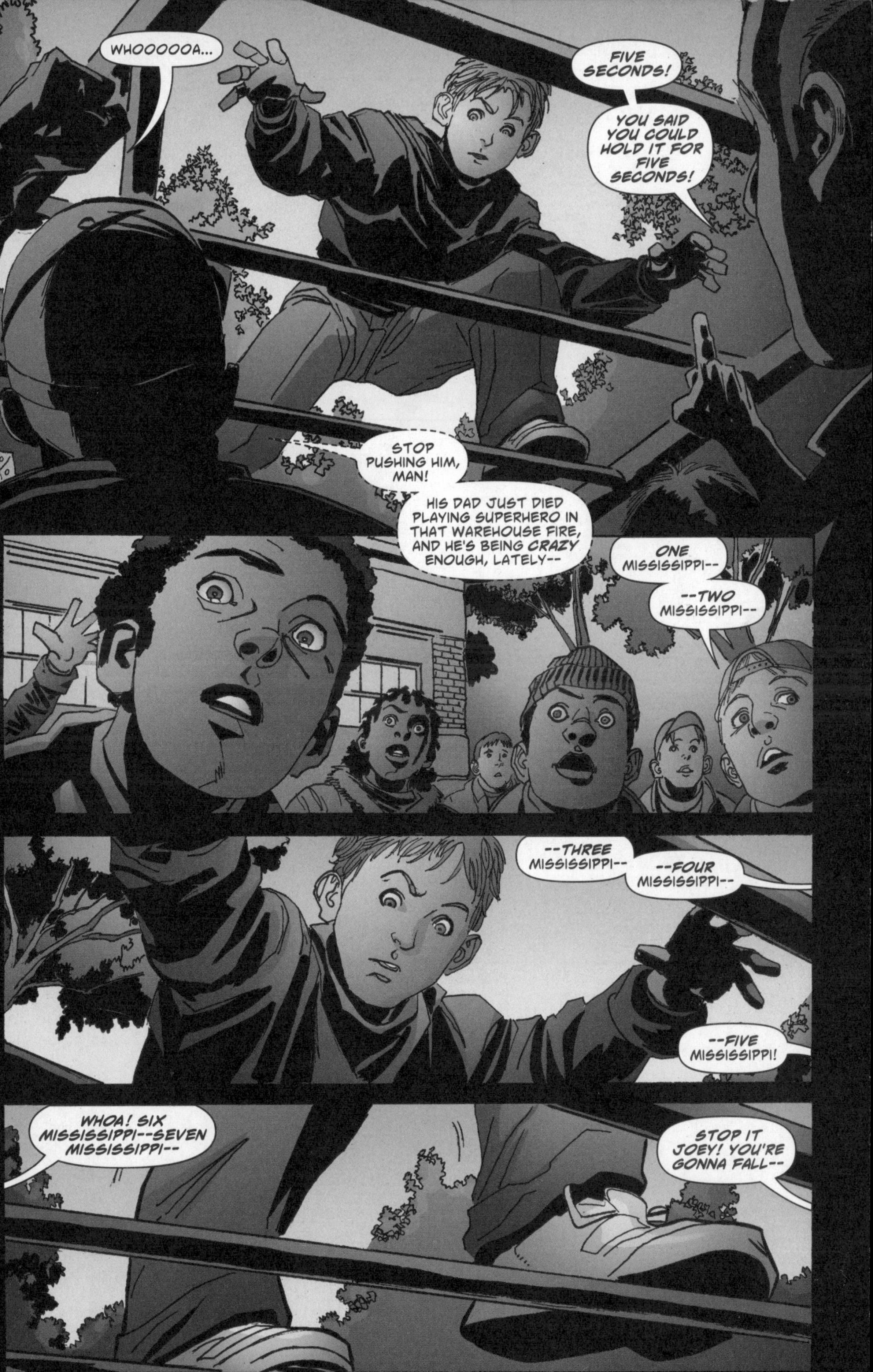
WHOOOOOA...
FIVE SECONDS!
YOU SAID YOU COULD HOLD IT FOR FIVE SECONDS!
STOP PUSHING HIM, MAN!
HIS DAD JUST DIED PLAYING SUPERHERO IN THAT WAREHOUSE FIRE, AND HE'S BEING CRAZY ENOUGH, LATELY--
ONE MISSISSIPPI--
--TWO MISSISSIPPI--
--THREE MISSISSIPPI--
--FOUR MISSISSIPPI--
--FIVE MISSISSIPPI!
WHOA! SIX MISSISSIPPI--SEVEN MISSISSIPPI--
STOP IT JOEY! YOU'RE GONNA FALL--

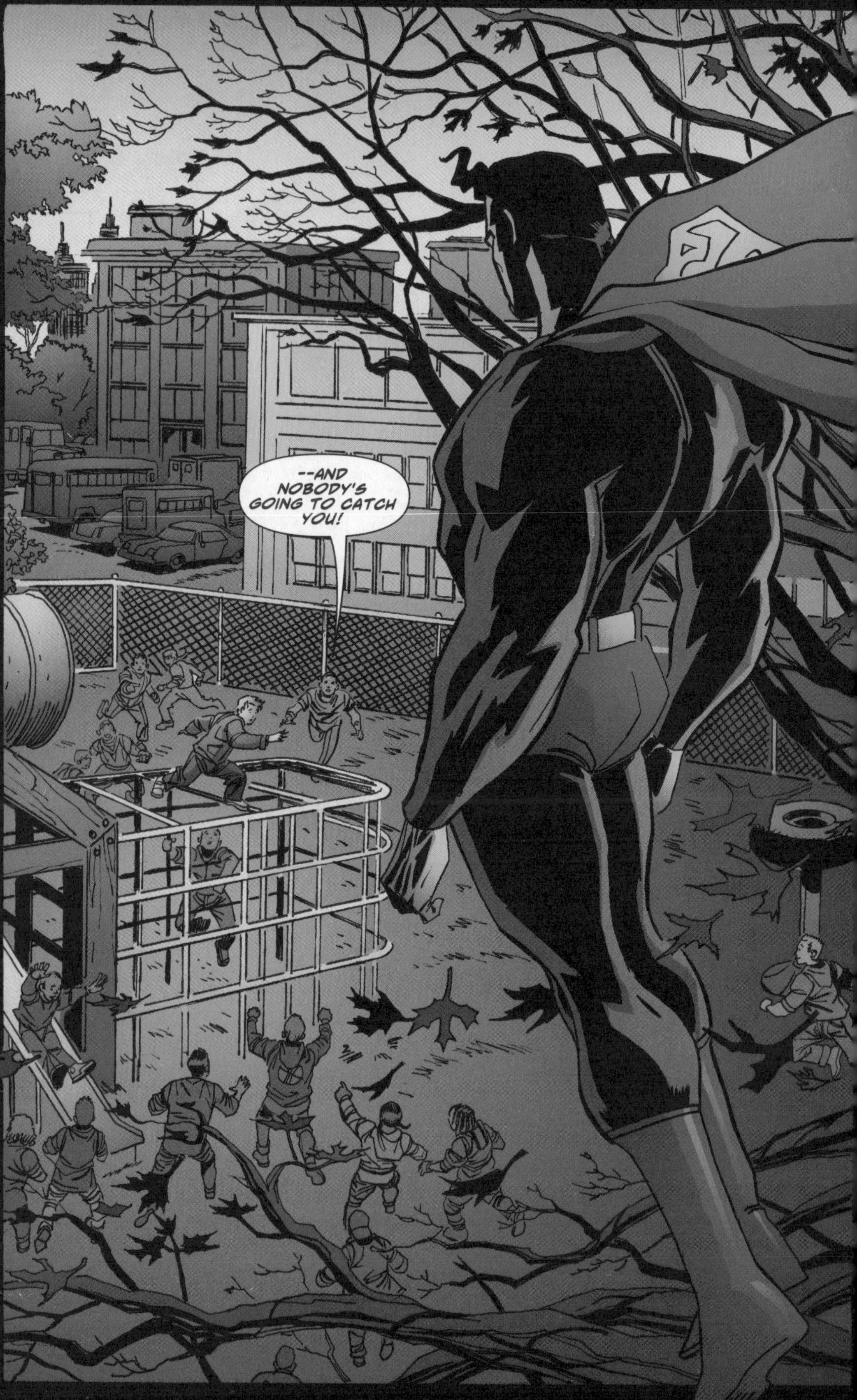
--AND NOBODY'S GOING TO CATCH YOU!

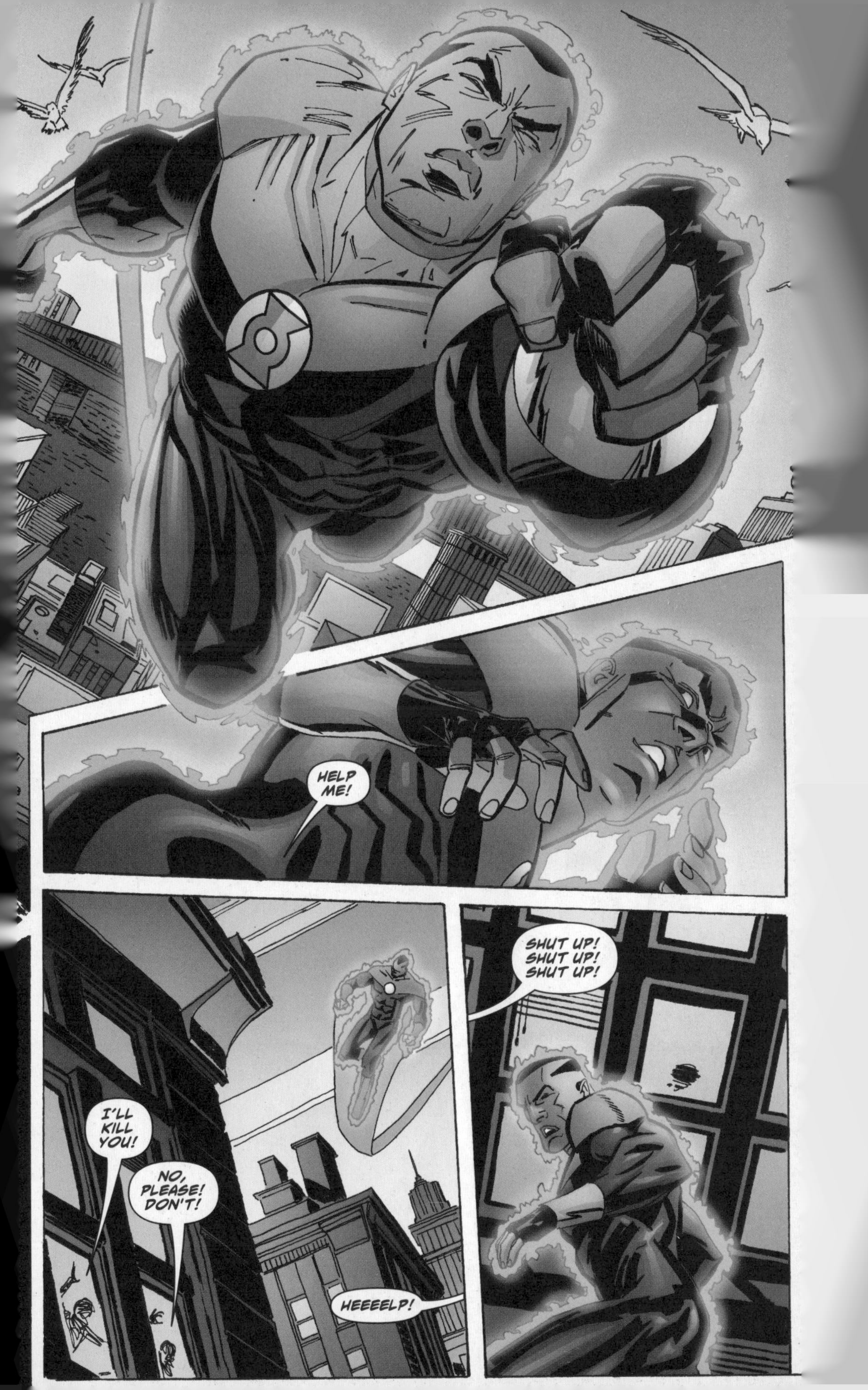
HELP ME!
I'LL KILL YOU!
NO, PLEASE! DON'T!
HEEEELP!
SHUT UP! SHUT UP! SHUT UP!

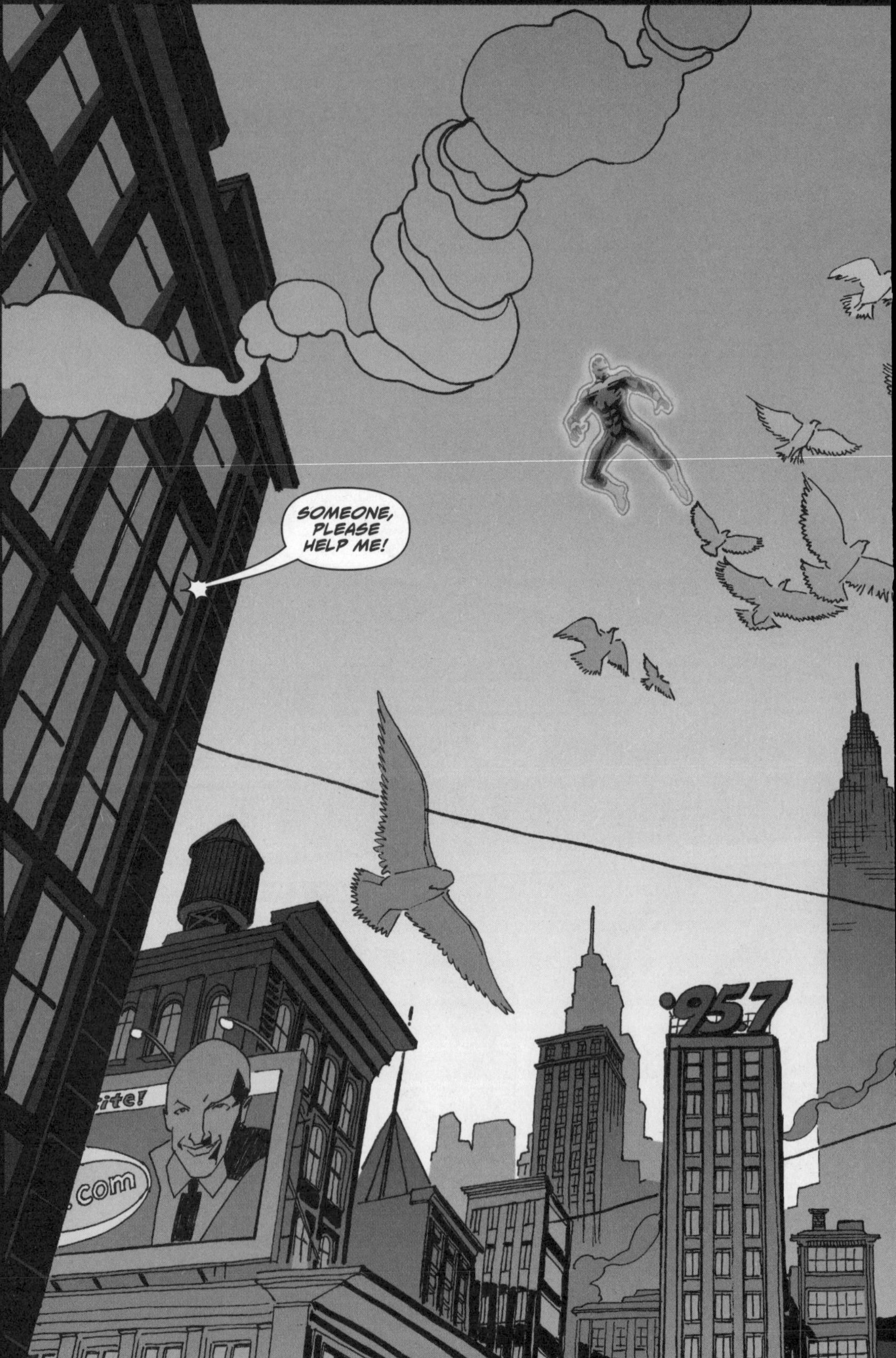
SOMEONE, PLEASE HELP ME!
95.7
.com

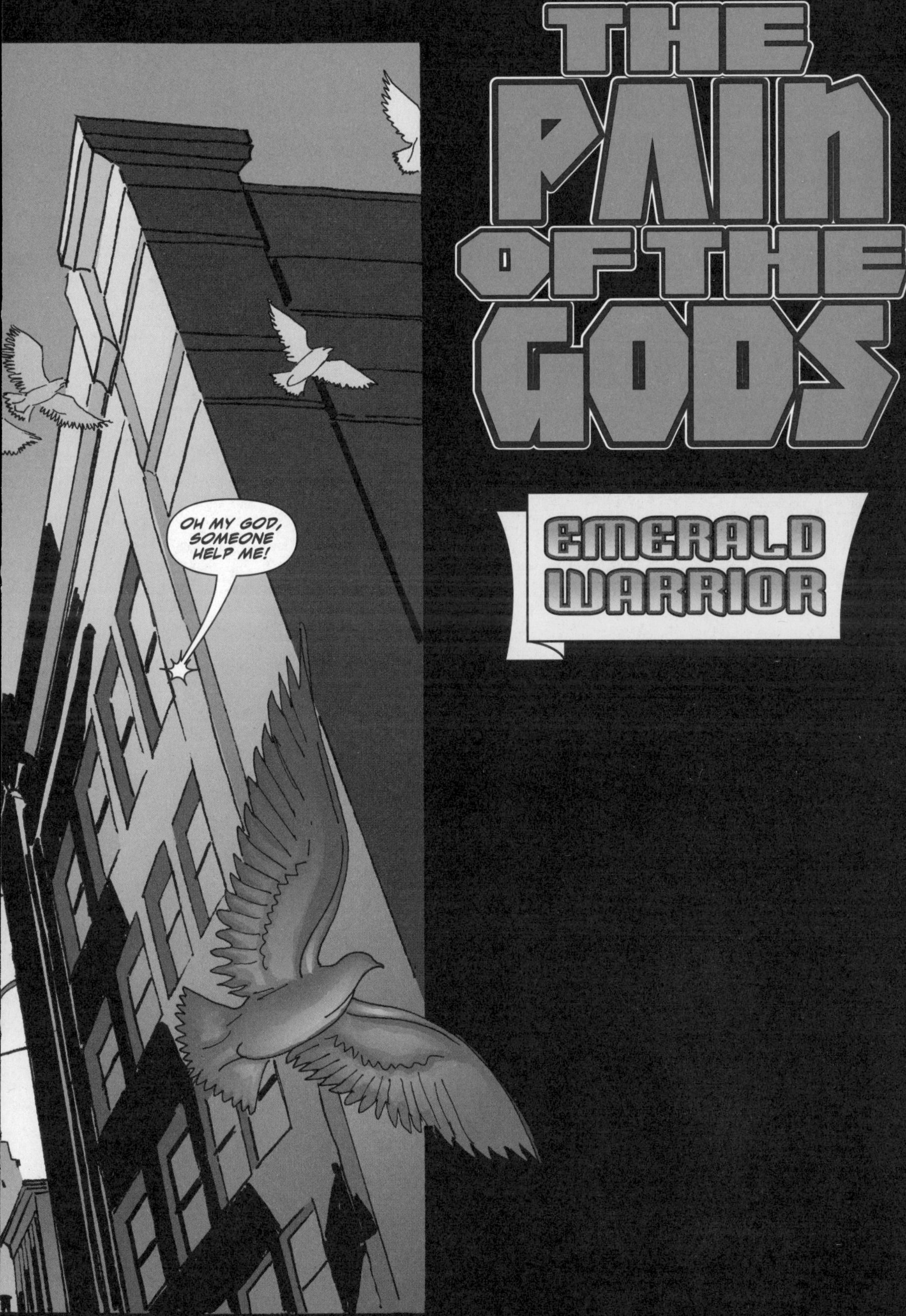
THE PAIN OF THE GODS
EMERALD WARRIOR
OH MY GOD, SOMEONE HELP ME!

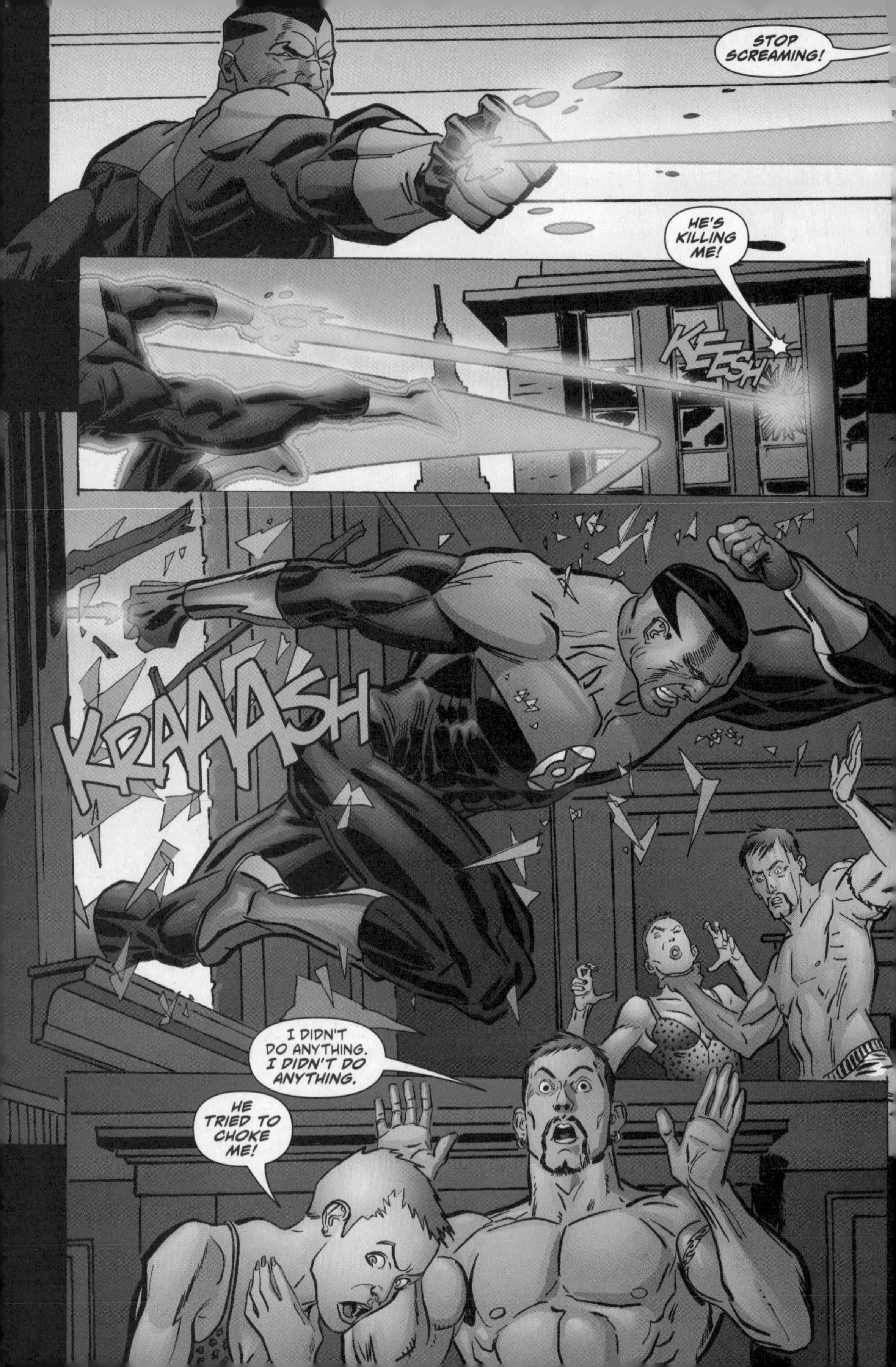
STOP SCREAMING!
HE'S KILLING ME!
KEESH
KRAAASH
I DIDN'T DO ANYTHING. I DIDN'T DO ANYTHING.
HE TRIED TO CHOKE ME!

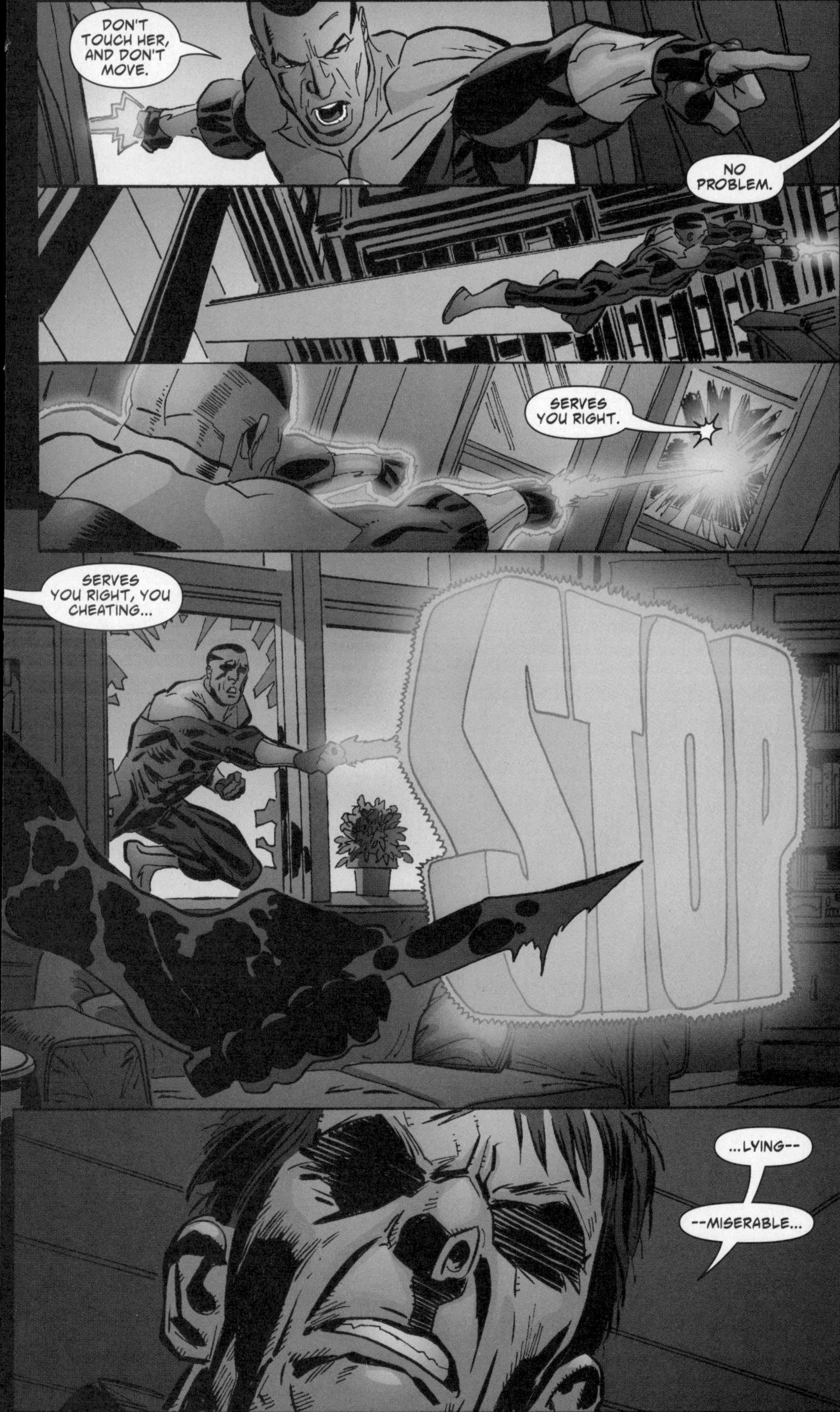
DON'T TOUCH HER, AND DON'T MOVE.
NO PROBLEM.
SERVES YOU RIGHT.
SERVES YOU RIGHT, YOU CHEATING...
STOP
...LYING--
--MISERABLE...

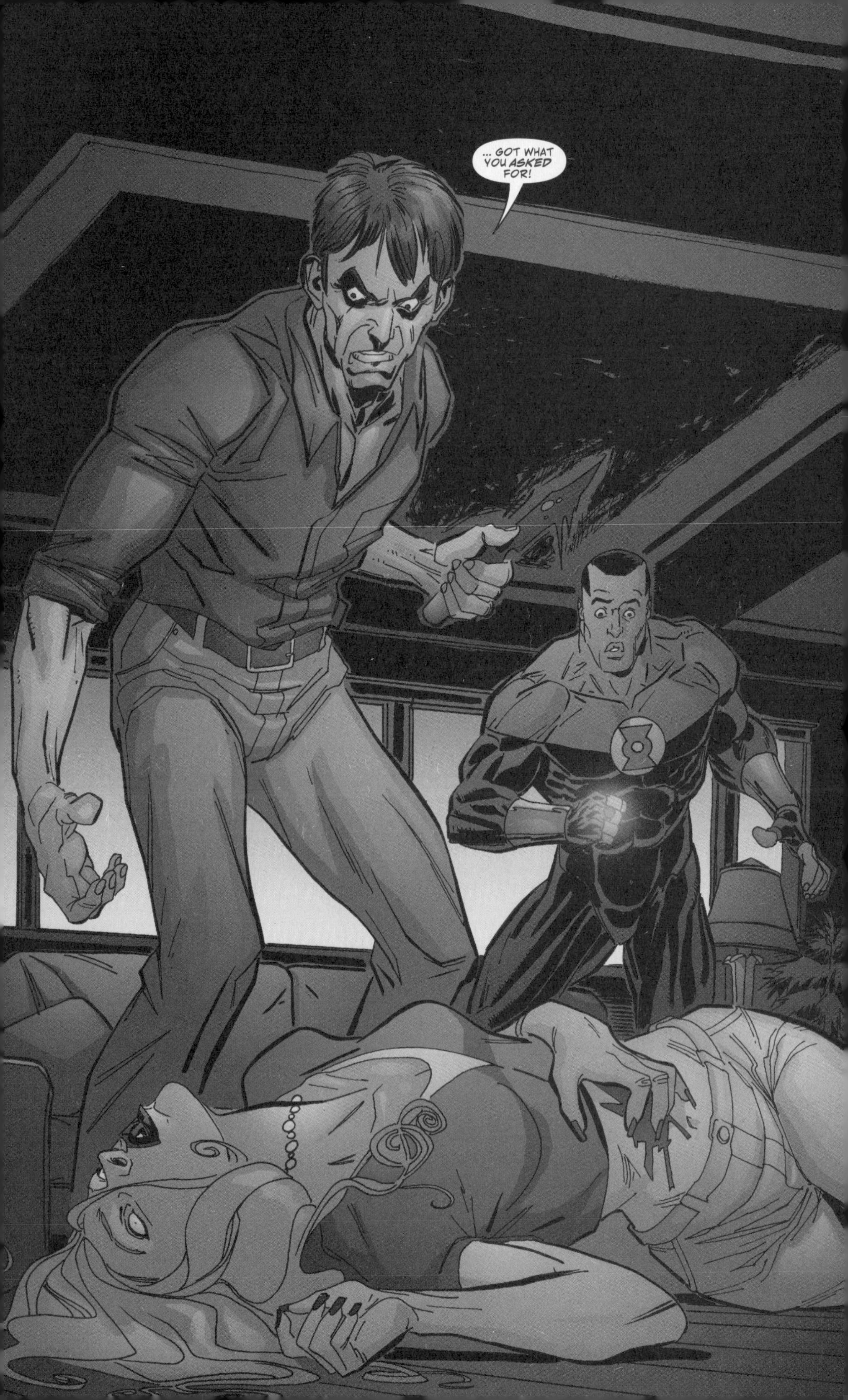
... GOT WHAT YOU ASKED FOR!

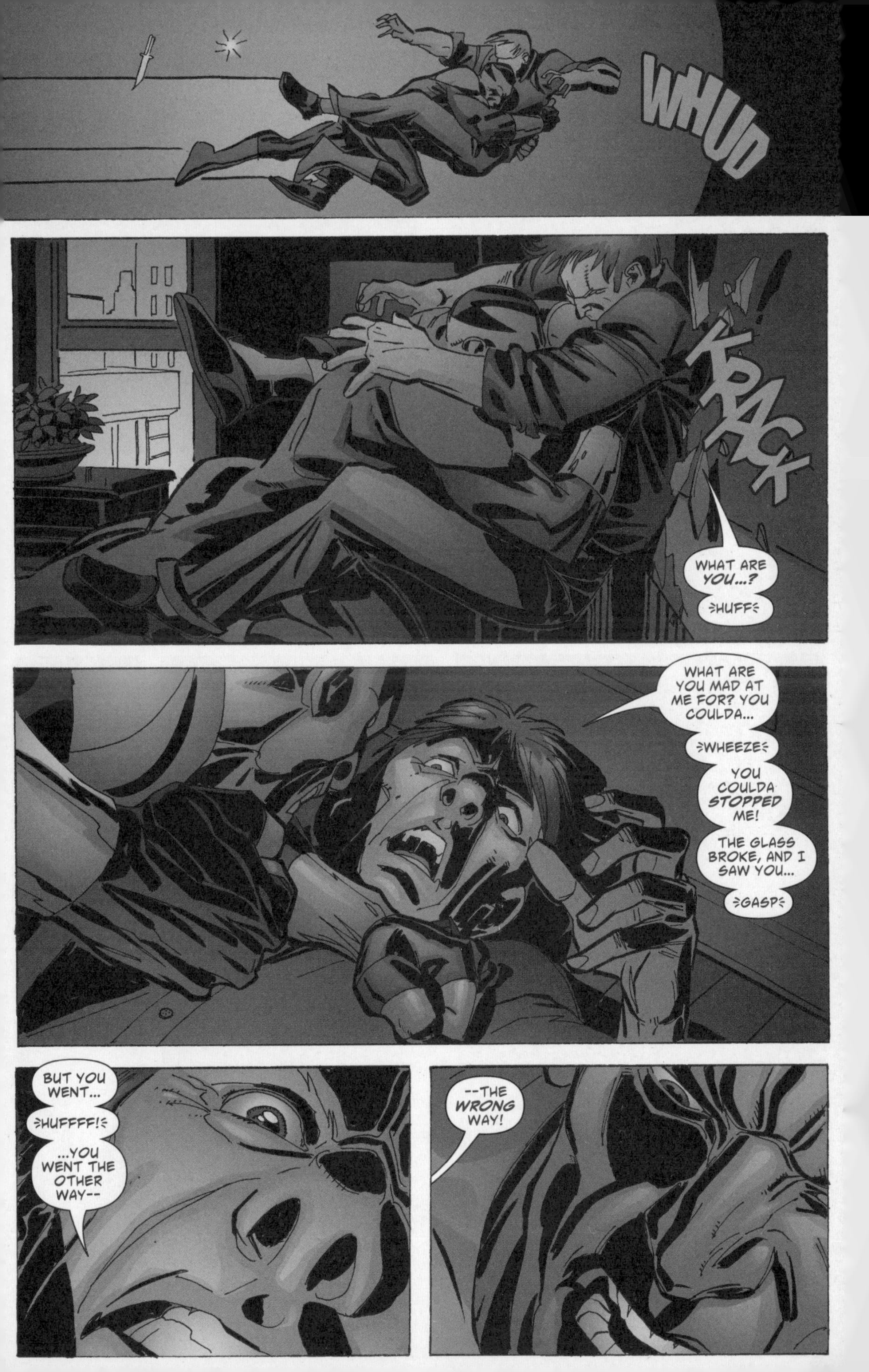
WHUD
KRACK
WHAT ARE YOU...?
HUFF
WHAT ARE YOU MAD AT ME FOR? YOU COULDA...
WHEEZE
YOU COULDA STOPPED ME!
THE GLASS BROKE, AND I SAW YOU...
GASP
BUT YOU WENT...
HUFFFF!
...YOU WENT THE OTHER WAY--
--THE WRONG WAY!

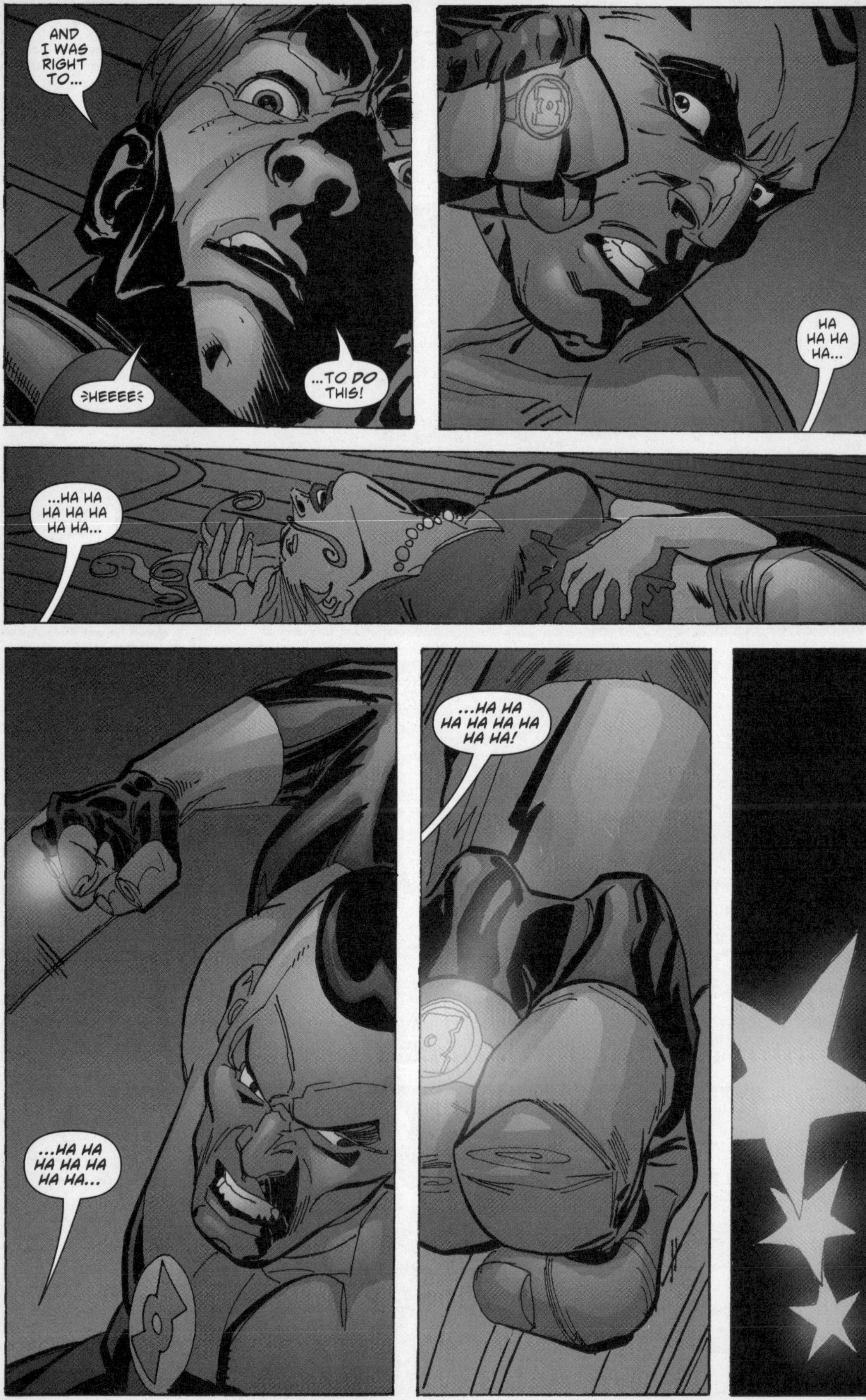
AND I WAS RIGHT TO...
HEEEE
...TO DO THIS!
HA HA HA HA...
...HA HA HA HA HA HA HA...
...HA HA HA HA HA HA HA...
...HA HA HA HA HA HA HA HA!

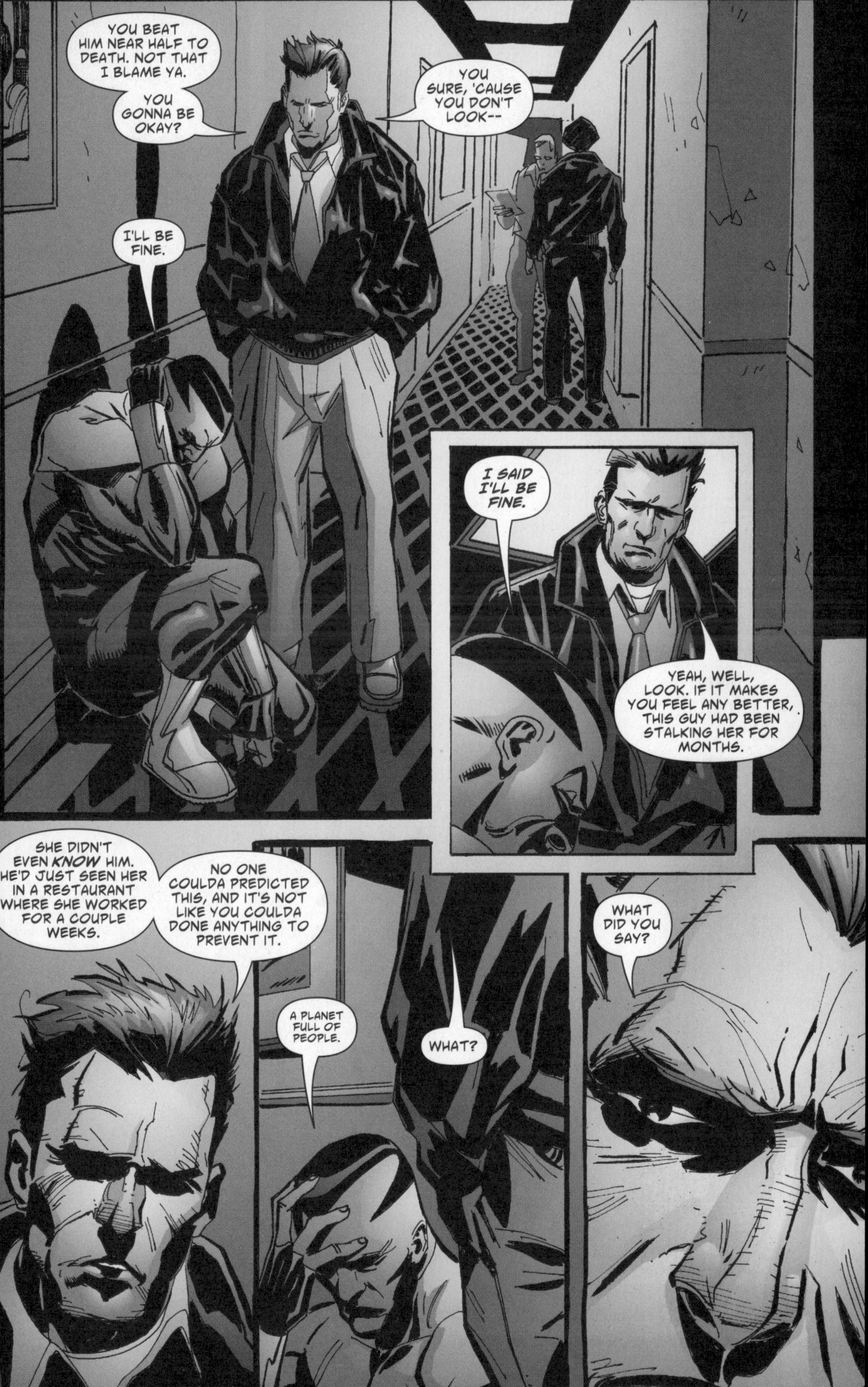
YOU BEAT HIM NEAR HALF TO DEATH. NOT THAT I BLAME YA.
YOU GONNA BE OKAY?
YOU SURE, 'CAUSE YOU DON'T LOOK--
I'LL BE FINE.
I SAID I'LL BE FINE.
YEAH, WELL, LOOK. IF IT MAKES YOU FEEL ANY BETTER, THIS GUY HAD BEEN STALKING HER FOR MONTHS.
SHE DIDN'T EVEN KNOW HIM. HE'D JUST SEEN HER IN A RESTAURANT WHERE SHE WORKED FOR A COUPLE WEEKS.
NO ONE COULDA PREDICTED THIS, AND IT'S NOT LIKE YOU COULDA DONE ANYTHING TO PREVENT IT.
A PLANET FULL OF PEOPLE.
WHAT?
WHAT DID YOU SAY?

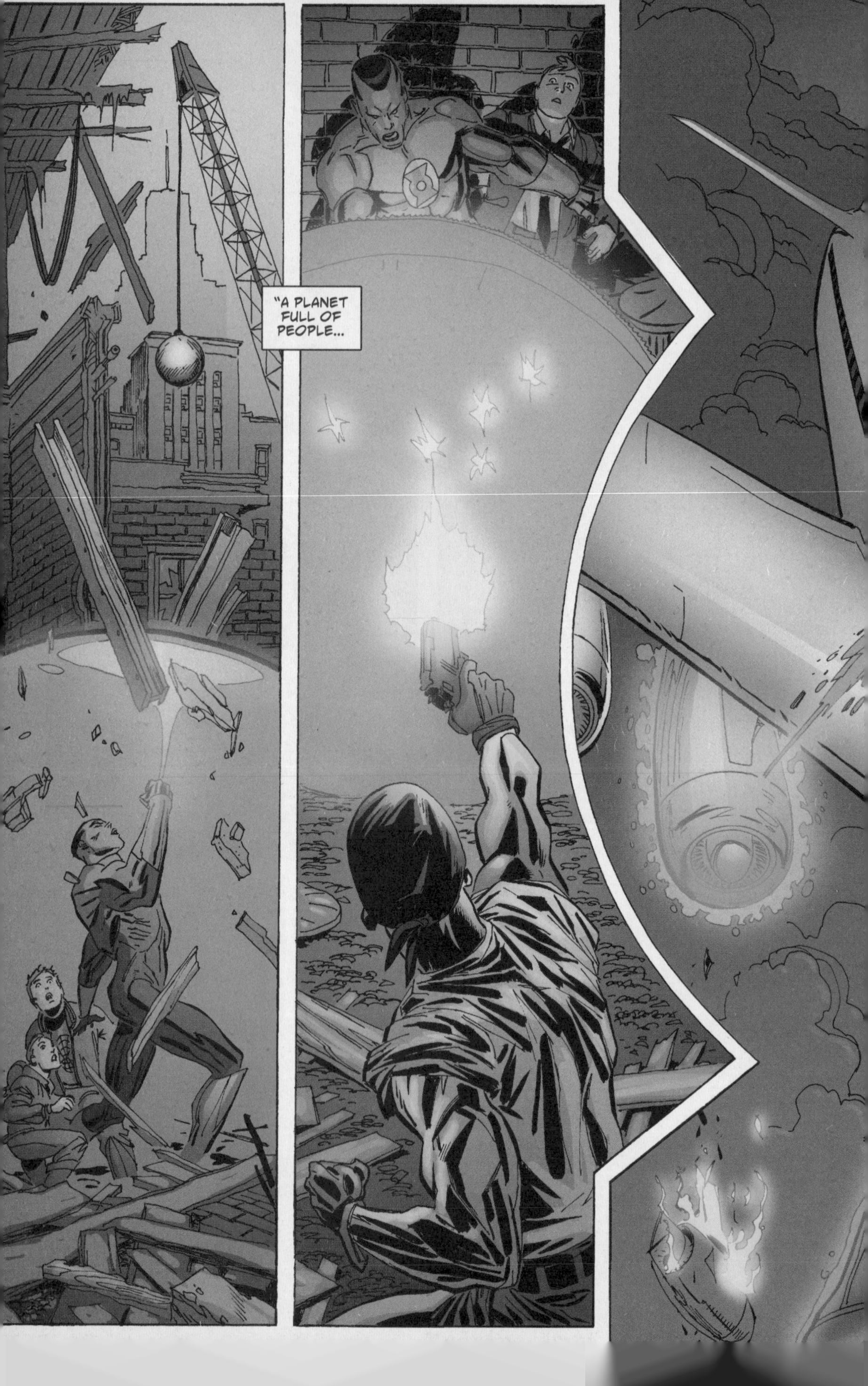
"A PLANET FULL OF PEOPLE...

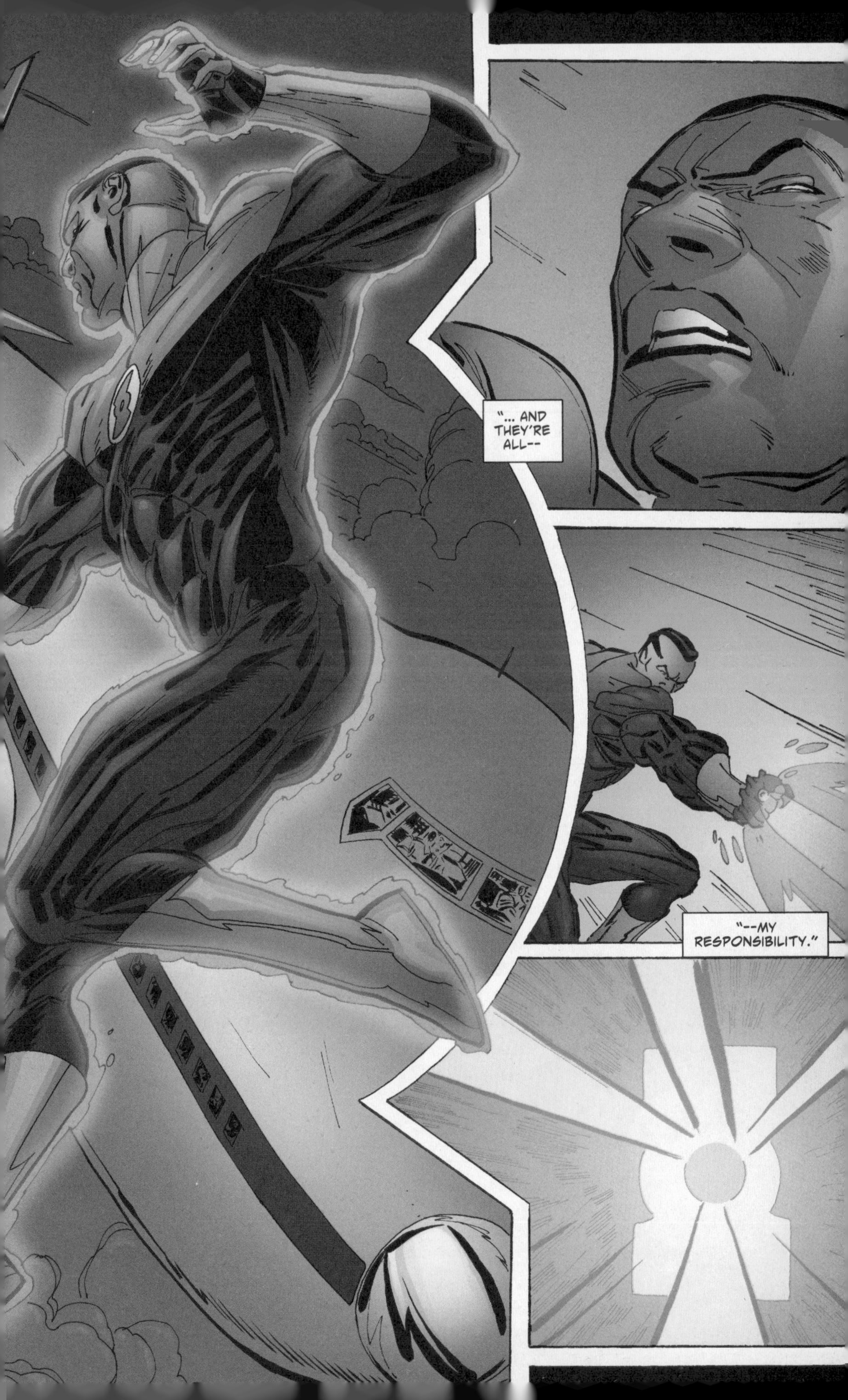
"... AND THEY'RE ALL--
"--MY RESPONSIBILITY."

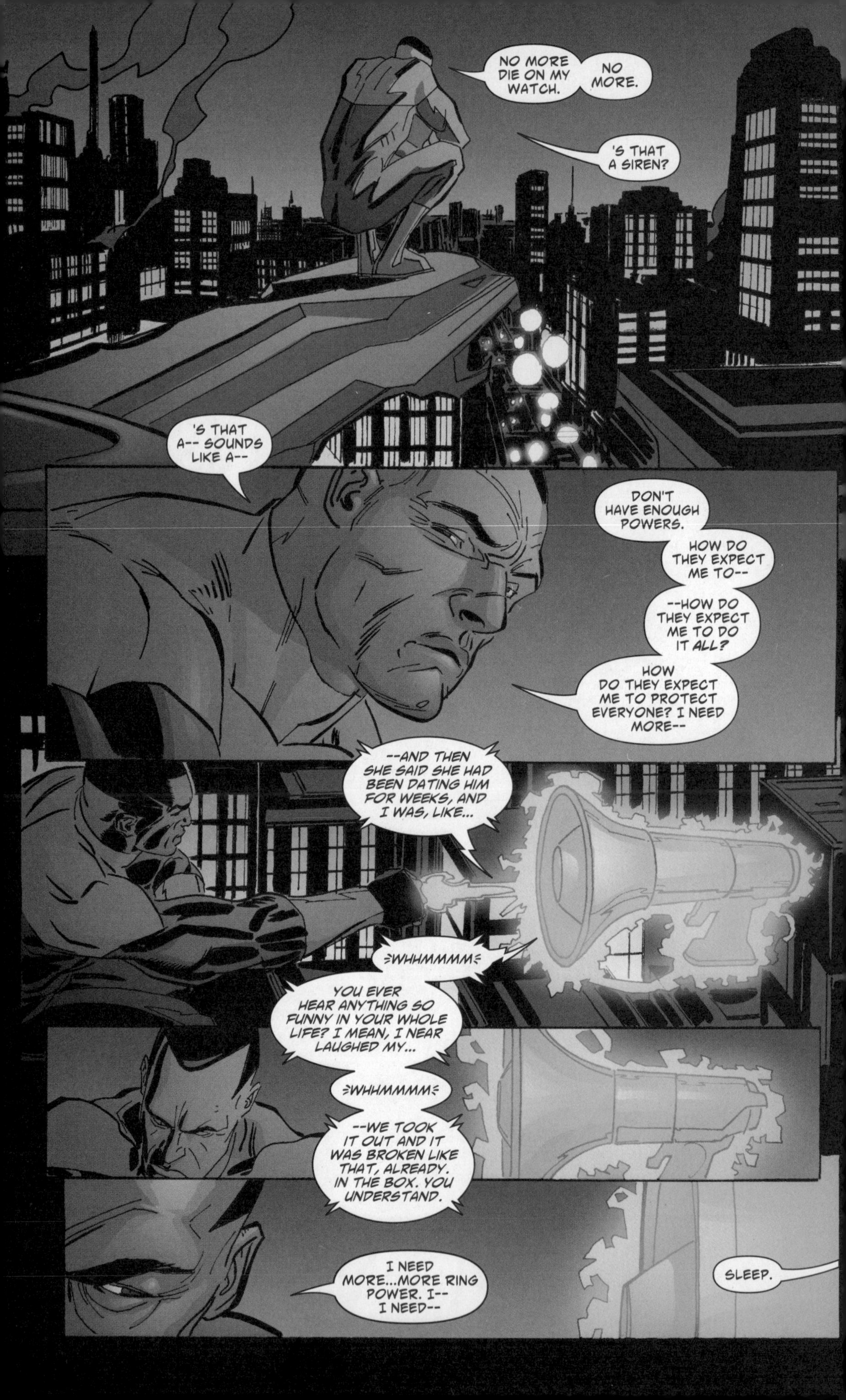
NO MORE DIE ON MY WATCH.
NO MORE.
'S THAT A SIREN?
'S THAT A-- SOUNDS LIKE A--
DON'T HAVE ENOUGH POWERS.
HOW DO THEY EXPECT ME TO--
--HOW DO THEY EXPECT ME TO DO IT ALL?
HOW DO THEY EXPECT ME TO PROTECT EVERYONE? I NEED MORE--
--AND THEN SHE SAID SHE HAD BEEN DATING HIM FOR WEEKS, AND I WAS, LIKE...
WHHMMMM
YOU EVER HEAR ANYTHING SO FUNNY IN YOUR WHOLE LIFE? I MEAN, I NEAR LAUGHED MY...
WHHMMMM
--WE TOOK IT OUT AND IT WAS BROKEN LIKE THAT, ALREADY. IN THE BOX. YOU UNDERSTAND.
I NEED MORE...MORE RING POWER. I-- I NEED--
SLEEP.

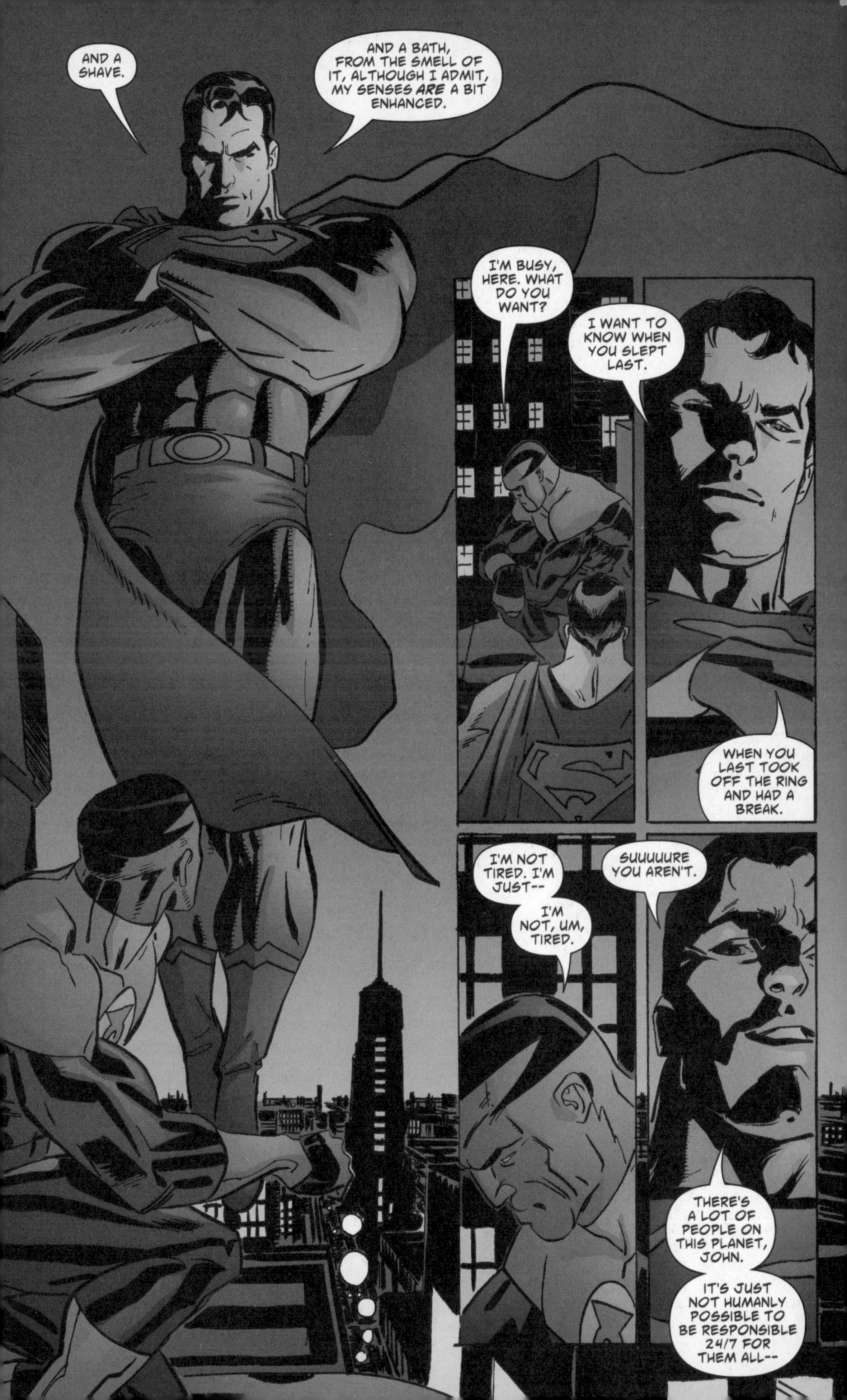
AND A SHAVE.
AND A BATH, FROM THE SMELL OF IT, ALTHOUGH I ADMIT, MY SENSES *ARE* A BIT ENHANCED.
I'M BUSY, HERE. WHAT DO YOU WANT?
I WANT TO KNOW WHEN YOU SLEPT LAST.
WHEN YOU LAST TOOK OFF THE RING AND HAD A BREAK.
I'M NOT TIRED. I'M JUST--
I'M NOT, UM, TIRED.
SUUUUURE YOU AREN'T.
THERE'S A LOT OF PEOPLE ON THIS PLANET, JOHN.
IT'S JUST NOT HUMANLY POSSIBLE TO BE RESPONSIBLE 24/7 FOR THEM ALL--

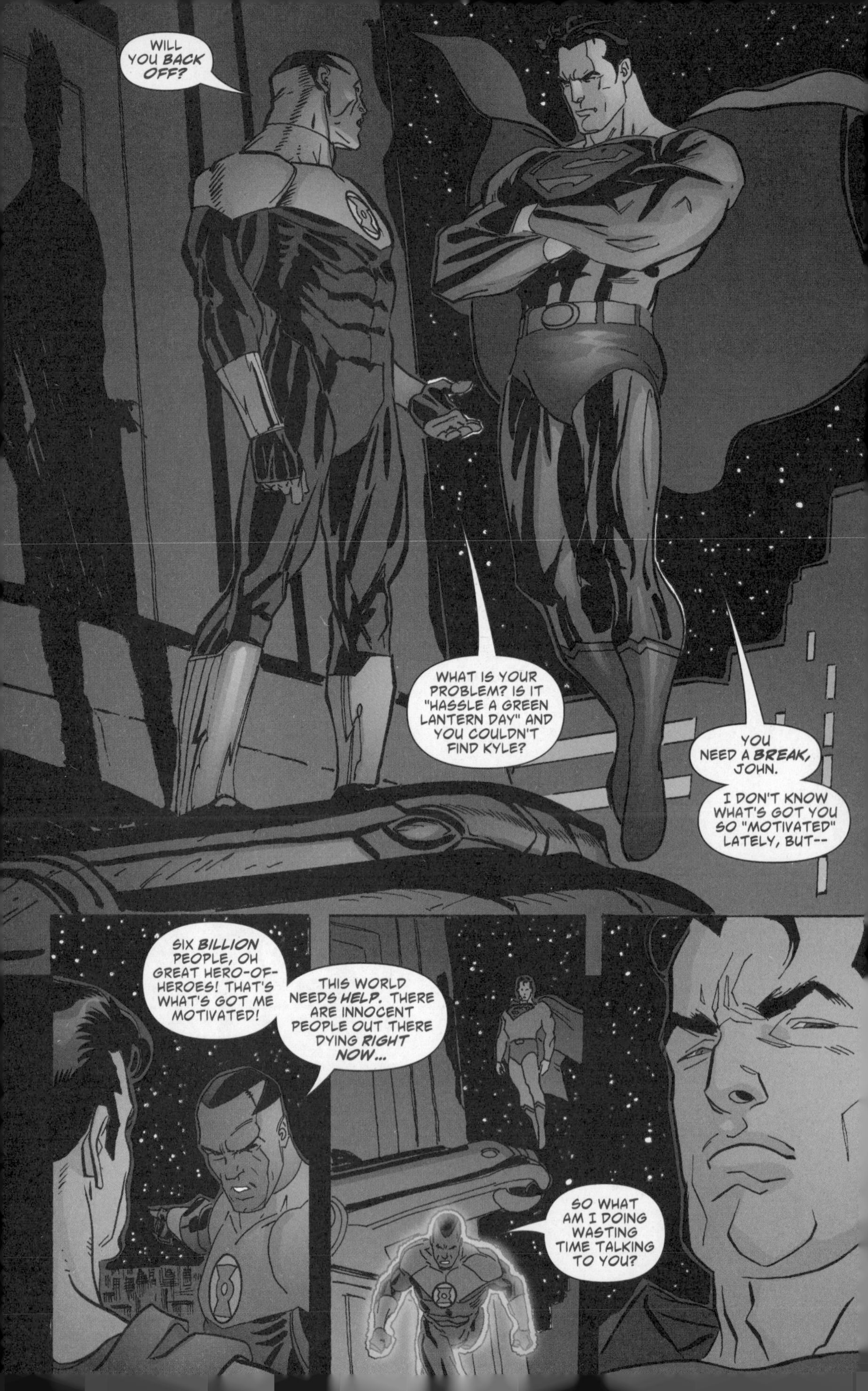
WILL YOU BACK OFF?
WHAT IS YOUR PROBLEM? IS IT "HASSLE A GREEN LANTERN DAY" AND YOU COULDN'T FIND KYLE?
YOU NEED A BREAK, JOHN.
I DON'T KNOW WHAT'S GOT YOU SO "MOTIVATED" LATELY, BUT--
SIX BILLION PEOPLE, OH GREAT HERO-OF-HEROES! THAT'S WHAT'S GOT ME MOTIVATED!
THIS WORLD NEEDS HELP. THERE ARE INNOCENT PEOPLE OUT THERE DYING RIGHT NOW...
SO WHAT AM I DOING WASTING TIME TALKING TO YOU?

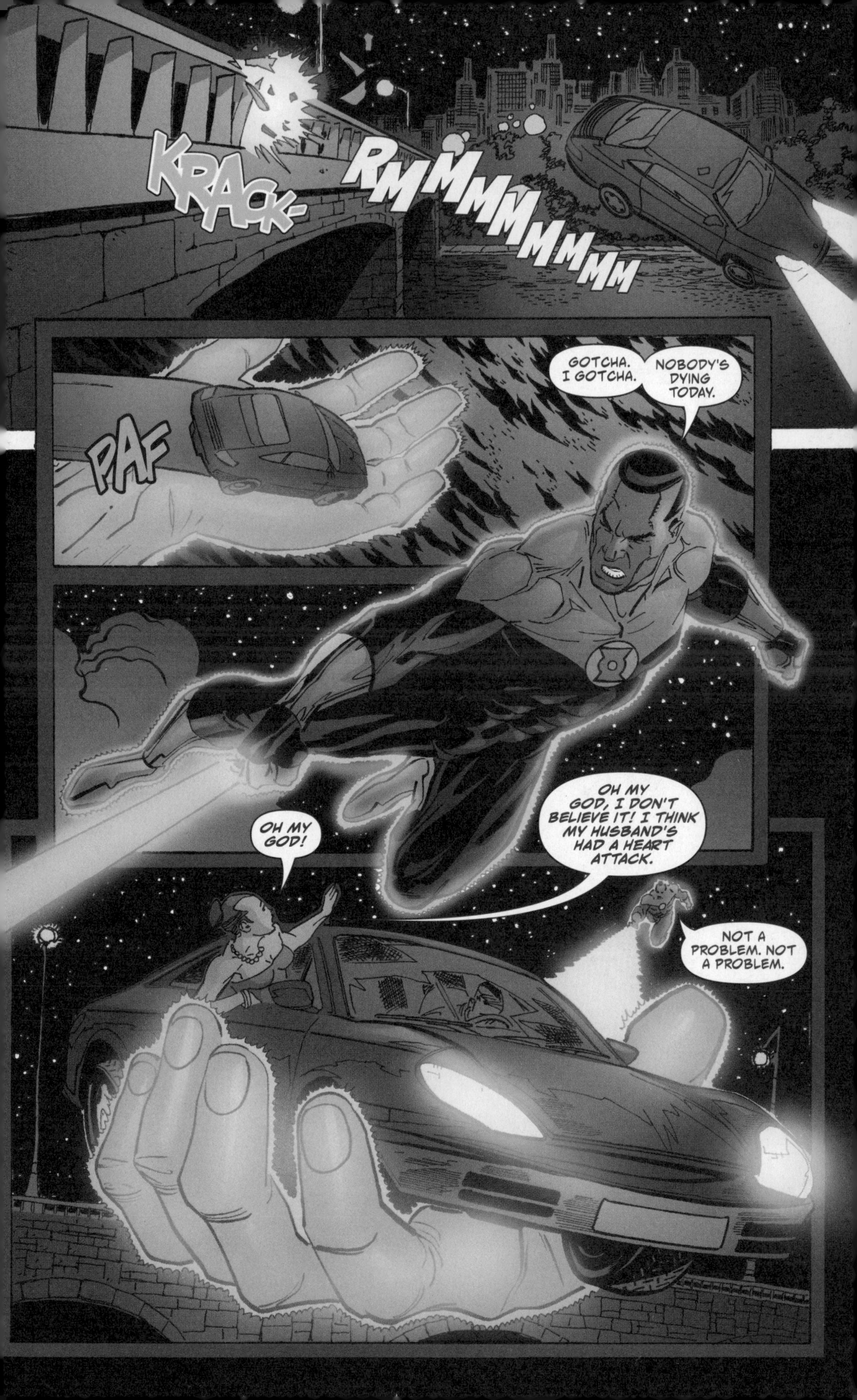
KRACK-
RMMMMMMMMMM
PAF
GOTCHA. I GOTCHA.
NOBODY'S DYING TODAY.
OH MY GOD!
OH MY GOD, I DON'T BELIEVE IT! I THINK MY HUSBAND'S HAD A HEART ATTACK.
NOT A PROBLEM. NOT A PROBLEM.

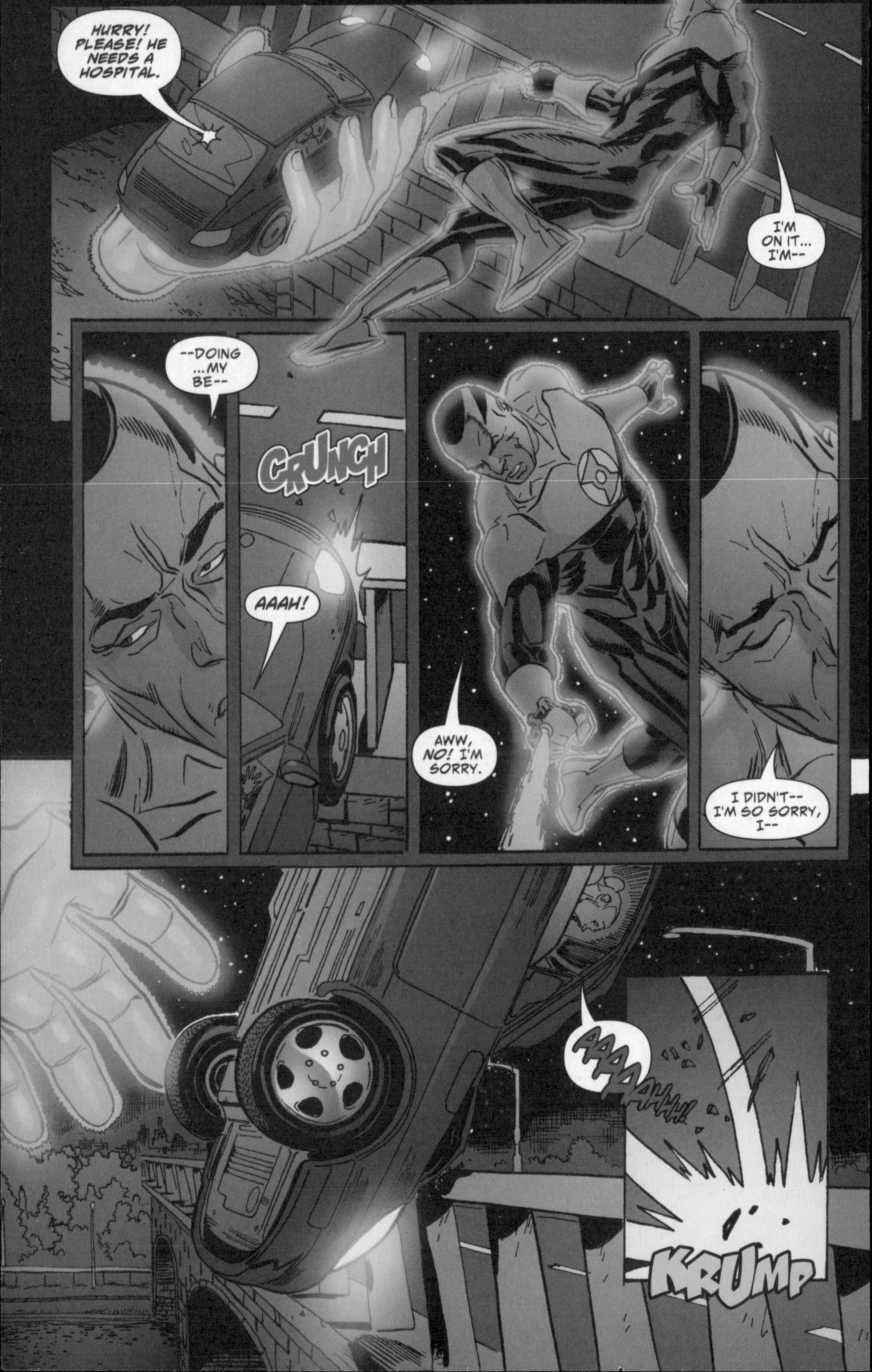
HURRY! PLEASE! HE NEEDS A HOSPITAL.
I'M ON IT... I'M--
--DOING ...MY BE--
CRUNCH
AAAH!
AWW, NO! I'M SORRY.
I DIDN'T-- I'M SO SORRY, I--
AAAAAHH!
KRUMP

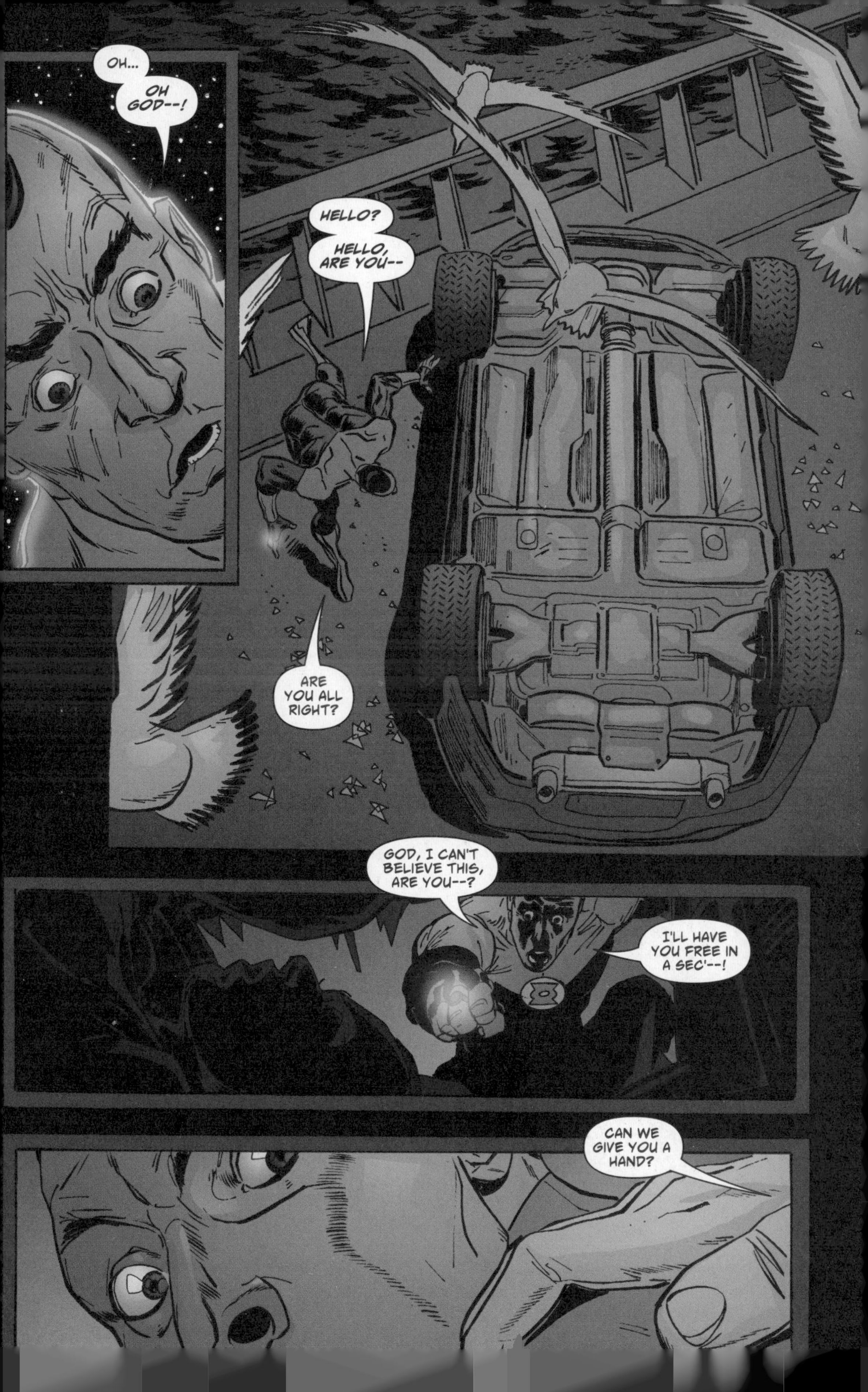
OH...
OH GOD--!
HELLO?
HELLO, ARE YOU--
ARE YOU ALL RIGHT?
GOD, I CAN'T BELIEVE THIS, ARE YOU--?
I'LL HAVE YOU FREE IN A SEC'--!
CAN WE GIVE YOU A HAND?

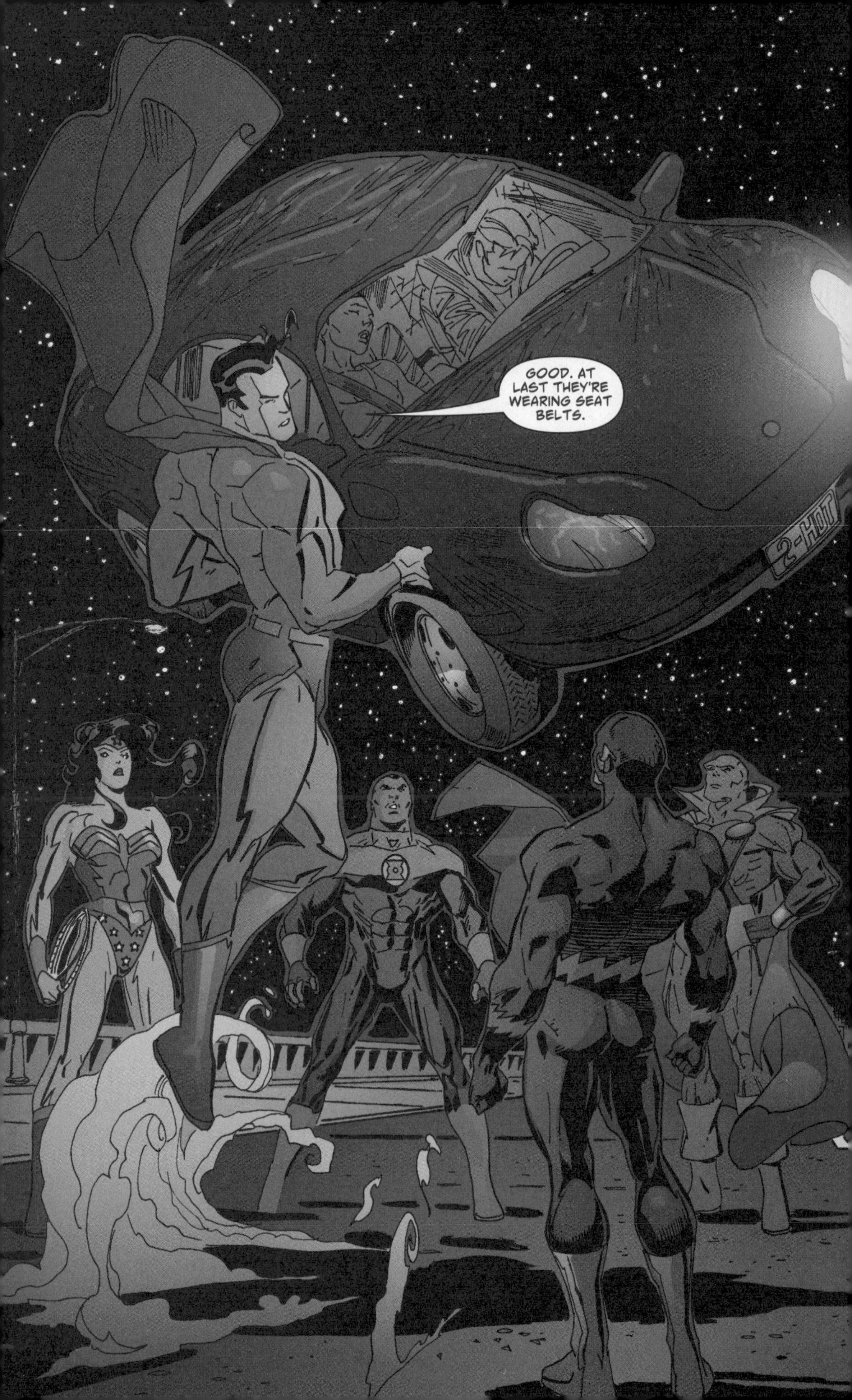
GOOD. AT LAST THEY'RE WEARING SEAT BELTS.
2-HOT

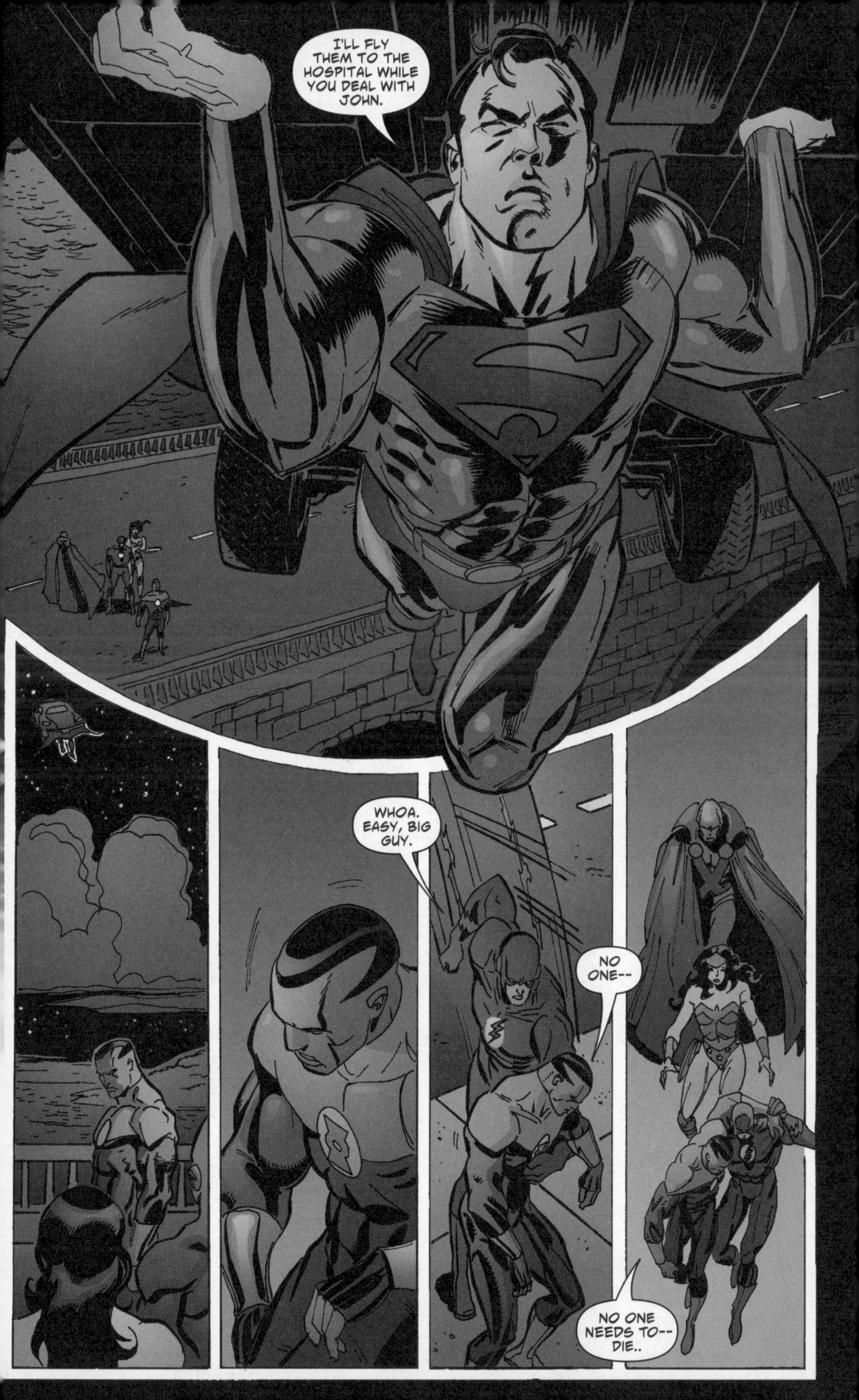
I'LL FLY THEM TO THE HOSPITAL WHILE YOU DEAL WITH JOHN.
WHOA. EASY, BIG GUY.
NO ONE--
NO ONE NEEDS TO-- DIE..

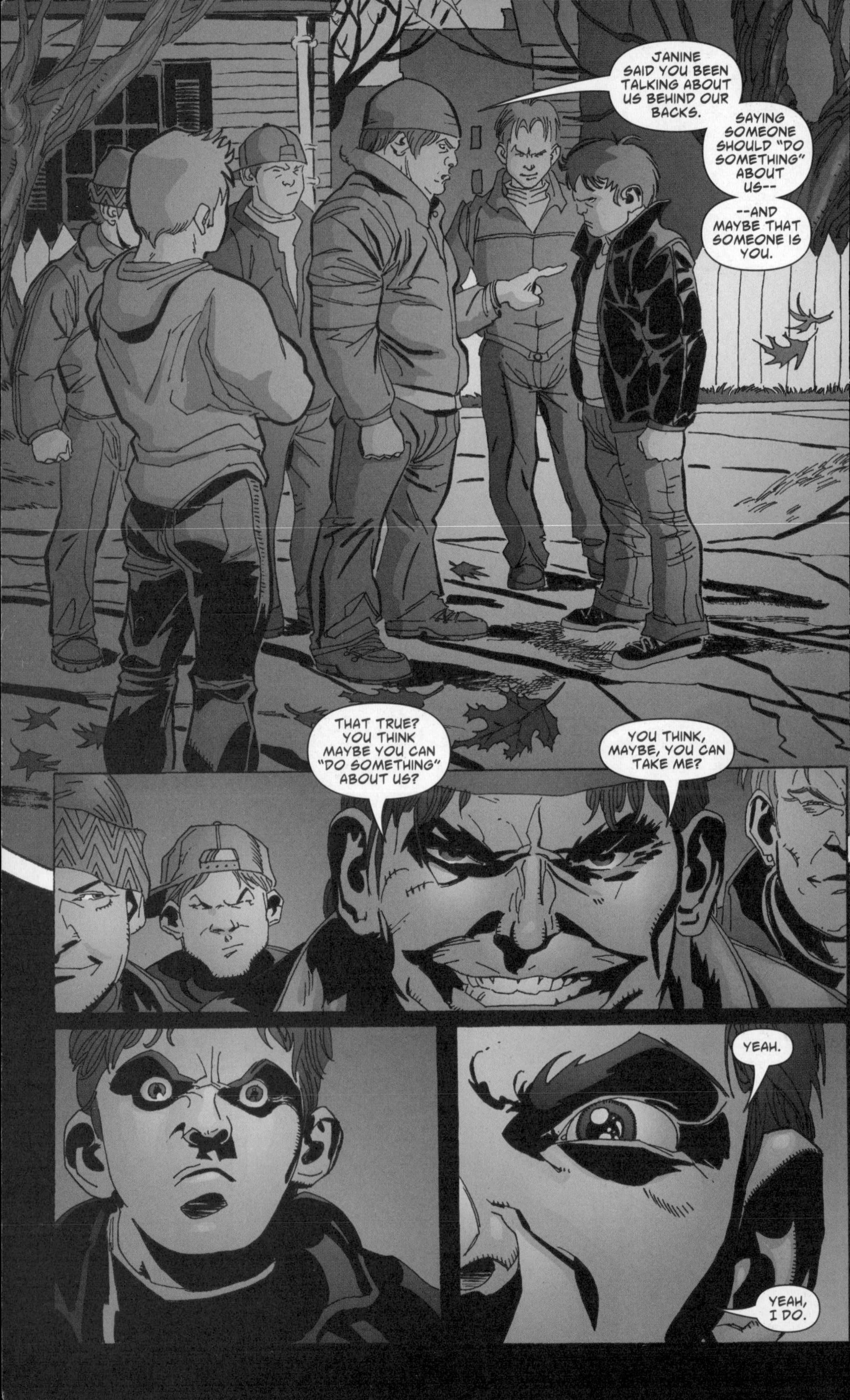
JANINE SAID YOU BEEN TALKING ABOUT US BEHIND OUR BACKS.
SAYING SOMEONE SHOULD "DO SOMETHING" ABOUT US--
--AND MAYBE THAT SOMEONE IS YOU.
THAT TRUE? YOU THINK MAYBE YOU CAN "DO SOMETHING" ABOUT US?
YOU THINK, MAYBE, YOU CAN TAKE ME?
YEAH.
YEAH, I DO.

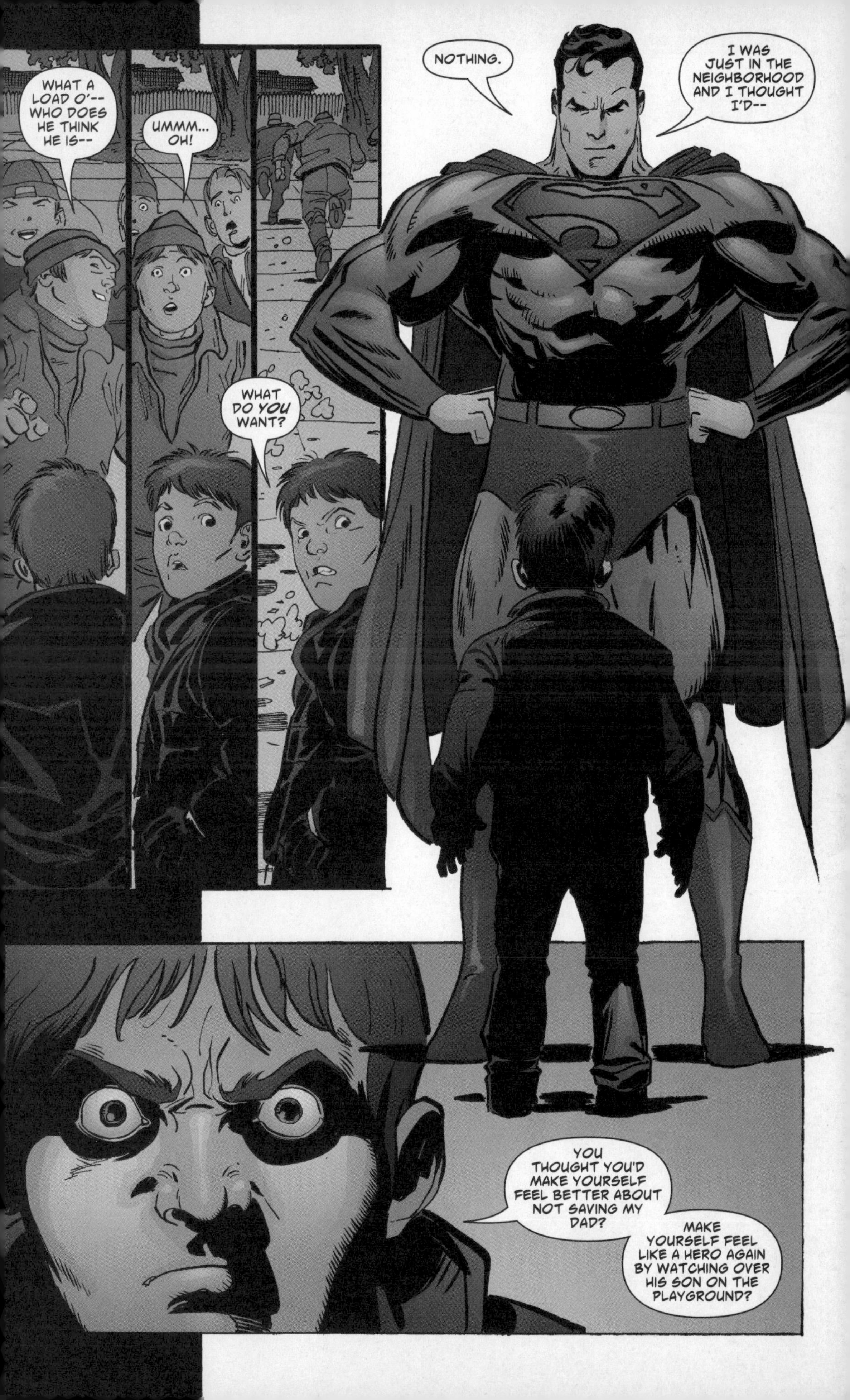
WHAT A LOAD O'-- WHO DOES HE THINK HE IS--
UMMM... OH!
WHAT DO YOU WANT?
NOTHING.
I WAS JUST IN THE NEIGHBORHOOD AND I THOUGHT I'D--
YOU THOUGHT YOU'D MAKE YOURSELF FEEL BETTER ABOUT NOT SAVING MY DAD?
MAKE YOURSELF FEEL LIKE A HERO AGAIN BY WATCHING OVER HIS SON ON THE PLAYGROUND?

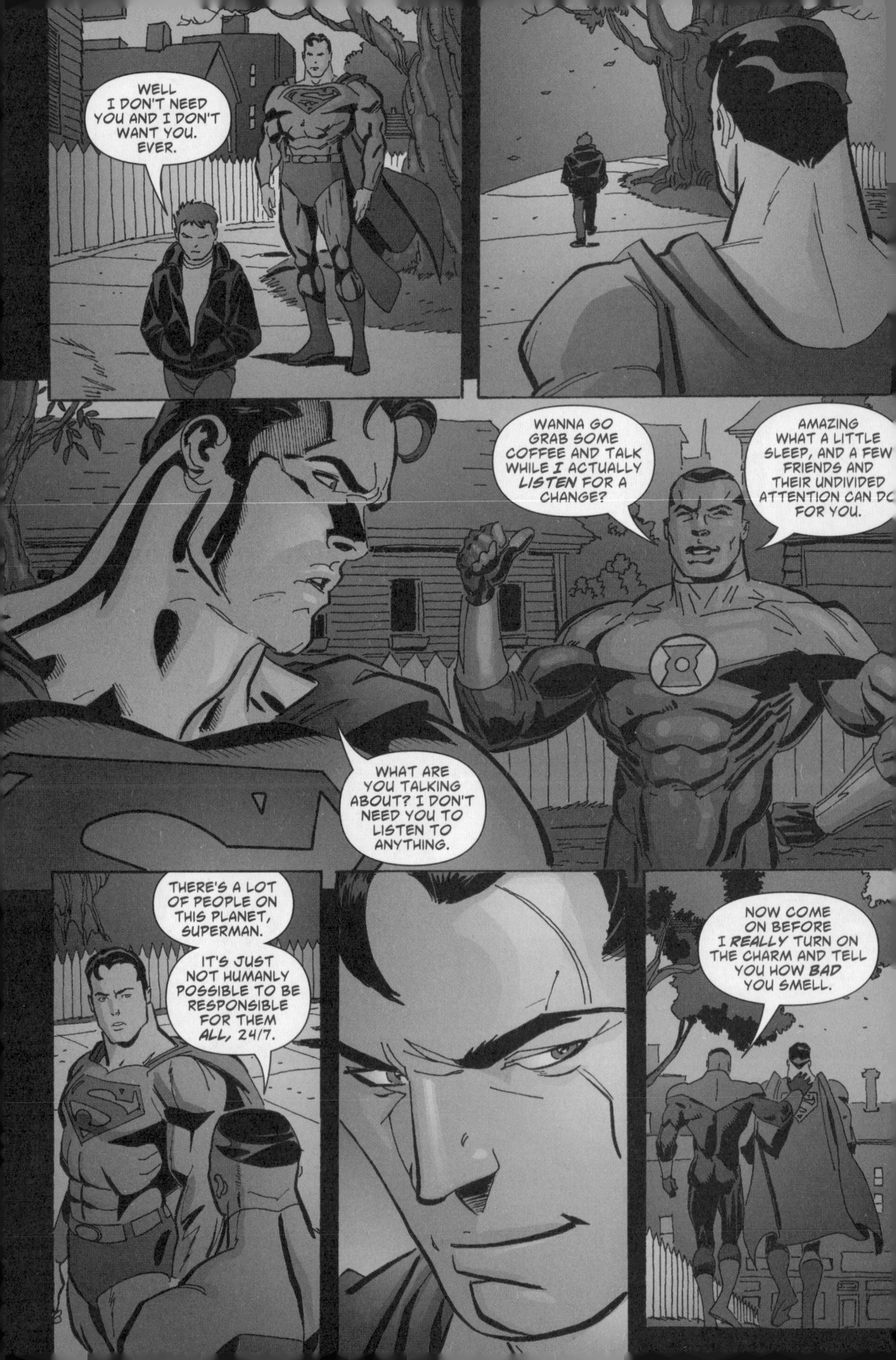
WELL I DON'T NEED YOU AND I DON'T WANT YOU. EVER.
WANNA GO GRAB SOME COFFEE AND TALK WHILE *I* ACTUALLY *LISTEN* FOR A CHANGE?
AMAZING WHAT A LITTLE SLEEP, AND A FEW FRIENDS AND THEIR UNDIVIDED ATTENTION CAN DO FOR YOU.
WHAT ARE YOU TALKING ABOUT? I DON'T NEED YOU TO LISTEN TO ANYTHING.
THERE'S A LOT OF PEOPLE ON THIS PLANET, SUPERMAN.
IT'S JUST NOT HUMANLY POSSIBLE TO BE RESPONSIBLE FOR THEM *ALL*, 24/7.
NOW COME ON BEFORE I *REALLY* TURN ON THE CHARM AND TELL YOU HOW *BAD* YOU SMELL.

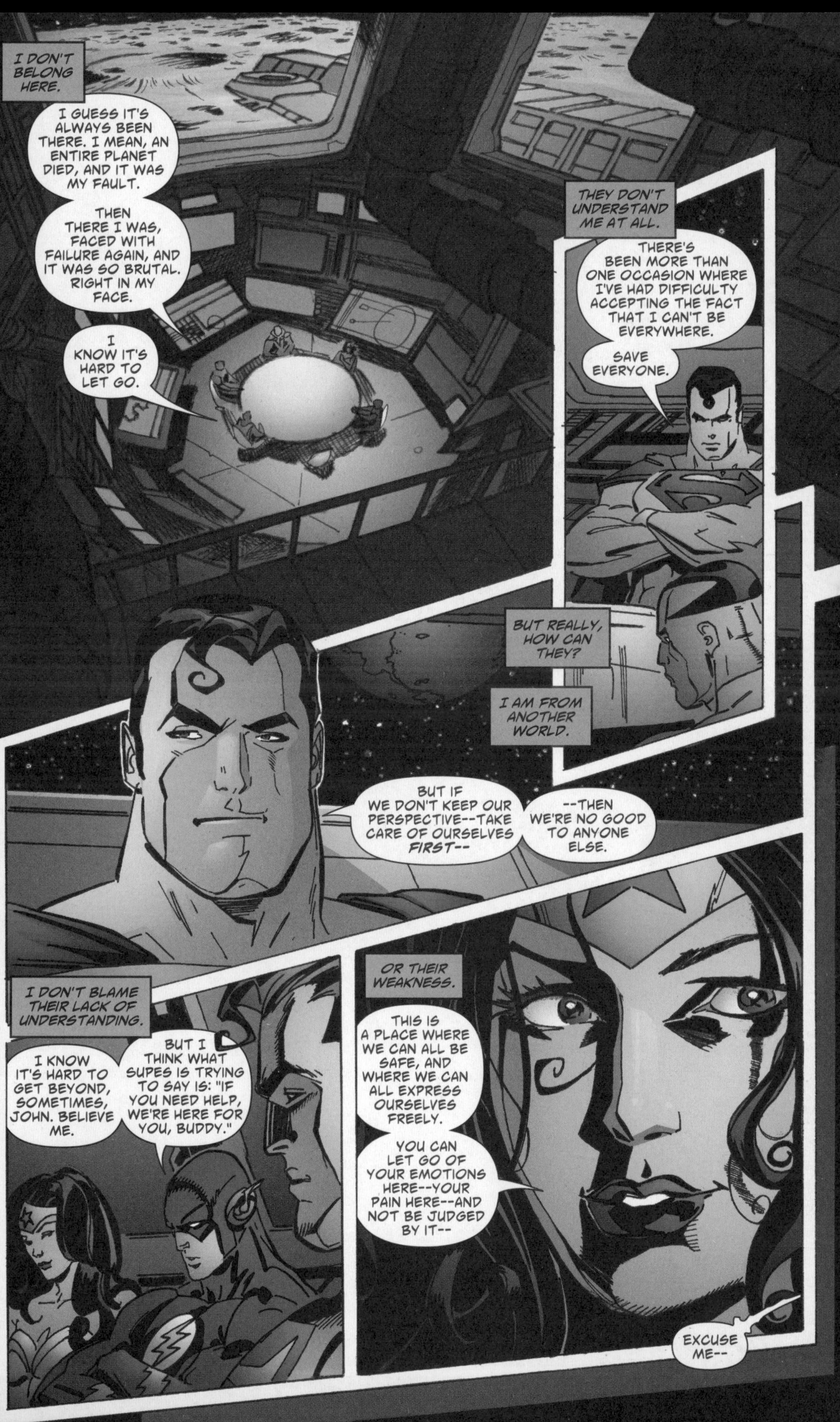
I DON'T BELONG HERE.
I GUESS IT'S ALWAYS BEEN THERE. I MEAN, AN ENTIRE PLANET DIED, AND IT WAS MY FAULT.
THEN THERE I WAS, FACED WITH FAILURE AGAIN, AND IT WAS SO BRUTAL. RIGHT IN MY FACE.
I KNOW IT'S HARD TO LET GO.
THEY DON'T UNDERSTAND ME AT ALL.
THERE'S BEEN MORE THAN ONE OCCASION WHERE I'VE HAD DIFFICULTY ACCEPTING THE FACT THAT I CAN'T BE EVERYWHERE.
SAVE EVERYONE.
BUT REALLY, HOW CAN THEY?
I AM FROM ANOTHER WORLD.
BUT IF WE DON'T KEEP OUR PERSPECTIVE--TAKE CARE OF OURSELVES *FIRST*--
--THEN WE'RE NO GOOD TO ANYONE ELSE.
I DON'T BLAME THEIR LACK OF UNDERSTANDING.
I KNOW IT'S HARD TO GET BEYOND, SOMETIMES, JOHN. BELIEVE ME.
BUT I THINK WHAT SUPES IS TRYING TO SAY IS: "IF YOU NEED HELP, WE'RE HERE FOR YOU, BUDDY."
OR THEIR WEAKNESS.
THIS IS A PLACE WHERE WE CAN ALL BE SAFE, AND WHERE WE CAN ALL EXPRESS OURSELVES FREELY.
YOU CAN LET GO OF YOUR EMOTIONS HERE--YOUR PAIN HERE--AND NOT BE JUDGED BY IT--
EXCUSE ME--

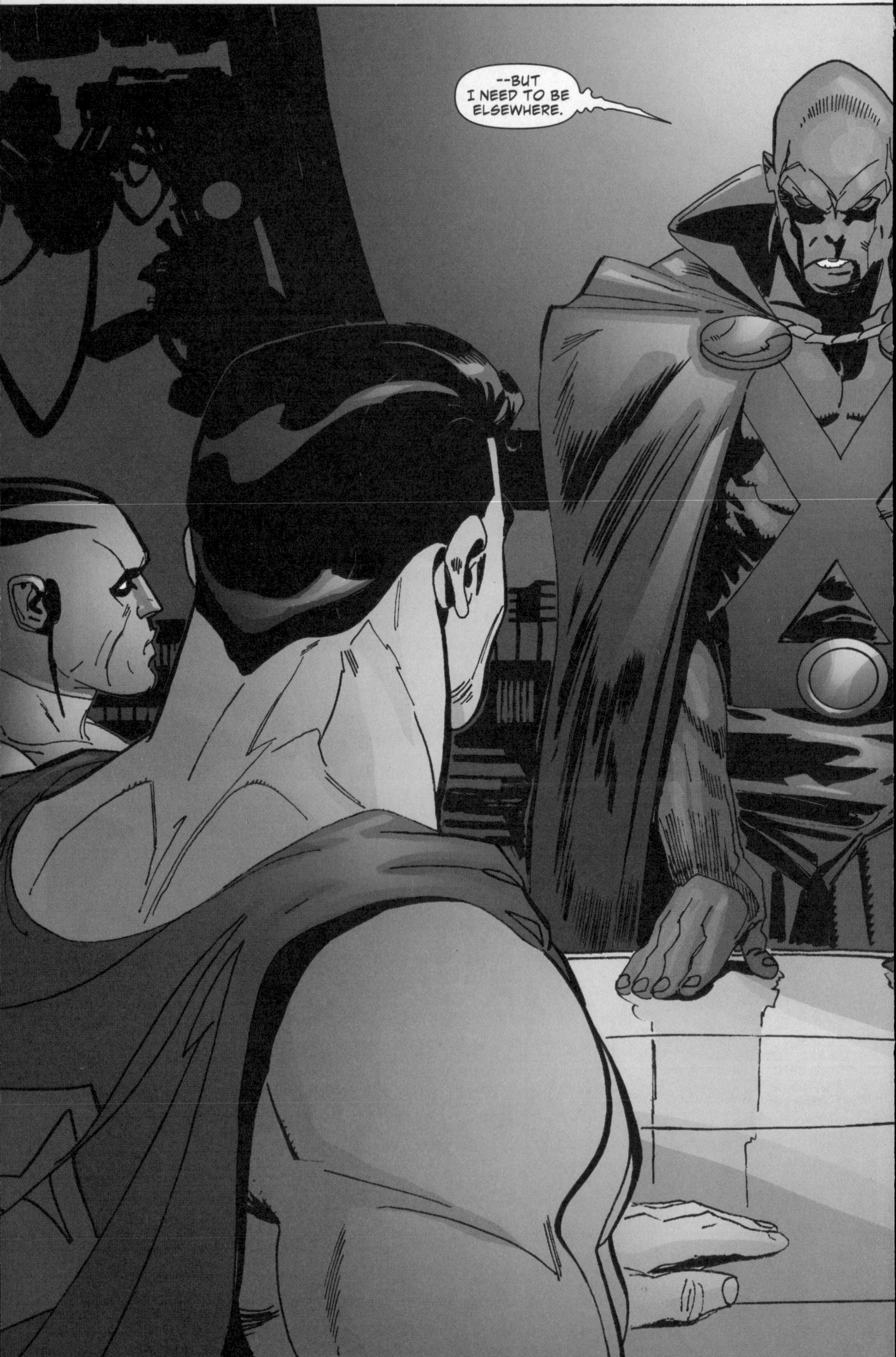
--BUT I NEED TO BE ELSEWHERE.

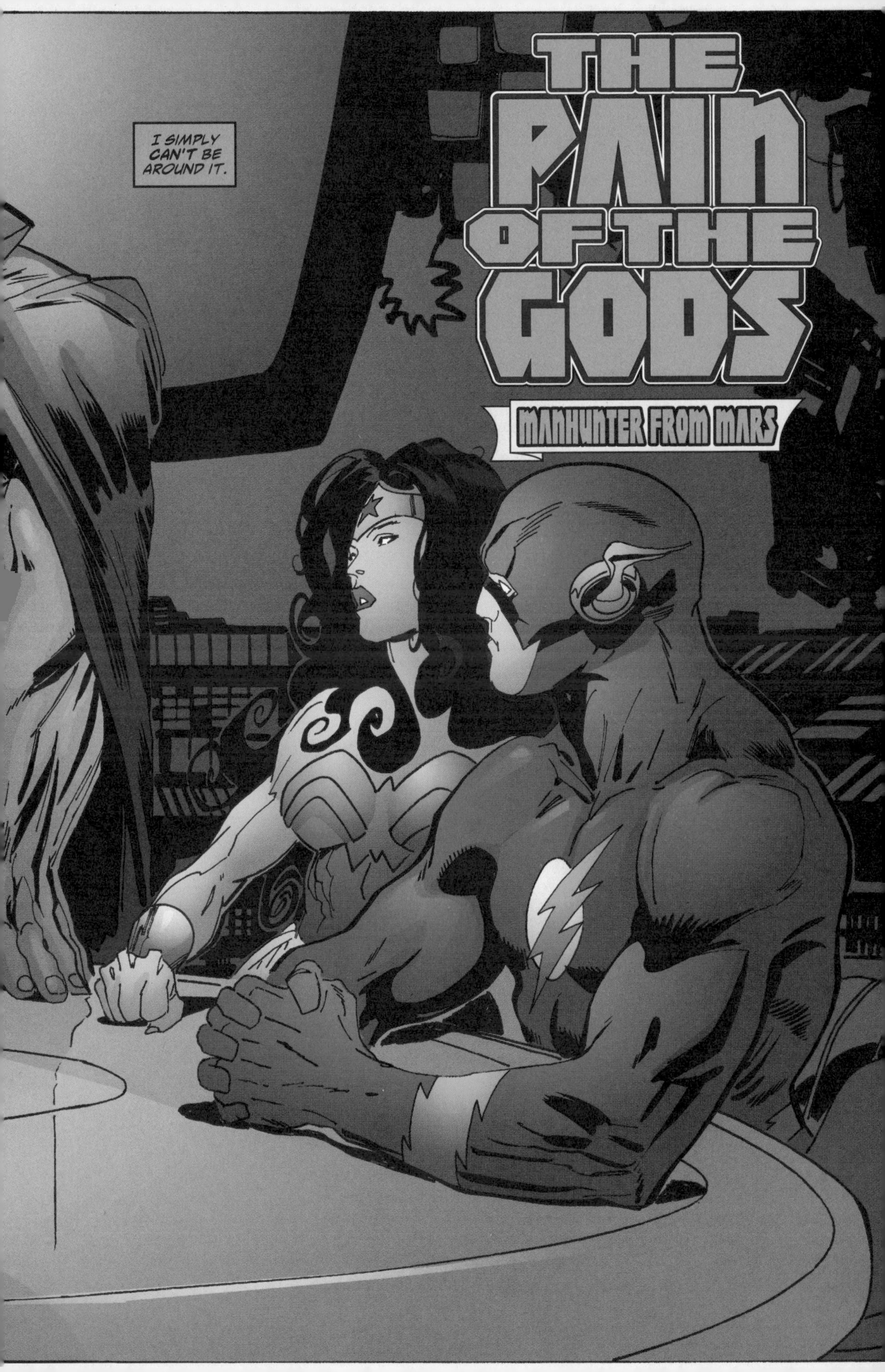
I SIMPLY CAN'T BE AROUND IT.
THE PAIN OF THE GODS
MANHUNTER FROM MARS

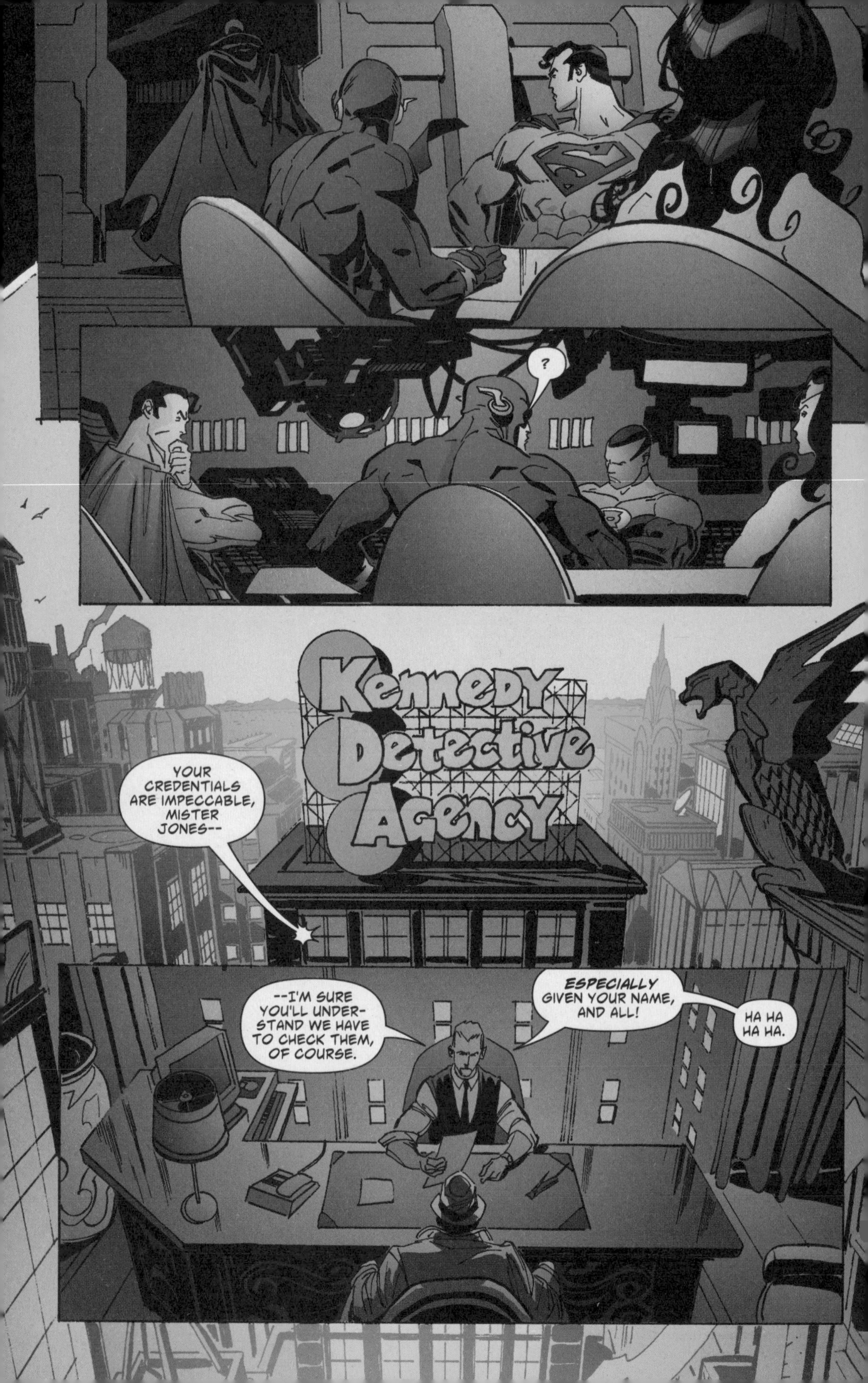
?
Kennedy Detective Agency
YOUR CREDENTIALS ARE IMPECCABLE, MISTER JONES--
--I'M SURE YOU'LL UNDERSTAND WE HAVE TO CHECK THEM, OF COURSE.
ESPECIALLY GIVEN YOUR NAME, AND ALL!
HA HA HA HA.

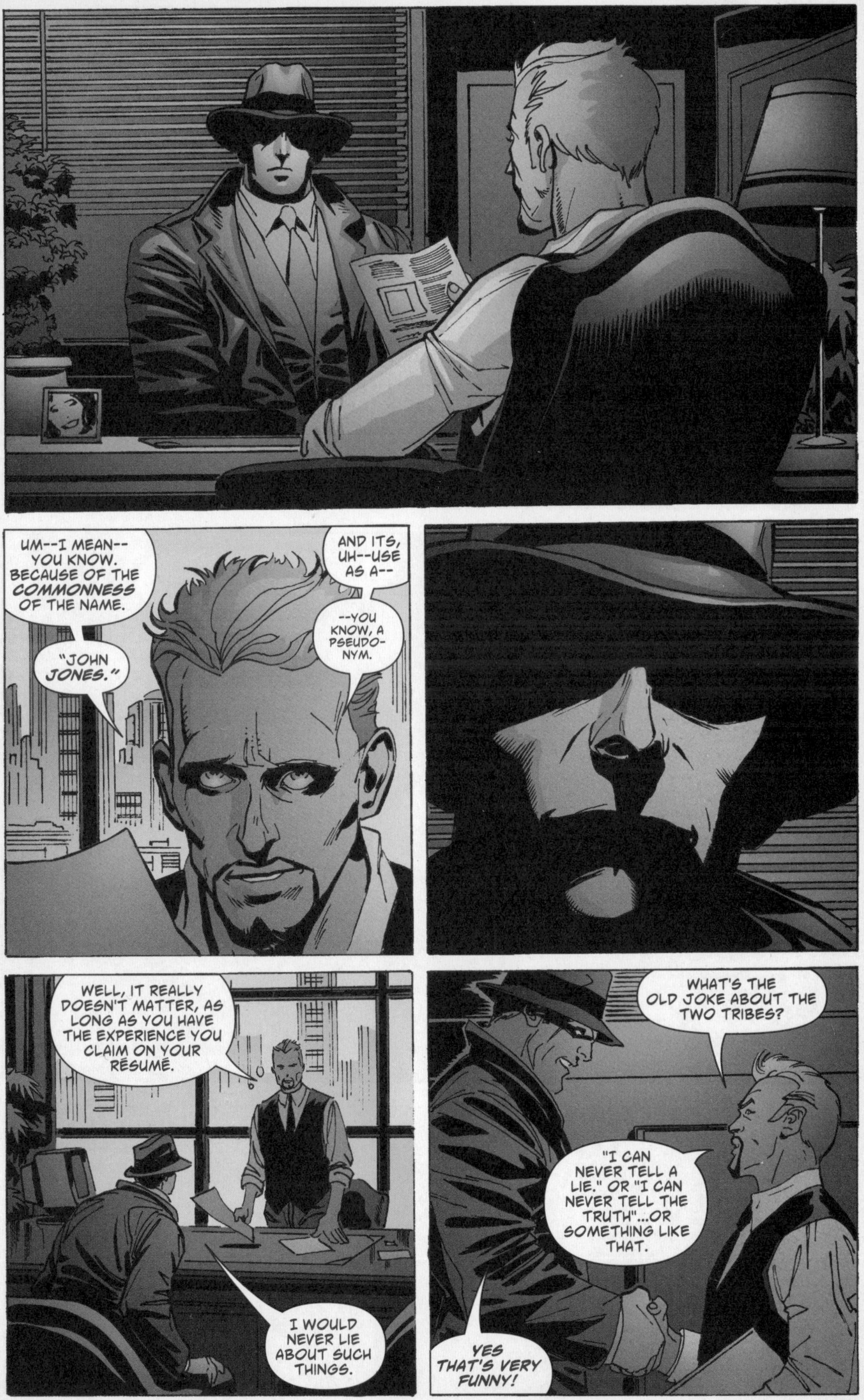
UM--I MEAN-- YOU KNOW. BECAUSE OF THE COMMONNESS OF THE NAME.
"JOHN JONES."
AND ITS, UH--USE AS A--
--YOU KNOW, A PSEUDONYM.
WELL, IT REALLY DOESN'T MATTER, AS LONG AS YOU HAVE THE EXPERIENCE YOU CLAIM ON YOUR RÉSUMÉ.
I WOULD NEVER LIE ABOUT SUCH THINGS.
WHAT'S THE OLD JOKE ABOUT THE TWO TRIBES?
"I CAN NEVER TELL A LIE." OR "I CAN NEVER TELL THE TRUTH"...OR SOMETHING LIKE THAT.
YES THAT'S VERY FUNNY!

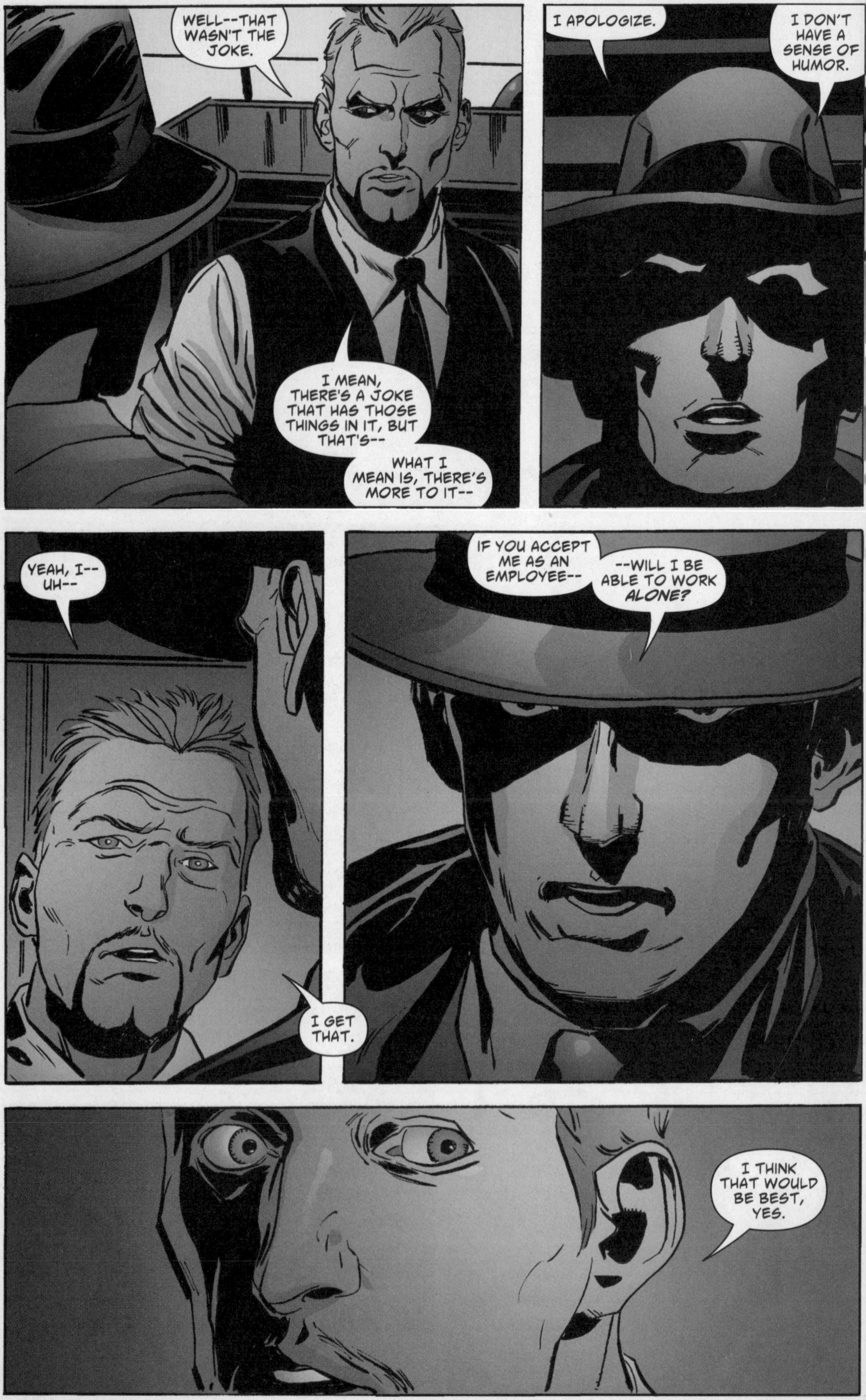
WELL--THAT WASN'T THE JOKE.
I MEAN, THERE'S A JOKE THAT HAS THOSE THINGS IN IT, BUT THAT'S--
WHAT I MEAN IS, THERE'S MORE TO IT--
I APOLOGIZE.
I DON'T HAVE A SENSE OF HUMOR.
YEAH, I-- UH--
I GET THAT.
IF YOU ACCEPT ME AS AN EMPLOYEE--
--WILL I BE ABLE TO WORK *ALONE?*
I THINK THAT WOULD BE BEST, YES.

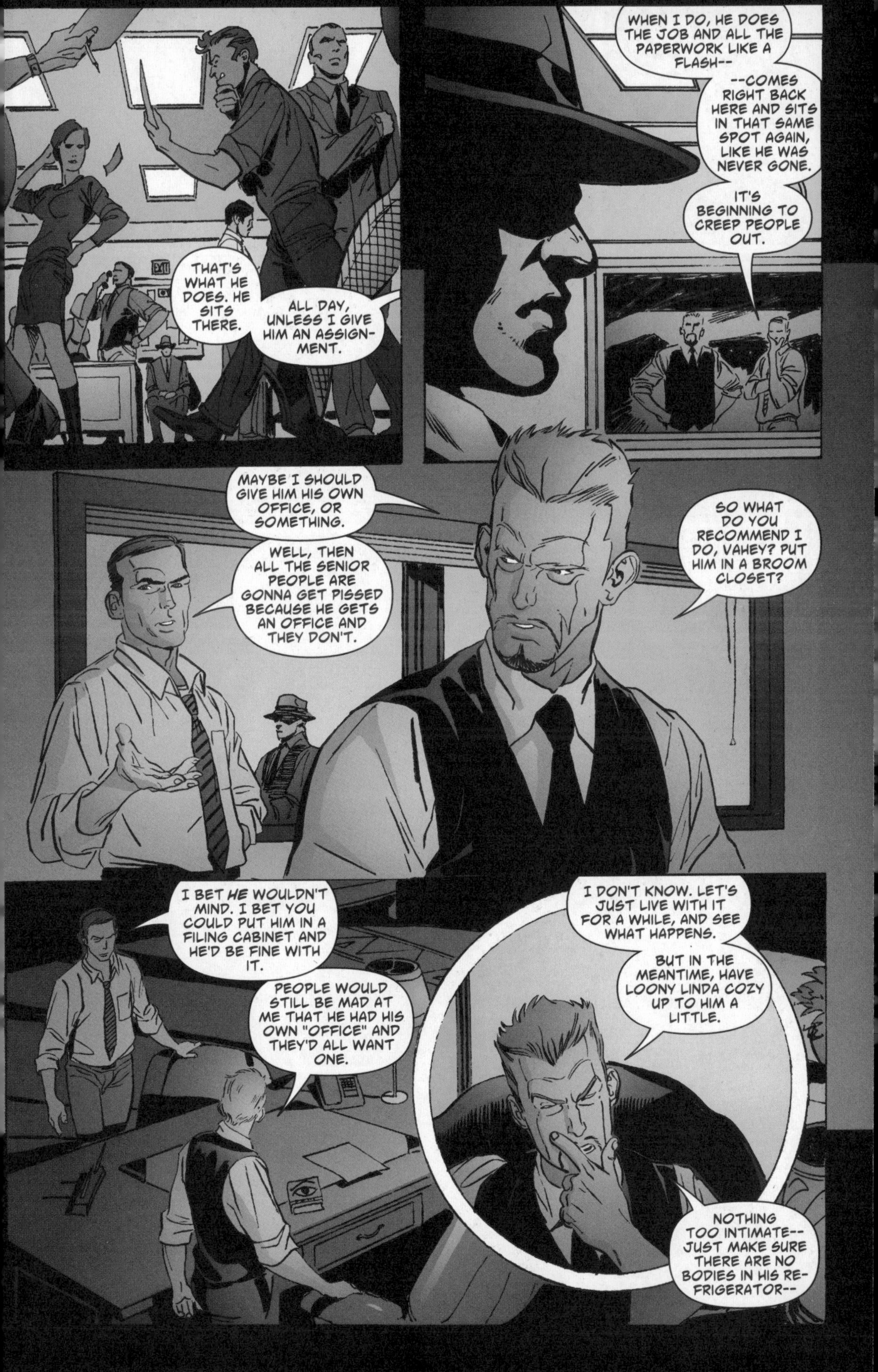
THAT'S WHAT HE DOES. HE SITS THERE.
ALL DAY, UNLESS I GIVE HIM AN ASSIGNMENT.
WHEN I DO, HE DOES THE JOB AND ALL THE PAPERWORK LIKE A FLASH--
--COMES RIGHT BACK HERE AND SITS IN THAT SAME SPOT AGAIN, LIKE HE WAS NEVER GONE.
IT'S BEGINNING TO CREEP PEOPLE OUT.
MAYBE I SHOULD GIVE HIM HIS OWN OFFICE, OR SOMETHING.
WELL, THEN ALL THE SENIOR PEOPLE ARE GONNA GET PISSED BECAUSE HE GETS AN OFFICE AND THEY DON'T.
SO WHAT DO YOU RECOMMEND I DO, VAHEY? PUT HIM IN A BROOM CLOSET?
I BET *HE* WOULDN'T MIND. I BET YOU COULD PUT HIM IN A FILING CABINET AND HE'D BE FINE WITH IT.
PEOPLE WOULD STILL BE MAD AT ME THAT HE HAD HIS OWN "OFFICE" AND THEY'D ALL WANT ONE.
I DON'T KNOW. LET'S JUST LIVE WITH IT FOR A WHILE, AND SEE WHAT HAPPENS.
BUT IN THE MEANTIME, HAVE LOONY LINDA COZY UP TO HIM A LITTLE.
NOTHING TOO INTIMATE--JUST MAKE SURE THERE ARE NO BODIES IN HIS RE-FRIGERATOR--

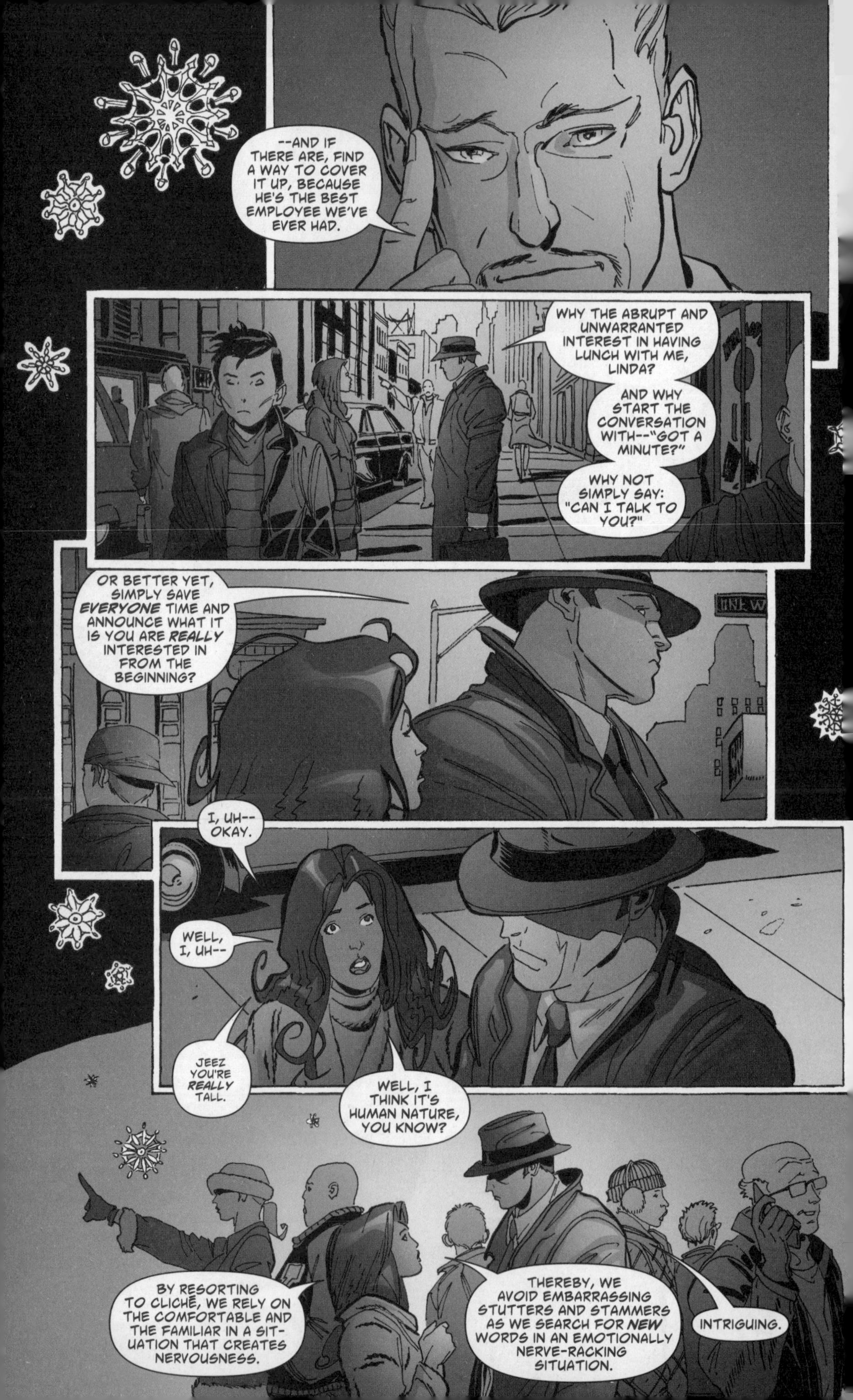
--AND IF THERE ARE, FIND A WAY TO COVER IT UP, BECAUSE HE'S THE BEST EMPLOYEE WE'VE EVER HAD.
WHY THE ABRUPT AND UNWARRANTED INTEREST IN HAVING LUNCH WITH ME, LINDA?
AND WHY START THE CONVERSATION WITH--"GOT A MINUTE?"
WHY NOT SIMPLY SAY: "CAN I TALK TO YOU?"
OR BETTER YET, SIMPLY SAVE EVERYONE TIME AND ANNOUNCE WHAT IT IS YOU ARE REALLY INTERESTED IN FROM THE BEGINNING?
I, UH-- OKAY.
WELL, I, UH--
JEEZ YOU'RE REALLY TALL.
WELL, I THINK IT'S HUMAN NATURE, YOU KNOW?
BY RESORTING TO CLICHÉ, WE RELY ON THE COMFORTABLE AND THE FAMILIAR IN A SIT-UATION THAT CREATES NERVOUSNESS.
THEREBY, WE AVOID EMBARRASSING STUTTERS AND STAMMERS AS WE SEARCH FOR NEW WORDS IN AN EMOTIONALLY NERVE-RACKING SITUATION.
INTRIGUING.

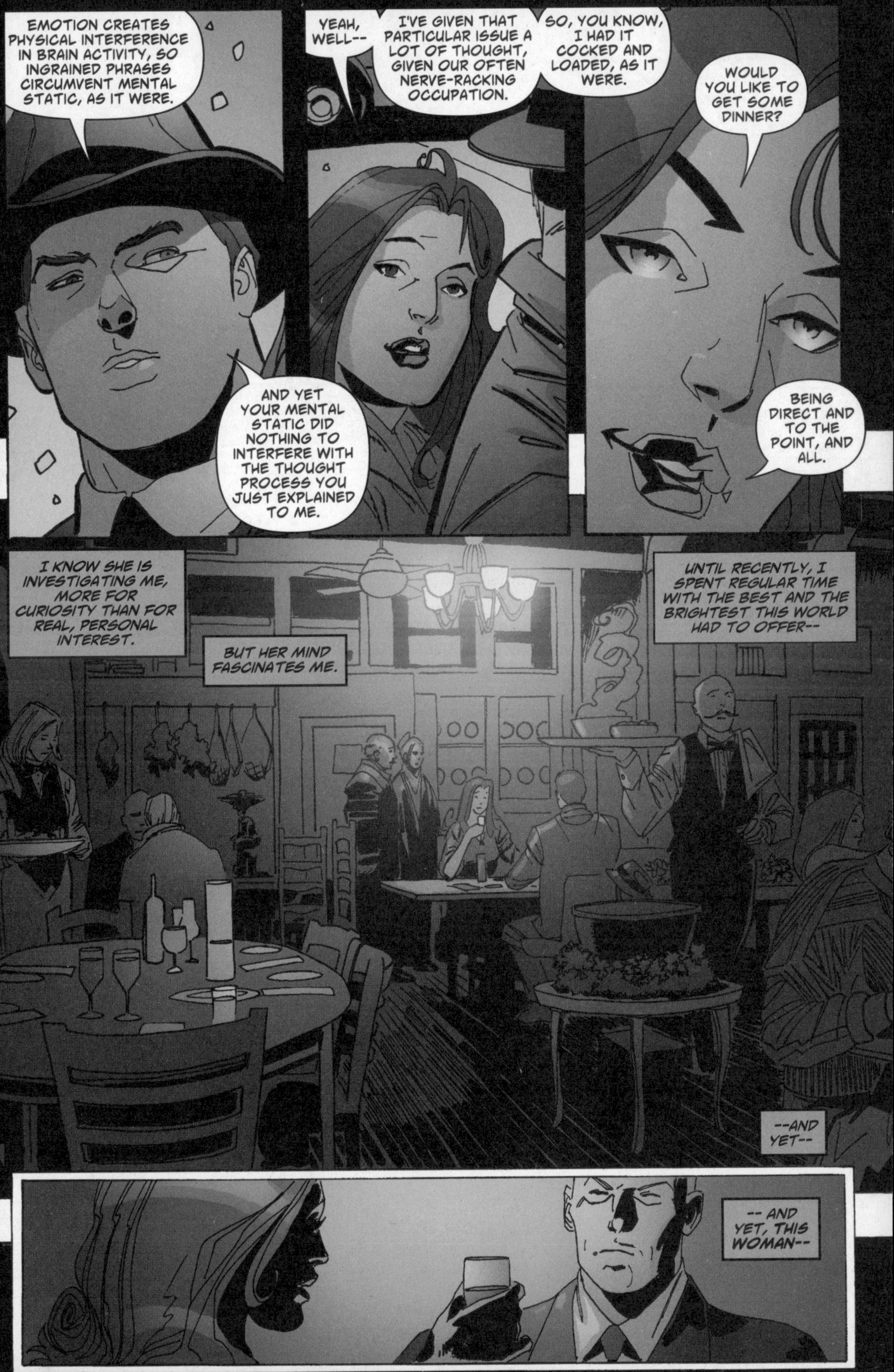
EMOTION CREATES PHYSICAL INTERFERENCE IN BRAIN ACTIVITY, SO INGRAINED PHRASES CIRCUMVENT MENTAL STATIC, AS IT WERE.
AND YET YOUR MENTAL STATIC DID NOTHING TO INTERFERE WITH THE THOUGHT PROCESS YOU JUST EXPLAINED TO ME.
YEAH, WELL--
I'VE GIVEN THAT PARTICULAR ISSUE A LOT OF THOUGHT, GIVEN OUR OFTEN NERVE-RACKING OCCUPATION.
SO, YOU KNOW, I HAD IT COCKED AND LOADED, AS IT WERE.
WOULD YOU LIKE TO GET SOME DINNER?
BEING DIRECT AND TO THE POINT, AND ALL.
I KNOW SHE IS INVESTIGATING ME, MORE FOR CURIOSITY THAN FOR REAL, PERSONAL INTEREST.
BUT HER MIND FASCINATES ME.
UNTIL RECENTLY, I SPENT REGULAR TIME WITH THE BEST AND THE BRIGHTEST THIS WORLD HAD TO OFFER--
--AND YET--
-- AND YET, THIS WOMAN--

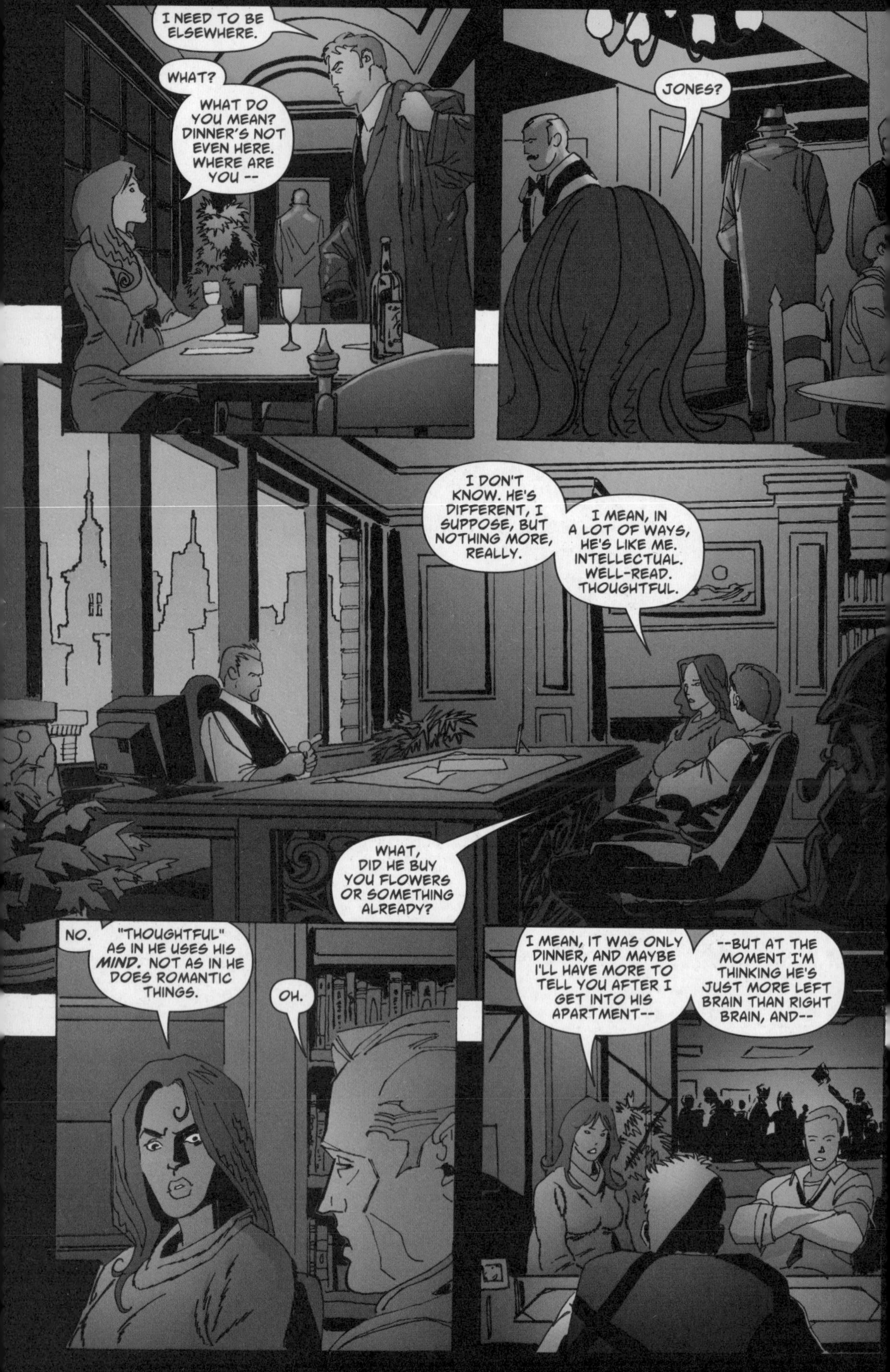

I NEED TO BE ELSEWHERE.
WHAT?
WHAT DO YOU MEAN? DINNER'S NOT EVEN HERE. WHERE ARE YOU --
JONES?
I DON'T KNOW. HE'S DIFFERENT, I SUPPOSE, BUT NOTHING MORE, REALLY.
I MEAN, IN A LOT OF WAYS, HE'S LIKE ME. INTELLECTUAL. WELL-READ. THOUGHTFUL.
WHAT, DID HE BUY YOU FLOWERS OR SOMETHING ALREADY?
NO.
"THOUGHTFUL" AS IN HE USES HIS *MIND*. NOT AS IN HE DOES ROMANTIC THINGS.
OH.
I MEAN, IT WAS ONLY DINNER, AND MAYBE I'LL HAVE MORE TO TELL YOU AFTER I GET INTO HIS APARTMENT--
--BUT AT THE MOMENT I'M THINKING HE'S JUST MORE LEFT BRAIN THAN RIGHT BRAIN, AND--

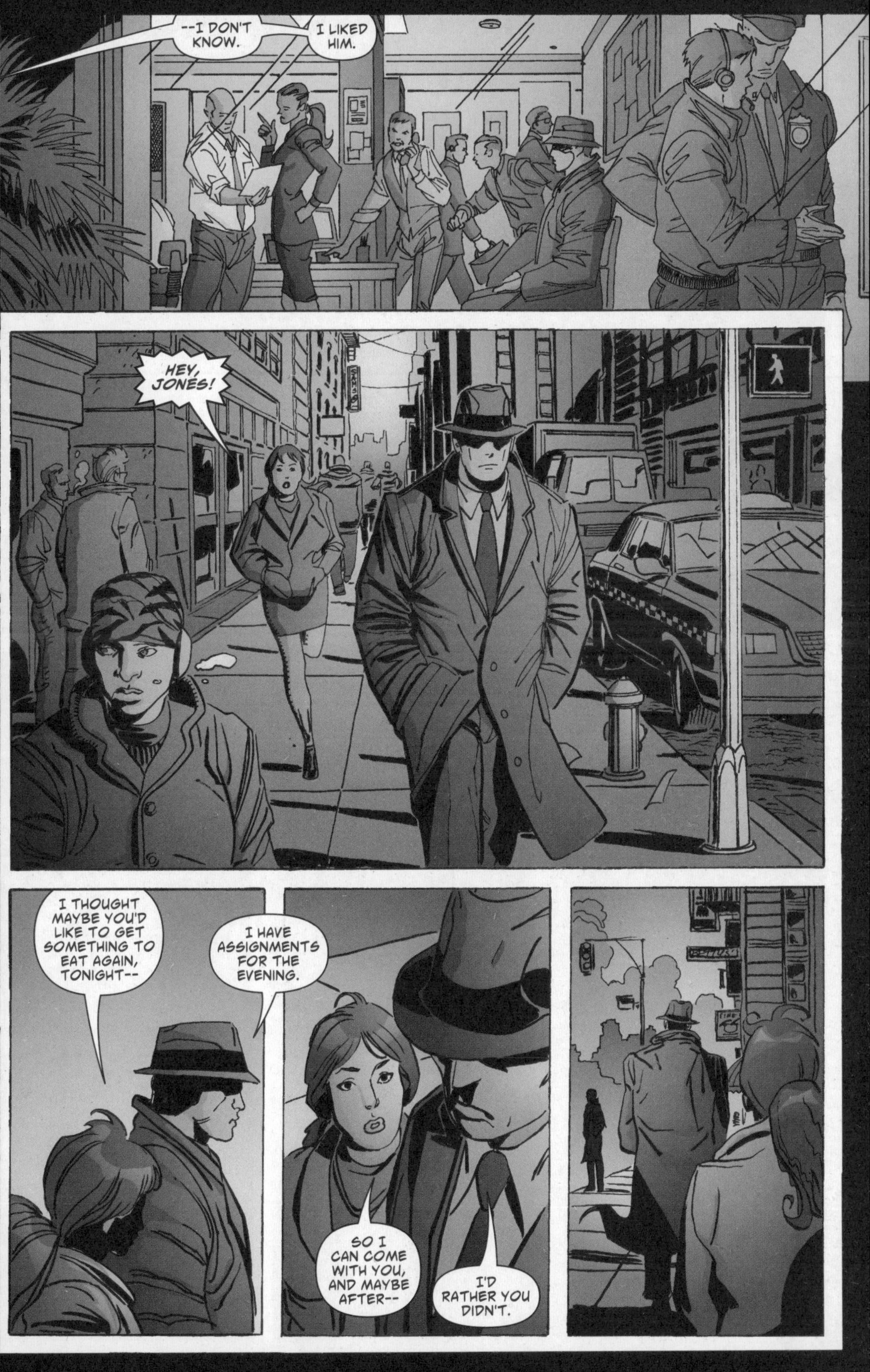
--I DON'T KNOW.
I LIKED HIM.
HEY, JONES!
I THOUGHT MAYBE YOU'D LIKE TO GET SOMETHING TO EAT AGAIN, TONIGHT--
I HAVE ASSIGNMENTS FOR THE EVENING.
SO I CAN COME WITH YOU, AND MAYBE AFTER--
I'D RATHER YOU DIDN'T.

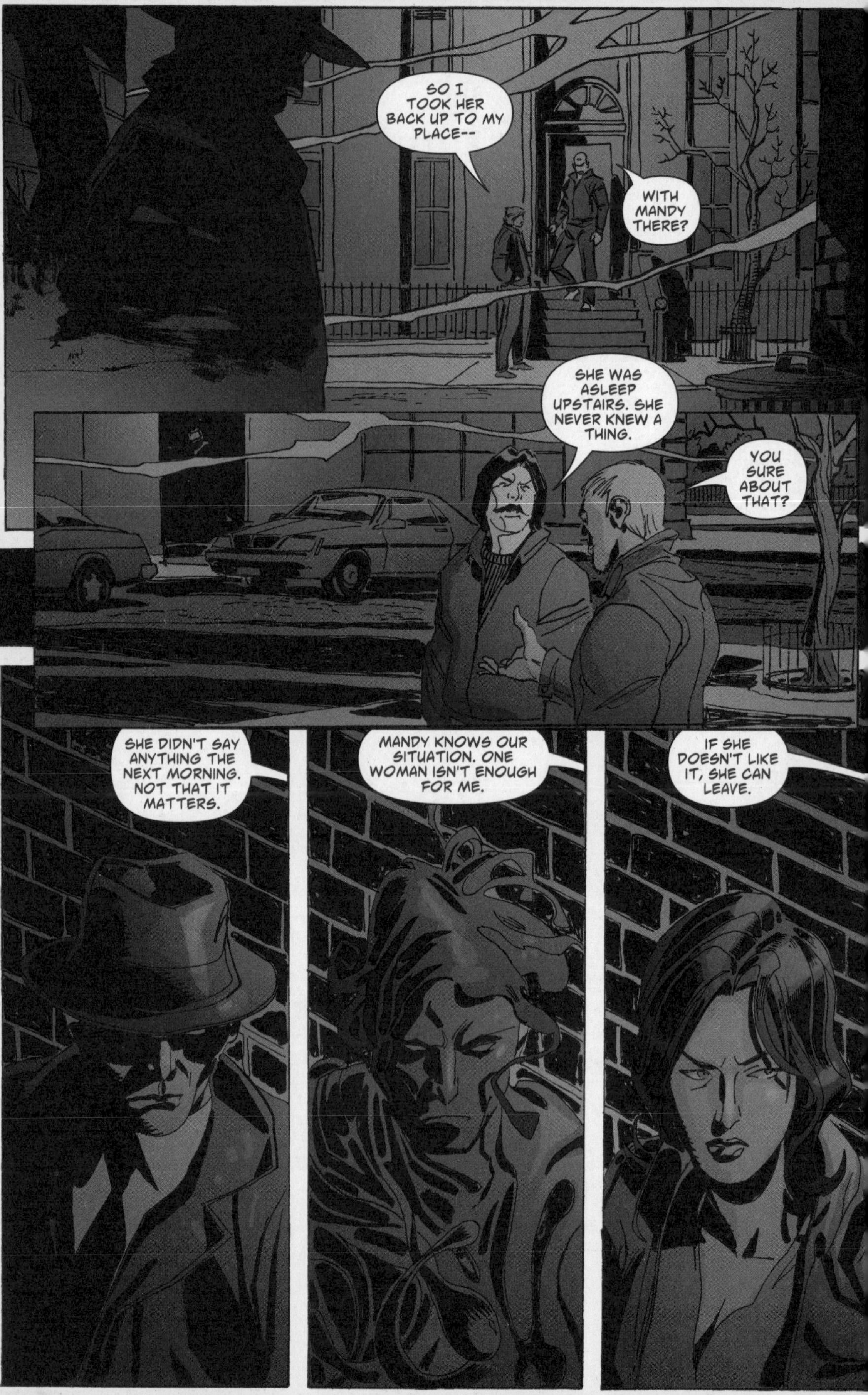
SO I TOOK HER BACK UP TO MY PLACE--
WITH MANDY THERE?
SHE WAS ASLEEP UPSTAIRS. SHE NEVER KNEW A THING.
YOU SURE ABOUT THAT?
SHE DIDN'T SAY ANYTHING THE NEXT MORNING. NOT THAT IT MATTERS.
MANDY KNOWS OUR SITUATION. ONE WOMAN ISN'T ENOUGH FOR ME.
IF SHE DOESN'T LIKE IT, SHE CAN LEAVE.

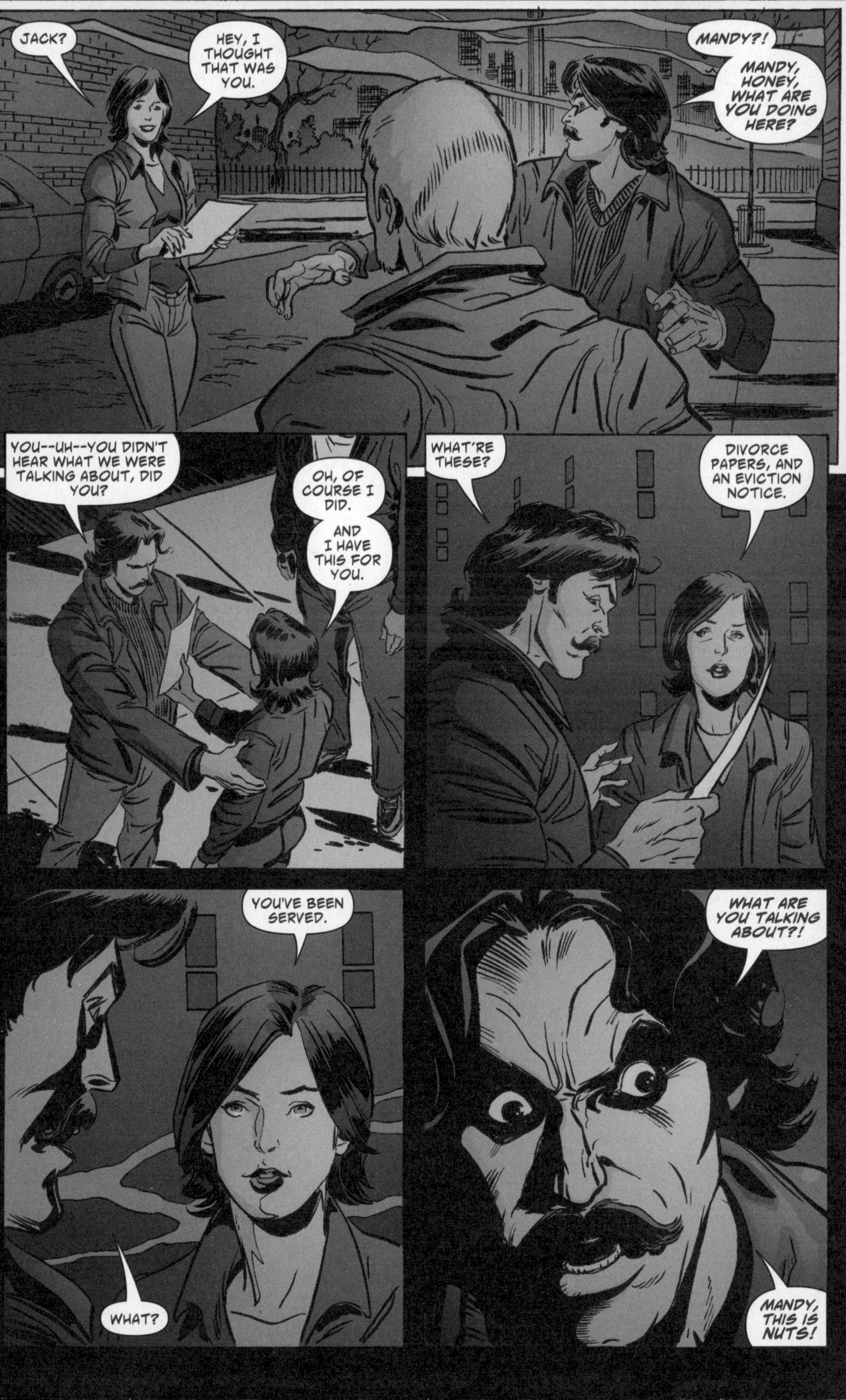
JACK?
HEY, I THOUGHT THAT WAS YOU.
MANDY?!
MANDY, HONEY, WHAT ARE YOU DOING HERE?
YOU--UH--YOU DIDN'T HEAR WHAT WE WERE TALKING ABOUT, DID YOU?
OH, OF COURSE I DID.
AND I HAVE THIS FOR YOU.
WHAT'RE THESE?
DIVORCE PAPERS, AND AN EVICTION NOTICE.
YOU'VE BEEN SERVED.
WHAT?
WHAT ARE YOU TALKING ABOUT?!
MANDY, THIS IS NUTS!

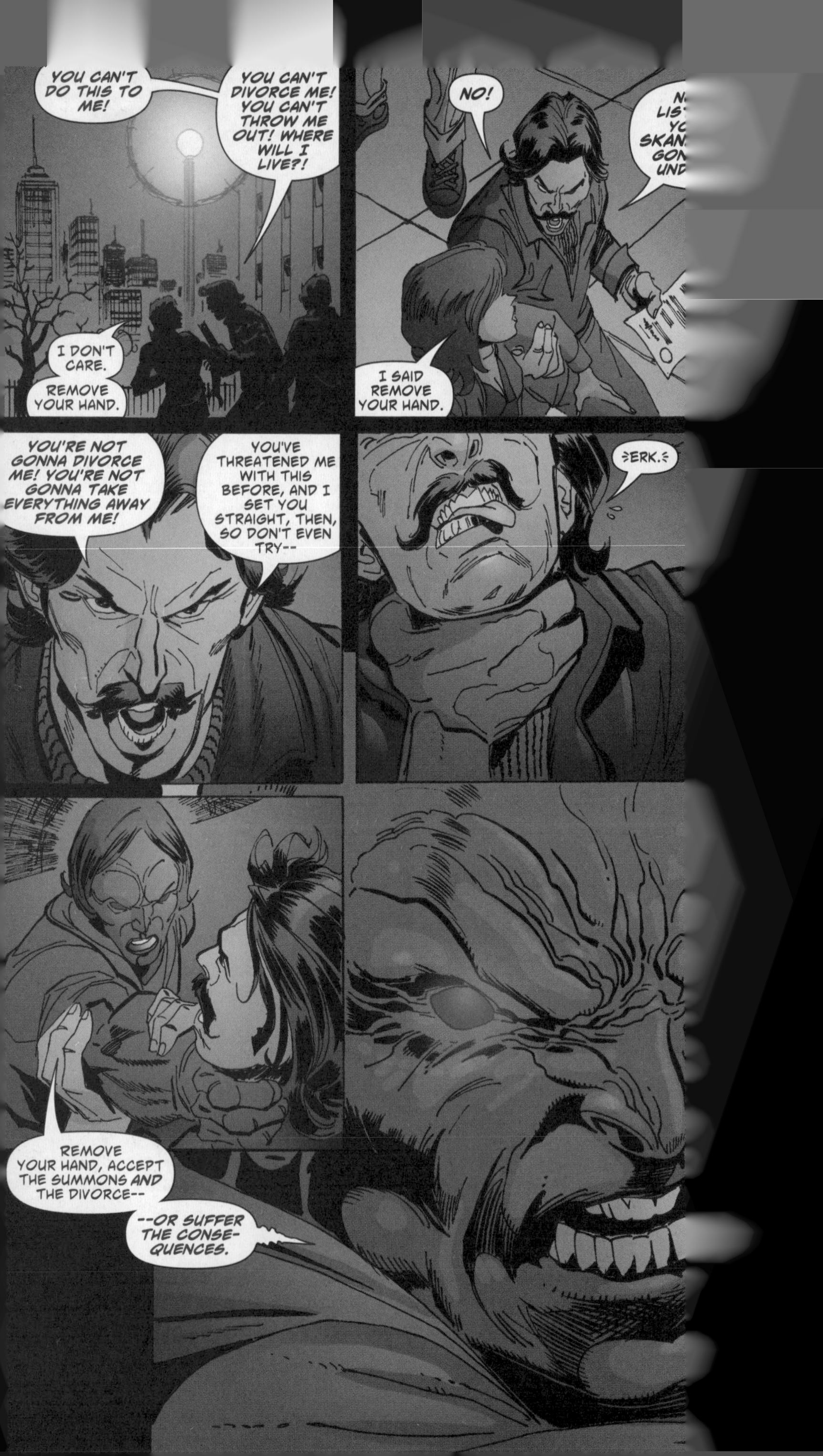
YOU CAN'T DO THIS TO ME!
YOU CAN'T DIVORCE ME! YOU CAN'T THROW ME OUT! WHERE WILL I LIVE?!
I DON'T CARE.
REMOVE YOUR HAND.
NO!
I SAID REMOVE YOUR HAND.
YOU'RE NOT GONNA DIVORCE ME! YOU'RE NOT GONNA TAKE EVERYTHING AWAY FROM ME!
YOU'VE THREATENED ME WITH THIS BEFORE, AND I SET YOU STRAIGHT, THEN, SO DON'T EVEN TRY--
ERK.
REMOVE YOUR HAND, ACCEPT THE SUMMONS AND THE DIVORCE--
--OR SUFFER THE CONSE-QUENCES.

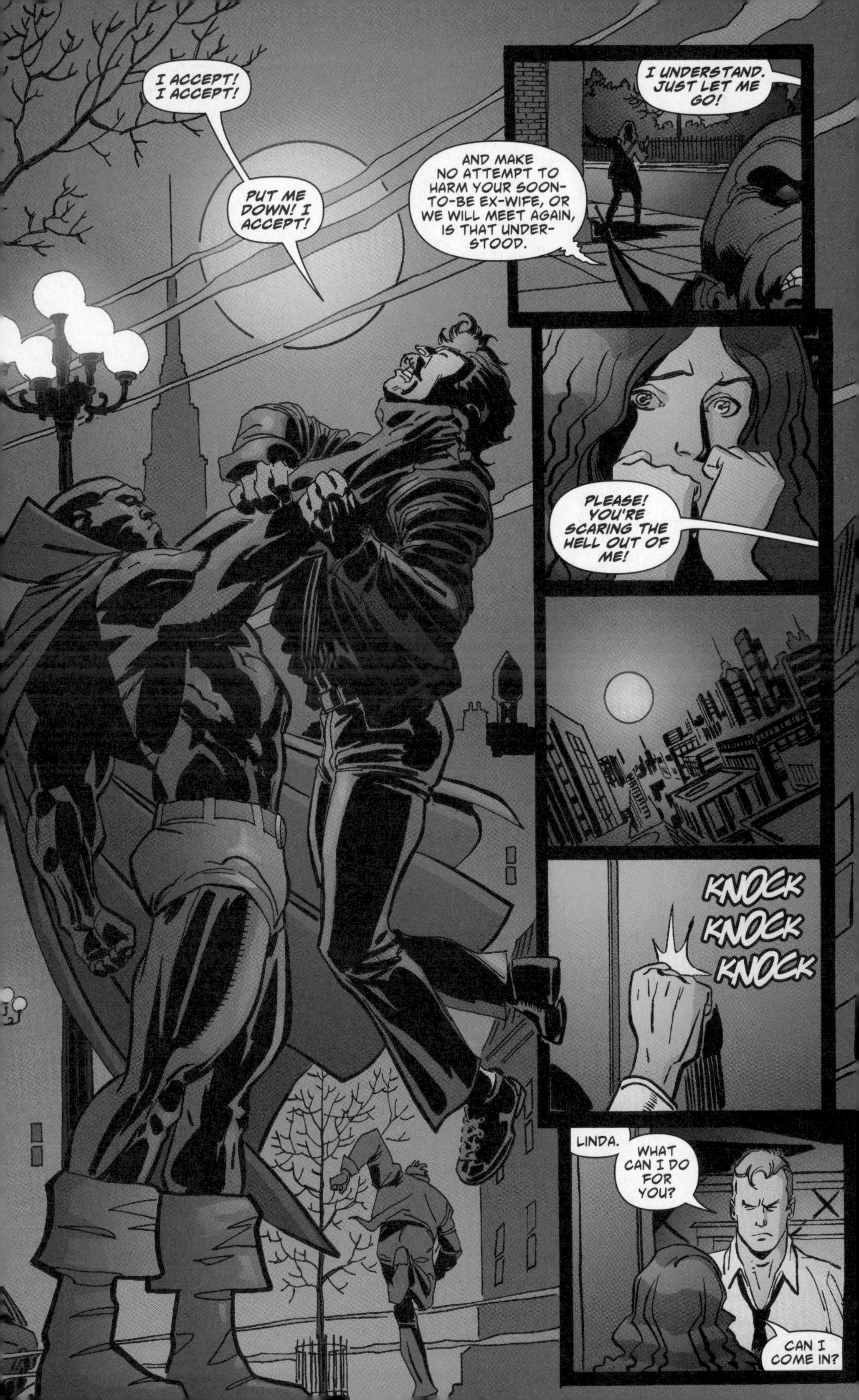
I ACCEPT! I ACCEPT!
PUT ME DOWN! I ACCEPT!
AND MAKE NO ATTEMPT TO HARM YOUR SOON-TO-BE EX-WIFE, OR WE WILL MEET AGAIN, IS THAT UNDER-STOOD.
I UNDERSTAND. JUST LET ME GO!
PLEASE! YOU'RE SCARING THE HELL OUT OF ME!
KNOCK KNOCK KNOCK
LINDA.
WHAT CAN I DO FOR YOU?
CAN I COME IN?

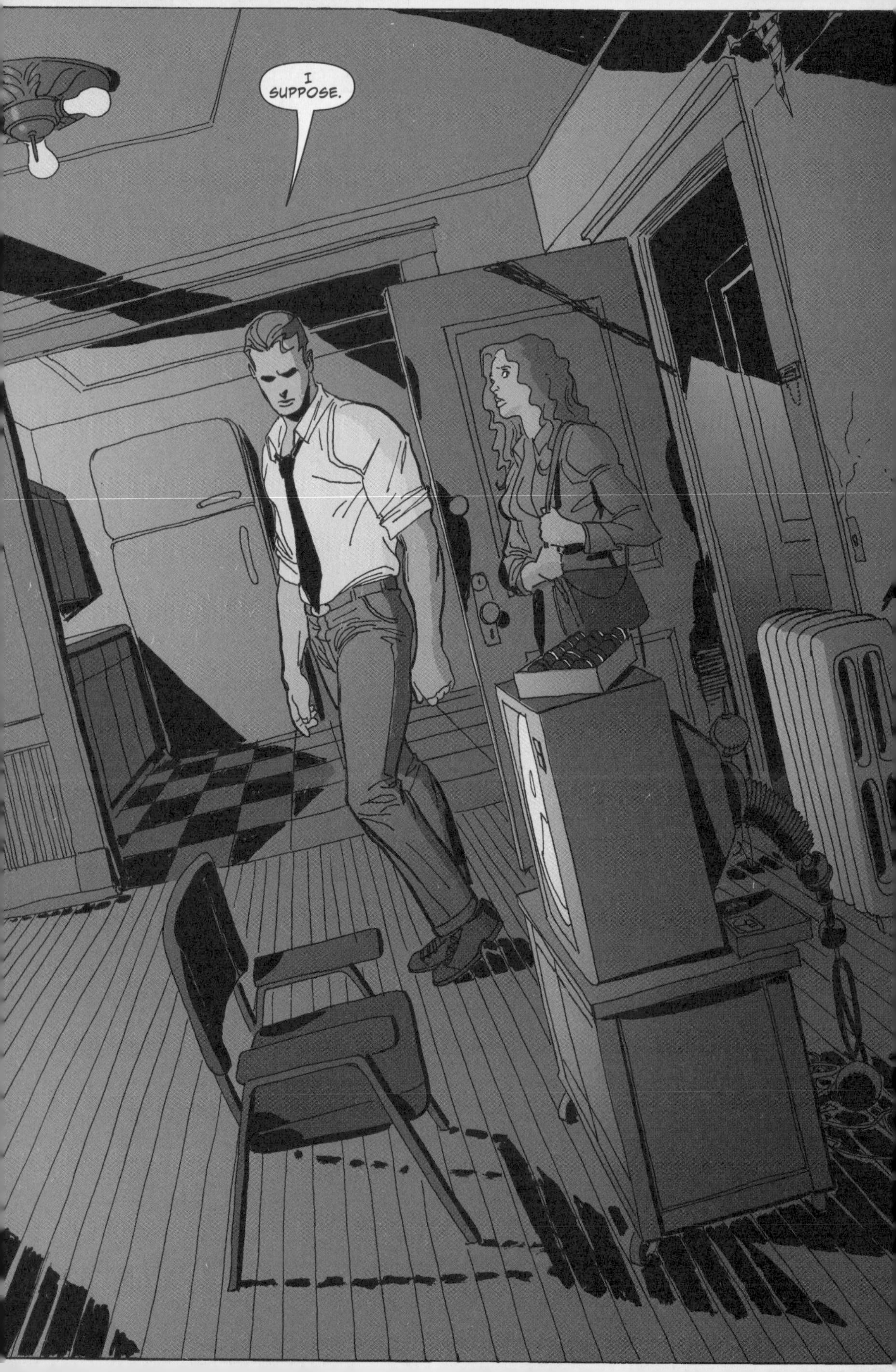
I SUPPOSE.

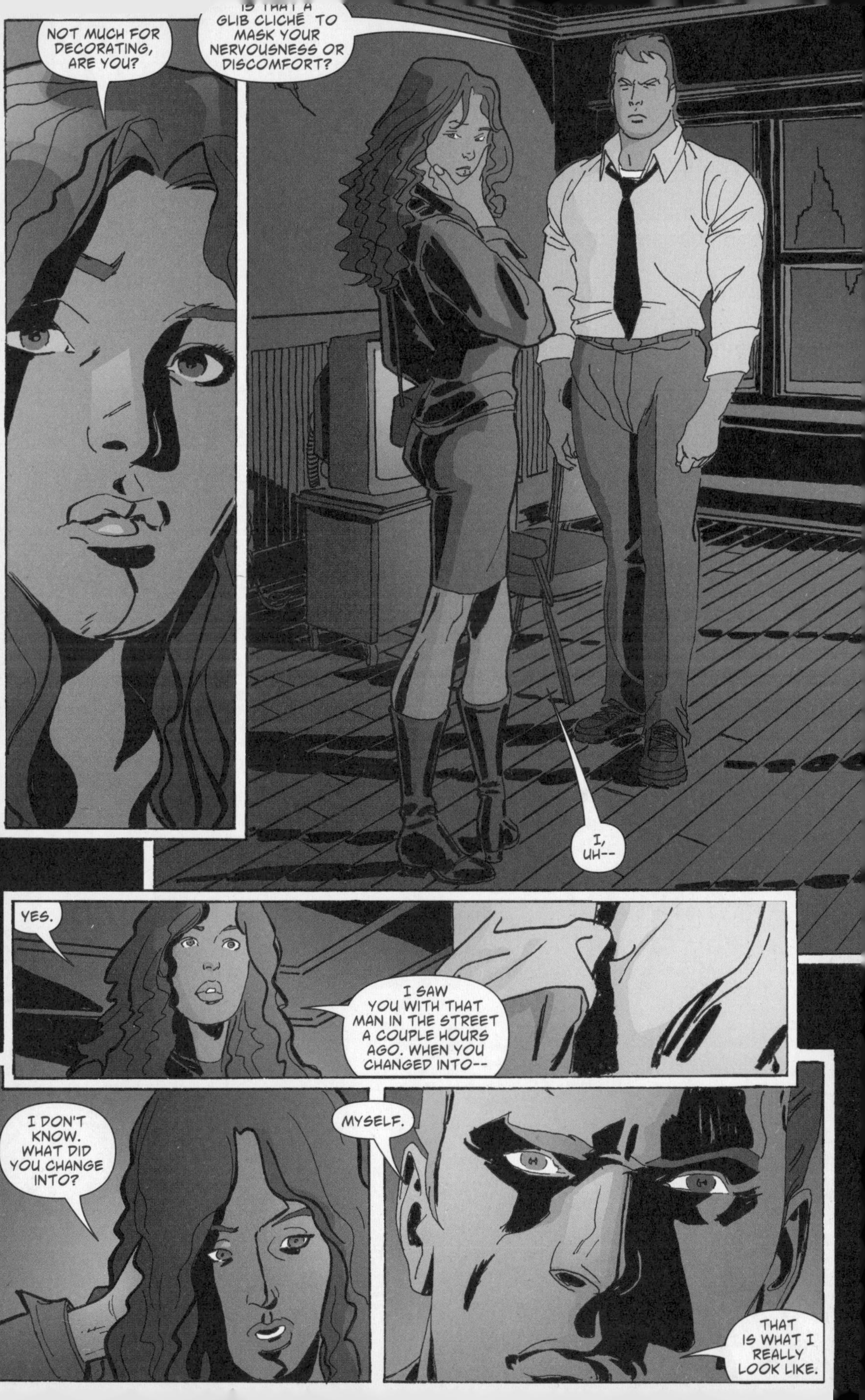
NOT MUCH FOR DECORATING, ARE YOU?
IS THAT A GLIB CLICHÉ TO MASK YOUR NERVOUSNESS OR DISCOMFORT?
I, UH--
YES.
I SAW YOU WITH THAT MAN IN THE STREET A COUPLE HOURS AGO. WHEN YOU CHANGED INTO--
I DON'T KNOW. WHAT DID YOU CHANGE INTO?
MYSELF.
THAT IS WHAT I REALLY LOOK LIKE.

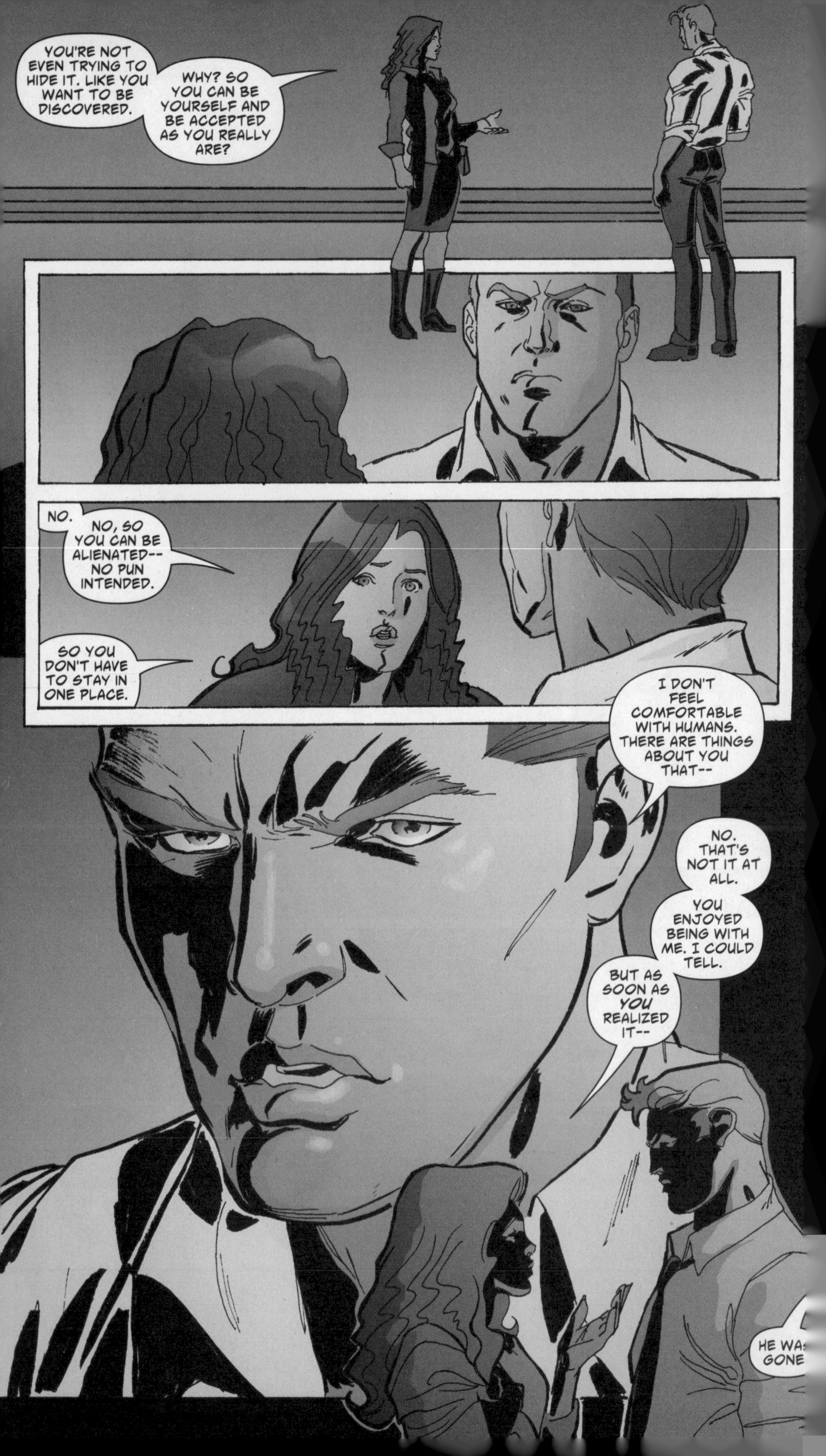
YOU'RE NOT EVEN TRYING TO HIDE IT. LIKE YOU WANT TO BE DISCOVERED.
WHY? SO YOU CAN BE YOURSELF AND BE ACCEPTED AS YOU REALLY ARE?
NO.
NO, SO YOU CAN BE ALIENATED-- NO PUN INTENDED.
SO YOU DON'T HAVE TO STAY IN ONE PLACE.
I DON'T FEEL COMFORTABLE WITH HUMANS. THERE ARE THINGS ABOUT YOU THAT--
NO. THAT'S NOT IT AT ALL.
YOU ENJOYED BEING WITH ME. I COULD TELL.
BUT AS SOON AS YOU REALIZED IT--

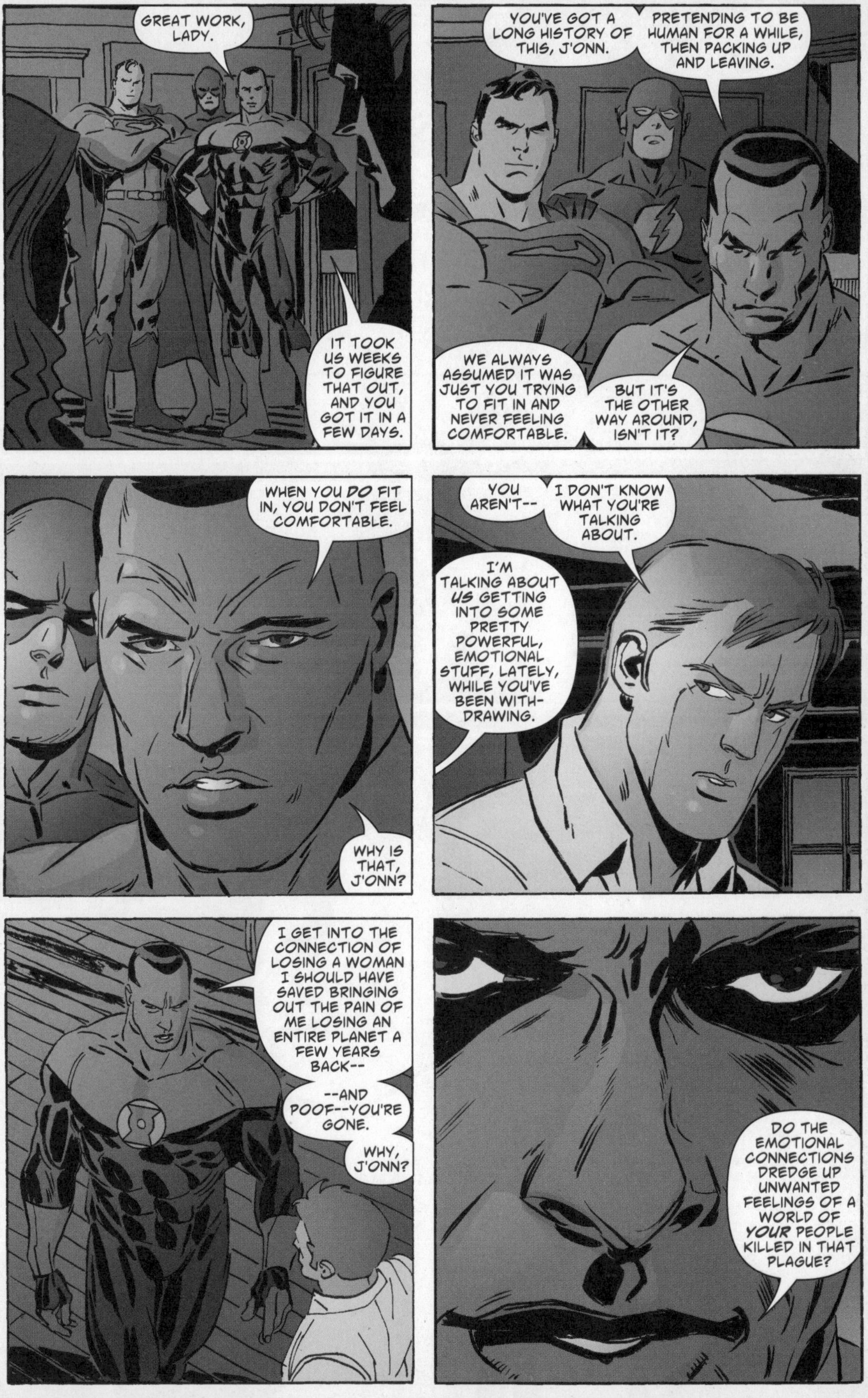
GREAT WORK, LADY.
IT TOOK US WEEKS TO FIGURE THAT OUT, AND YOU GOT IT IN A FEW DAYS.
YOU'VE GOT A LONG HISTORY OF THIS, J'ONN.
PRETENDING TO BE HUMAN FOR A WHILE, THEN PACKING UP AND LEAVING.
WE ALWAYS ASSUMED IT WAS JUST YOU TRYING TO FIT IN AND NEVER FEELING COMFORTABLE.
BUT IT'S THE OTHER WAY AROUND, ISN'T IT?
WHEN YOU *DO* FIT IN, YOU DON'T FEEL COMFORTABLE.
WHY IS THAT, J'ONN?
YOU AREN'T--
I DON'T KNOW WHAT YOU'RE TALKING ABOUT.
I'M TALKING ABOUT *US* GETTING INTO SOME PRETTY POWERFUL, EMOTIONAL STUFF, LATELY, WHILE YOU'VE BEEN WITH-DRAWING.
I GET INTO THE CONNECTION OF LOSING A WOMAN I SHOULD HAVE SAVED BRINGING OUT THE PAIN OF ME LOSING AN ENTIRE PLANET A FEW YEARS BACK--
--AND POOF--YOU'RE GONE.
WHY, J'ONN?
DO THE EMOTIONAL CONNECTIONS DREDGE UP UNWANTED FEELINGS OF A WORLD OF *YOUR* PEOPLE KILLED IN THAT PLAGUE?

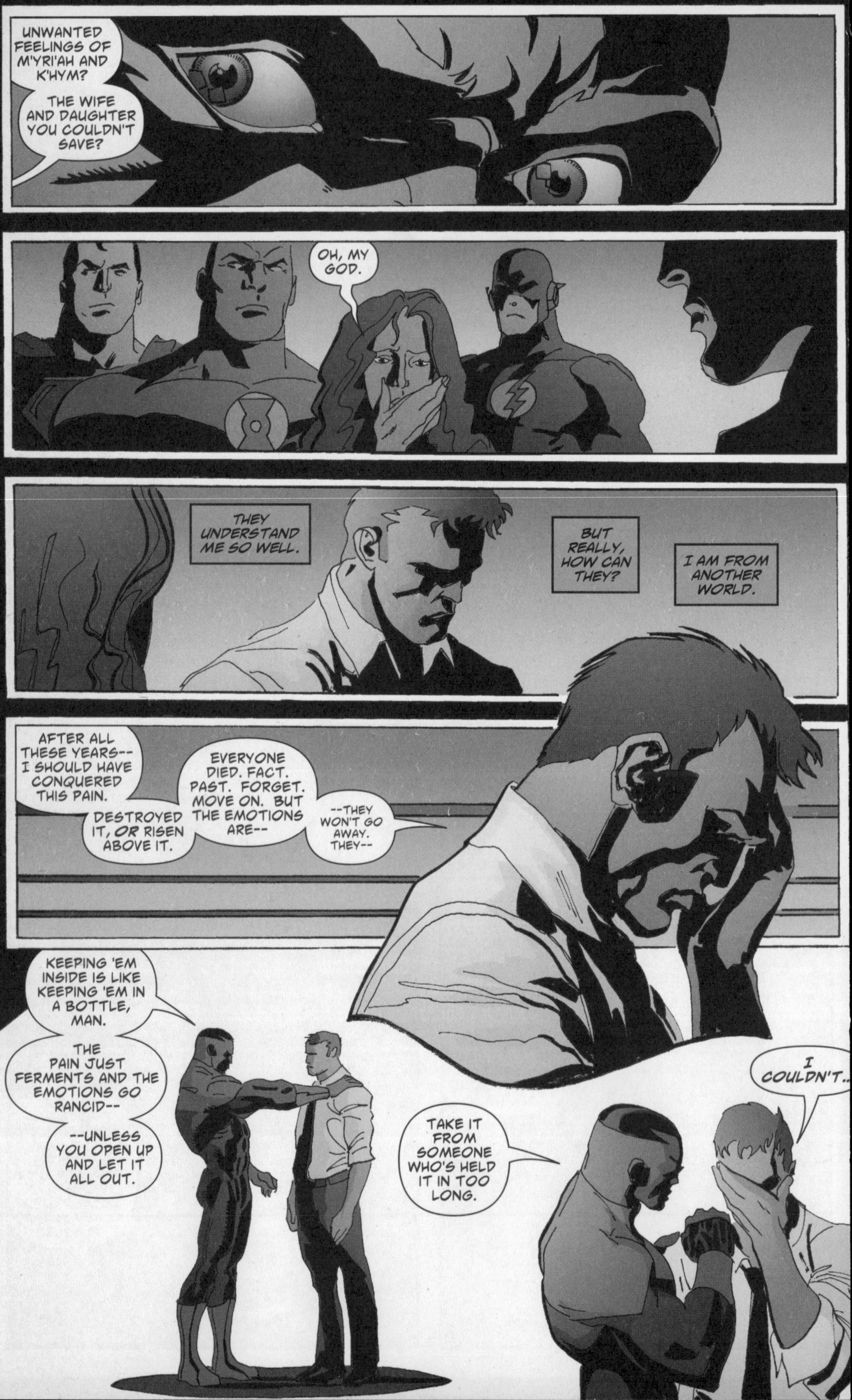
UNWANTED FEELINGS OF M'YRI'AH AND K'HYM?
THE WIFE AND DAUGHTER YOU COULDN'T SAVE?
OH, MY GOD.
THEY UNDERSTAND ME SO WELL.
BUT REALLY, HOW CAN THEY?
I AM FROM ANOTHER WORLD.
AFTER ALL THESE YEARS-- I SHOULD HAVE CONQUERED THIS PAIN.
DESTROYED IT, OR RISEN ABOVE IT.
EVERYONE DIED. FACT. PAST. FORGET. MOVE ON. BUT THE EMOTIONS ARE--
--THEY WON'T GO AWAY. THEY--
KEEPING 'EM INSIDE IS LIKE KEEPING 'EM IN A BOTTLE, MAN.
THE PAIN JUST FERMENTS AND THE EMOTIONS GO RANCID--
--UNLESS YOU OPEN UP AND LET IT ALL OUT.
TAKE IT FROM SOMEONE WHO'S HELD IT IN TOO LONG.
I COULDN'T...

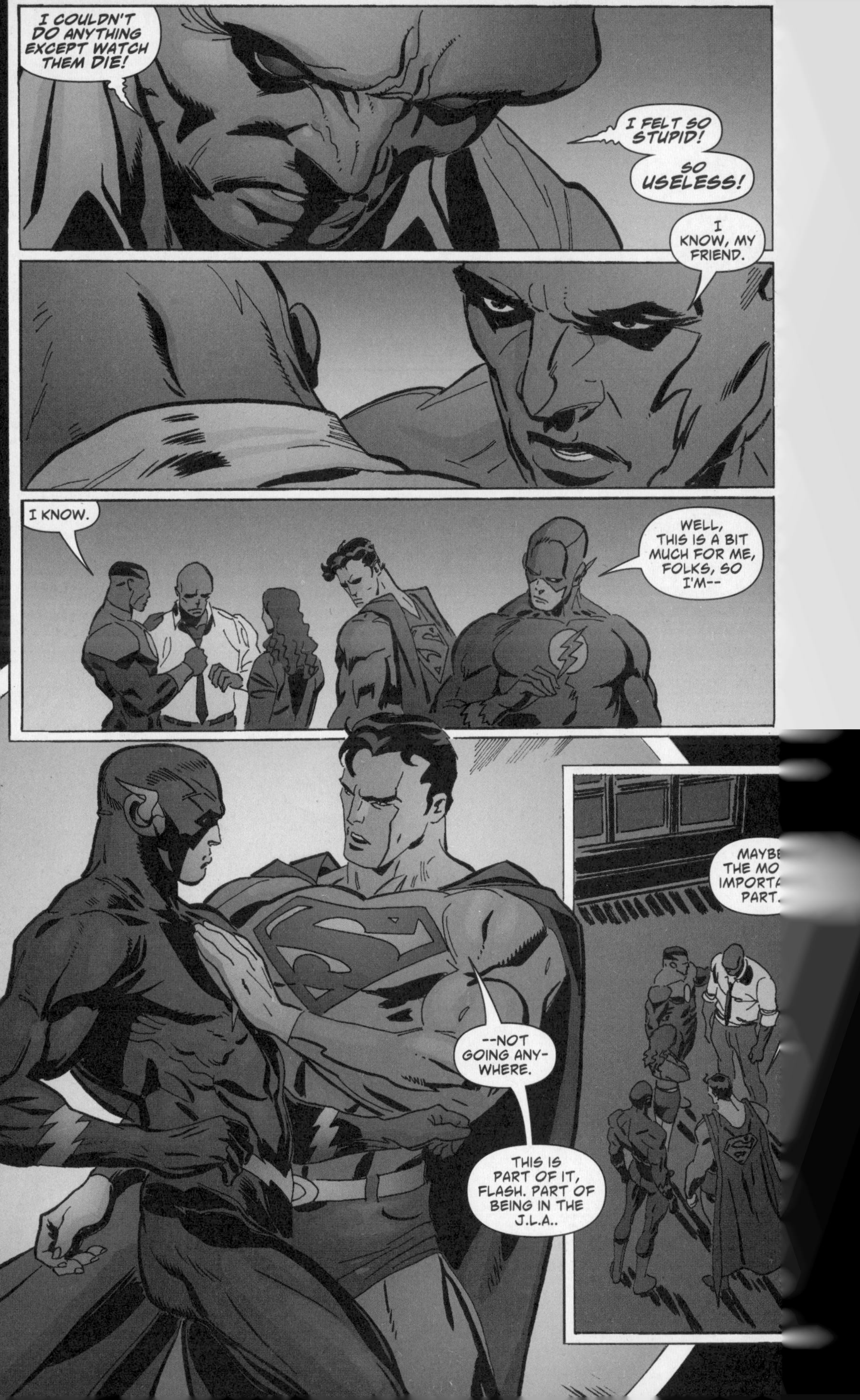
I COULDN'T DO ANYTHING EXCEPT WATCH THEM DIE!
I FELT SO STUPID!
SO USELESS!
I KNOW, MY FRIEND.
I KNOW.
WELL, THIS IS A BIT MUCH FOR ME, FOLKS, SO I'M--
--NOT GOING ANY-WHERE.
THIS IS PART OF IT, FLASH. PART OF BEING IN THE J.L.A..

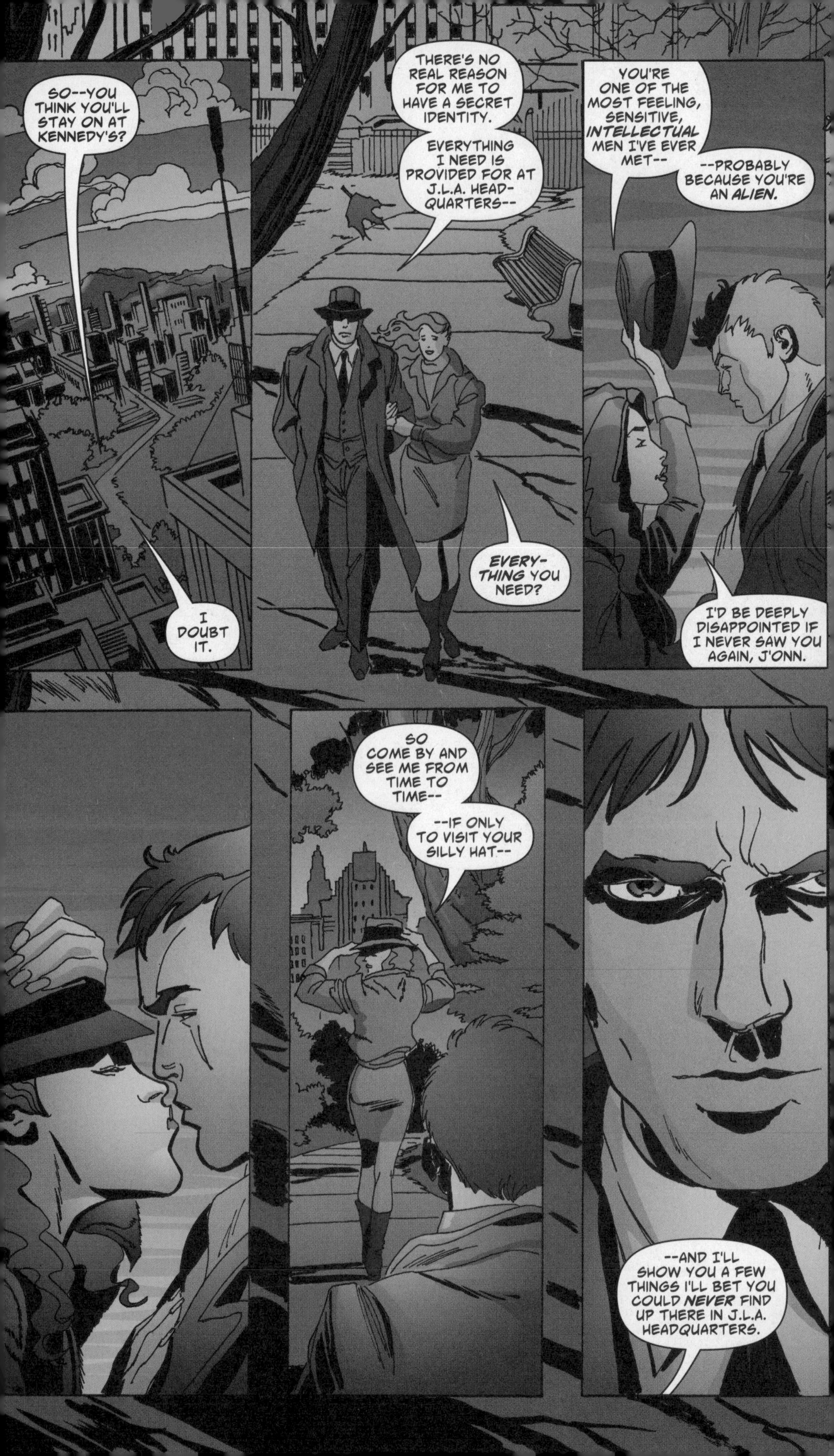
SO--YOU THINK YOU'LL STAY ON AT KENNEDY'S?
I DOUBT IT.
THERE'S NO REAL REASON FOR ME TO HAVE A SECRET IDENTITY.
EVERYTHING I NEED IS PROVIDED FOR AT J.L.A. HEAD-QUARTERS--
EVERY-THING YOU NEED?
YOU'RE ONE OF THE MOST FEELING, SENSITIVE, INTELLECTUAL MEN I'VE EVER MET--
--PROBABLY BECAUSE YOU'RE AN ALIEN.
I'D BE DEEPLY DISAPPOINTED IF I NEVER SAW YOU AGAIN, J'ONN.
SO COME BY AND SEE ME FROM TIME TO TIME--
--IF ONLY TO VISIT YOUR SILLY HAT--
--AND I'LL SHOW YOU A FEW THINGS I'LL BET YOU COULD NEVER FIND UP THERE IN J.L.A. HEADQUARTERS.

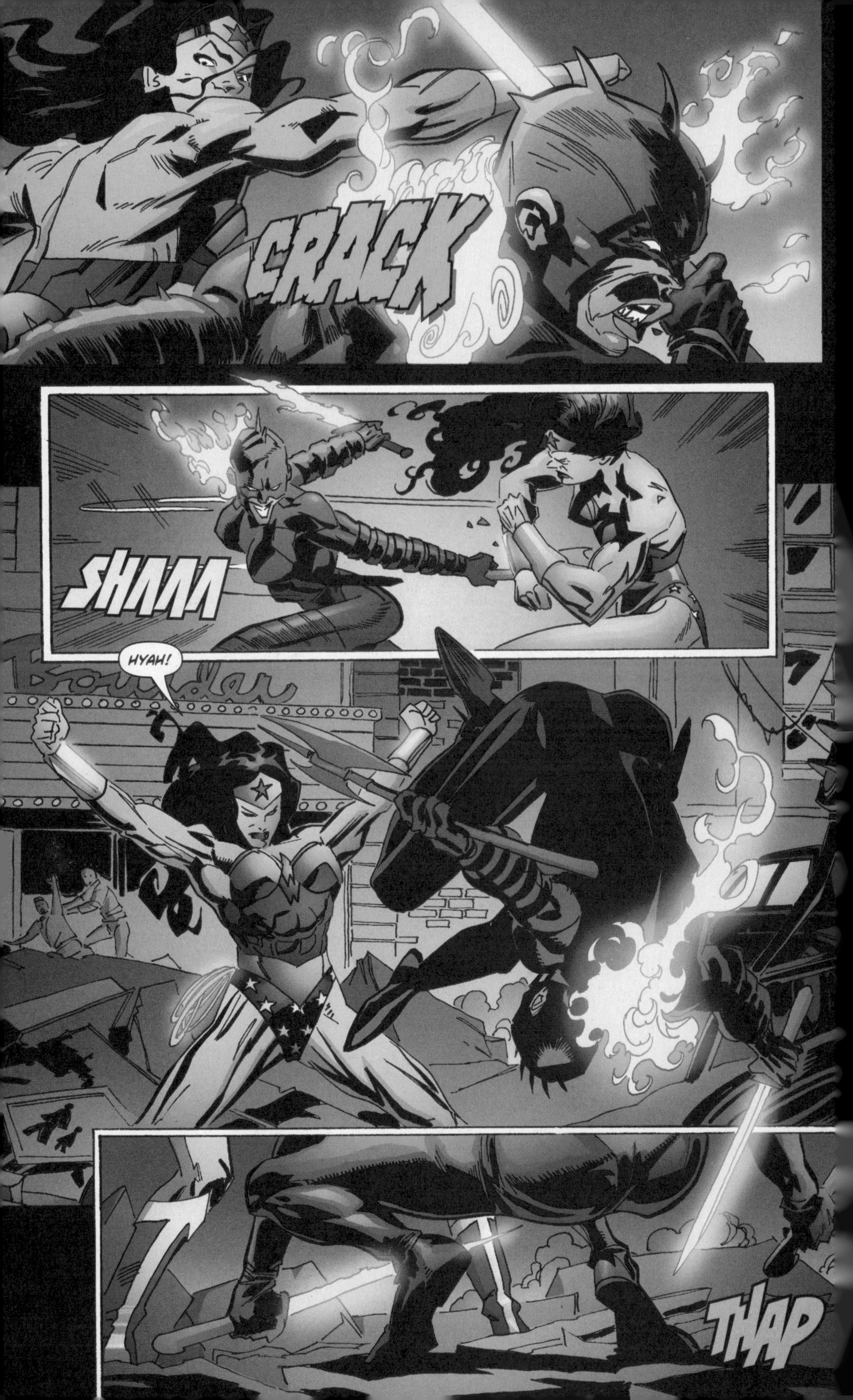
CRACK
SHAAA
HYAH!
THAP

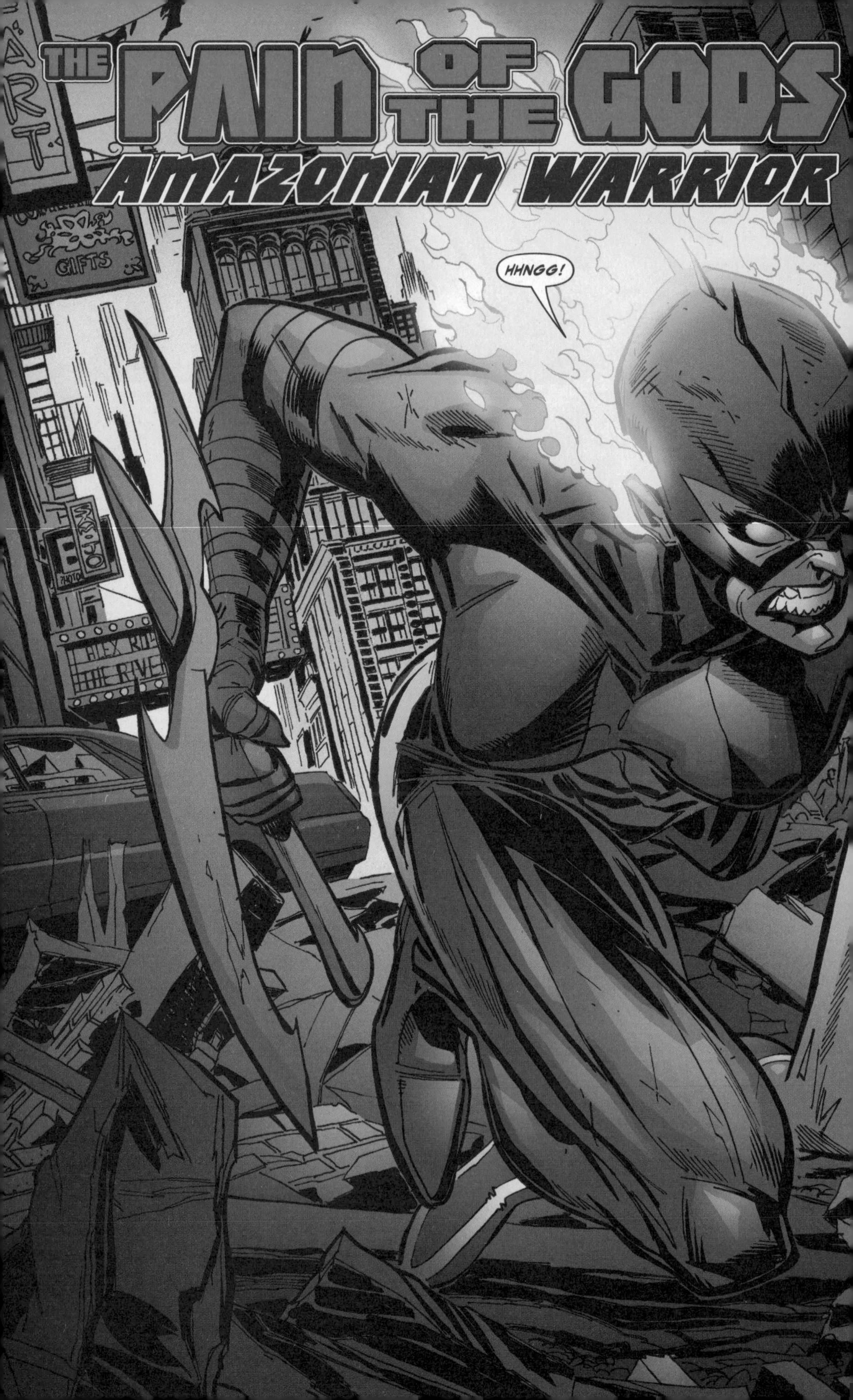
THE PAIN OF THE GODS
AMAZONIAN WARRIOR
HHNGG!

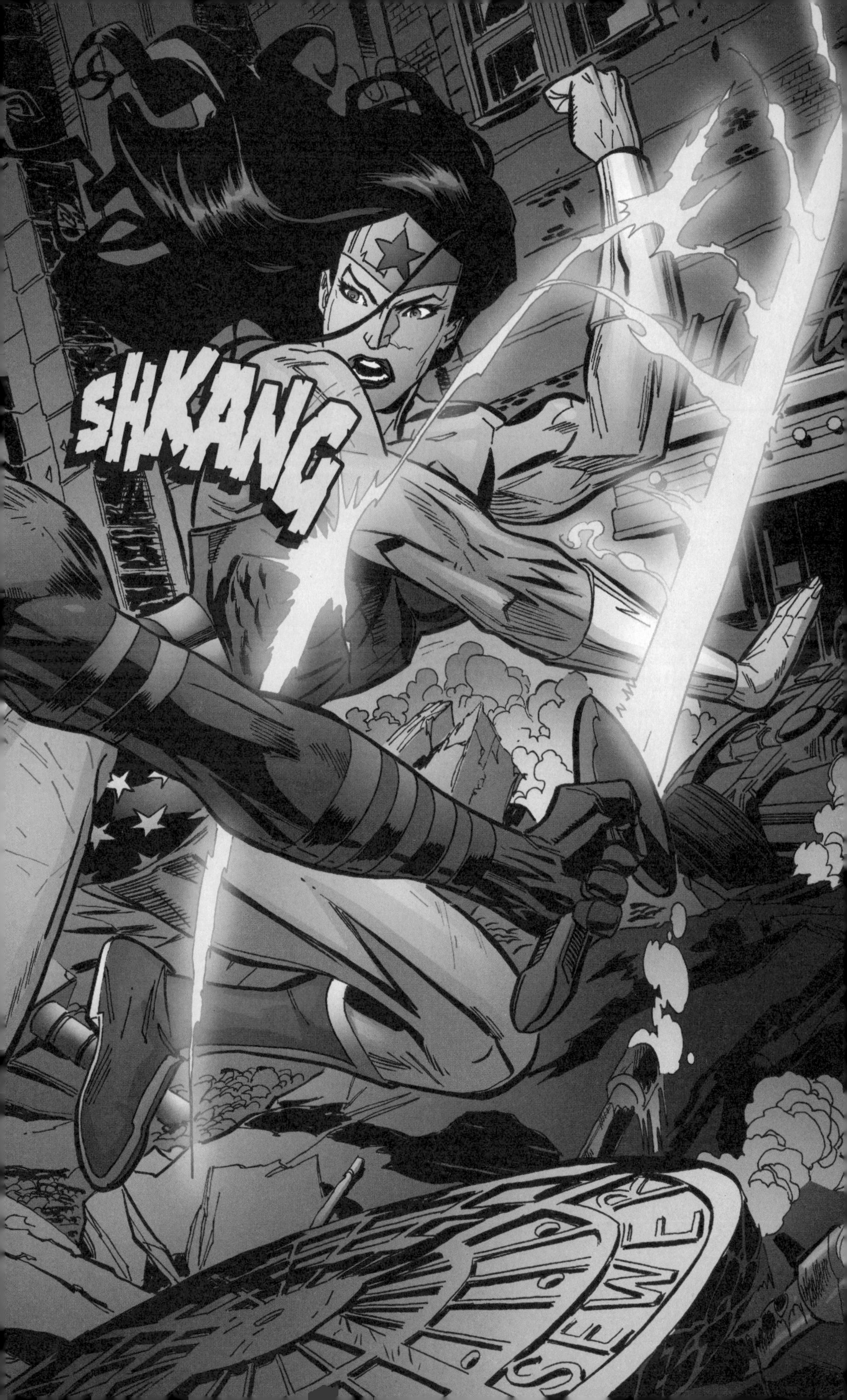
SHKANG

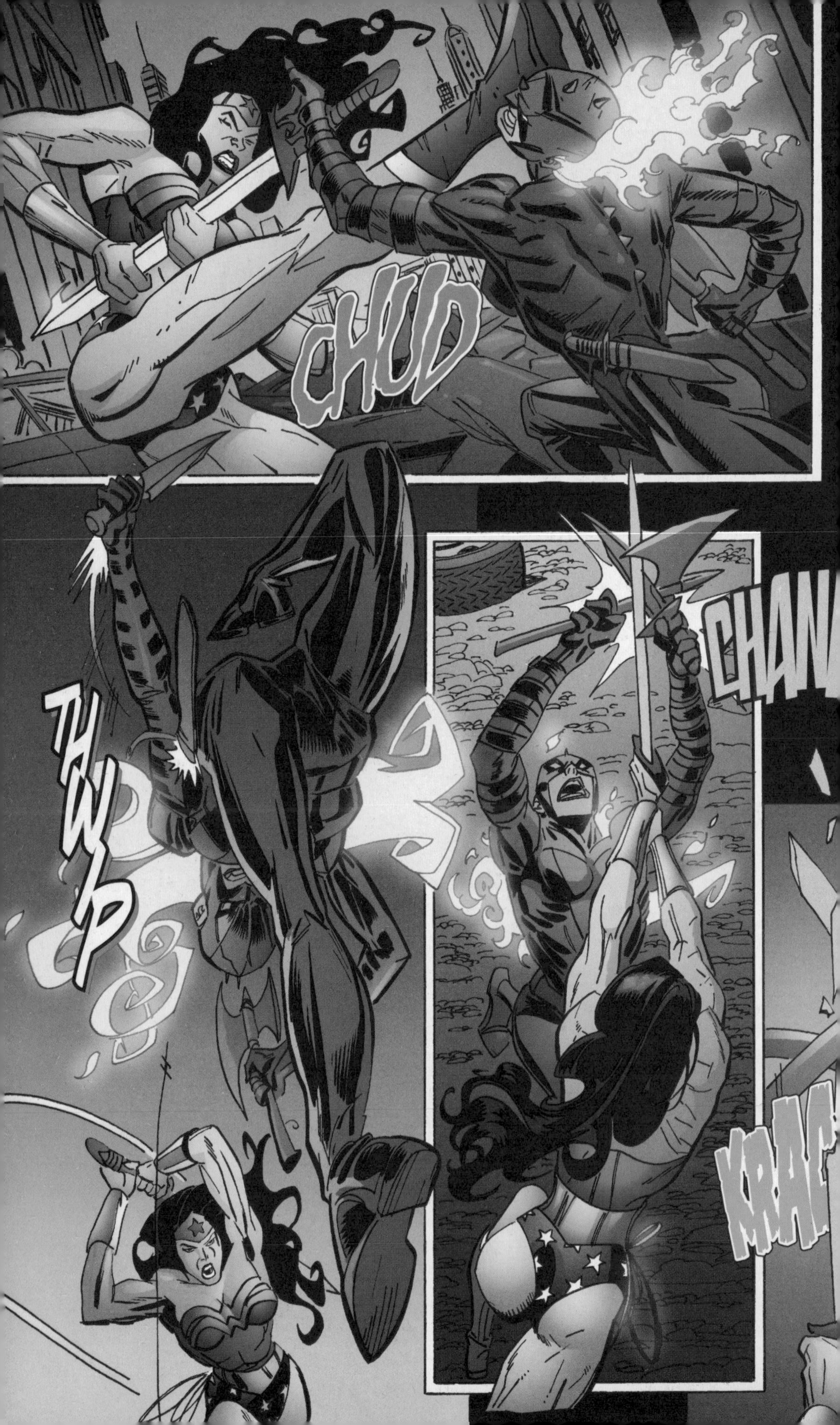
CHUD
THWIP

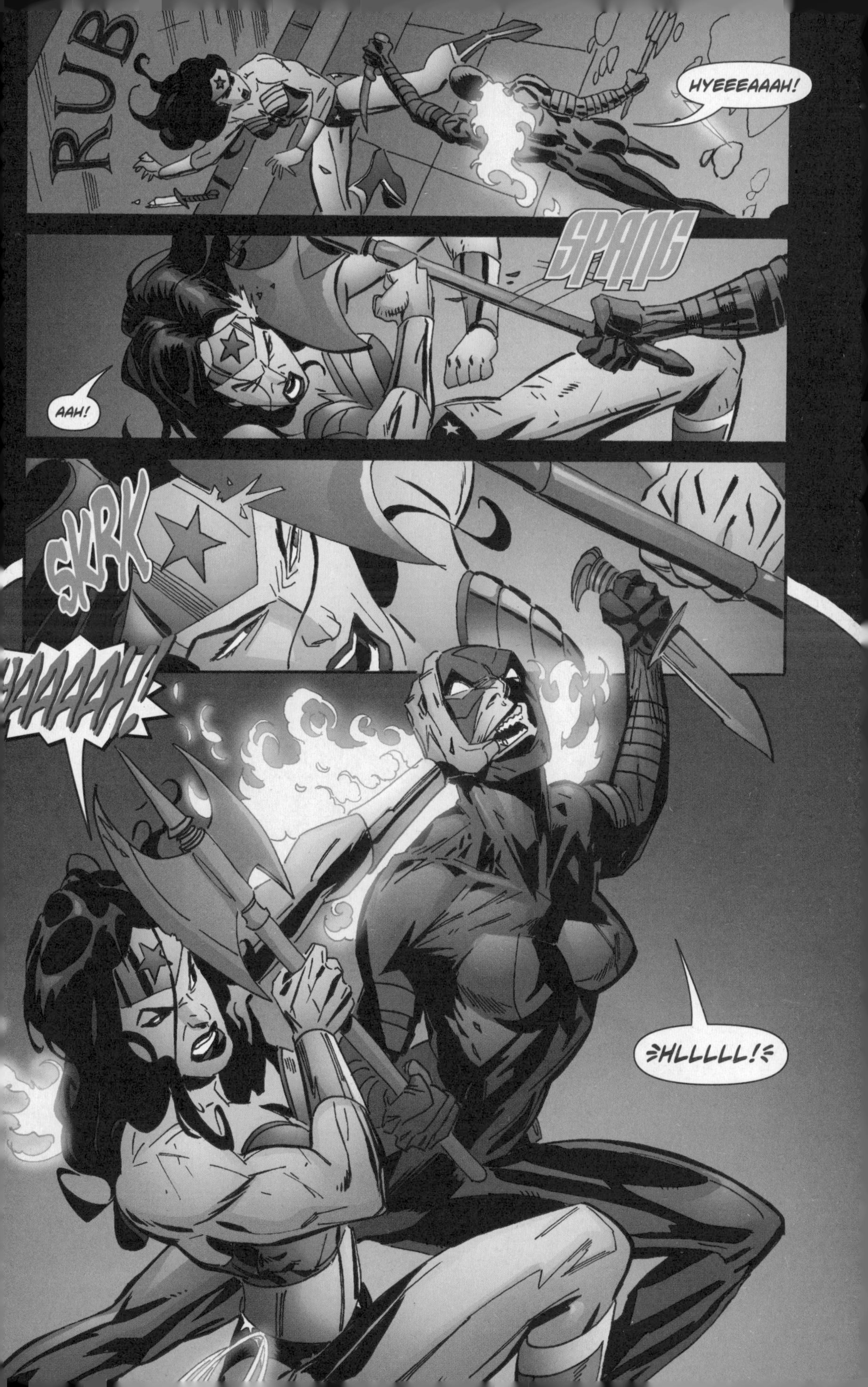
RUB
HYEEEAAAH!
SPANG
AAH!
SKRK
AAAAAH!
HLLLLL!

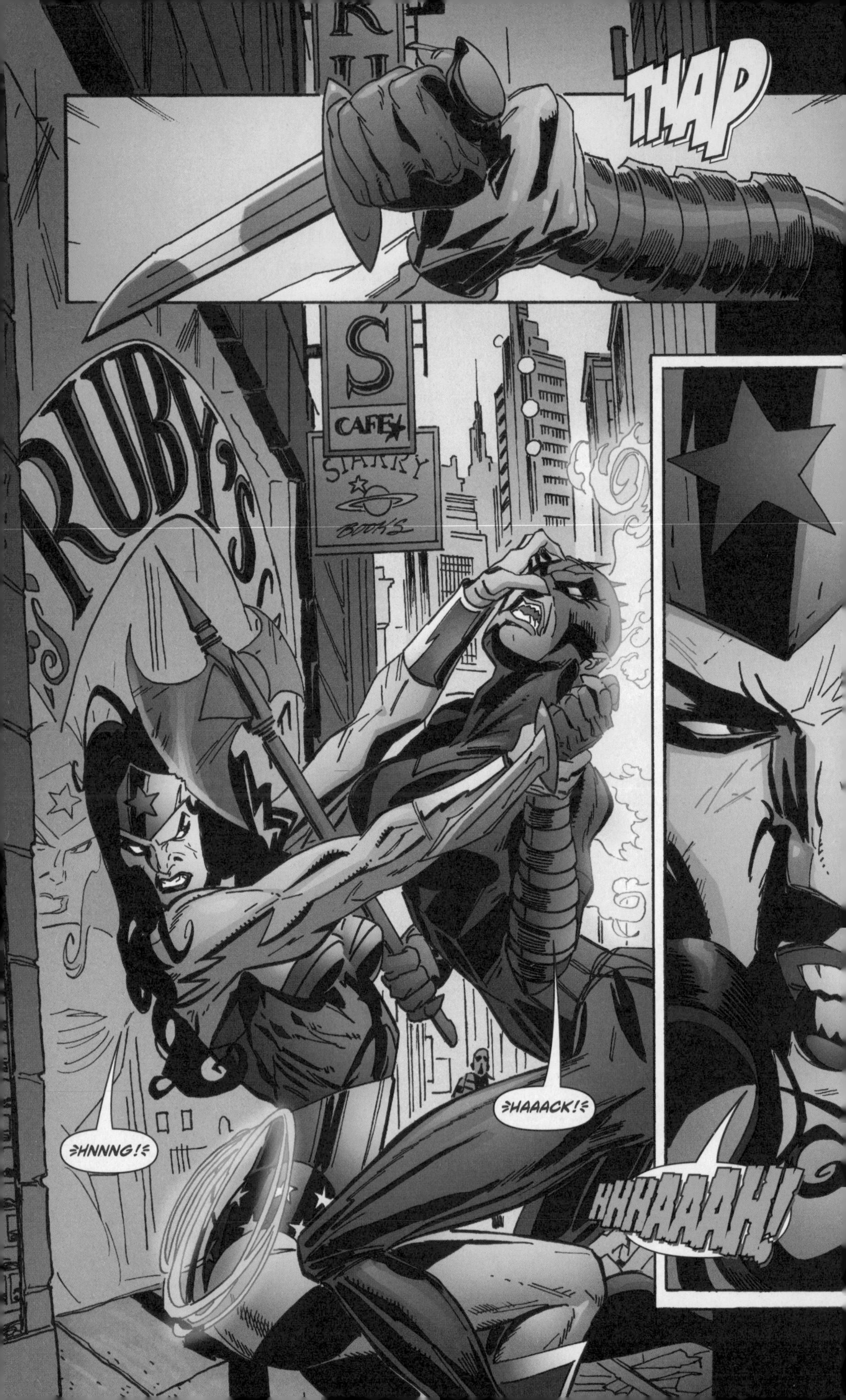

THAP
RUBY'S
S
CAFE
STARRY
BOOKS
HNNNG!
HAAACK!
HHHAAAAH!

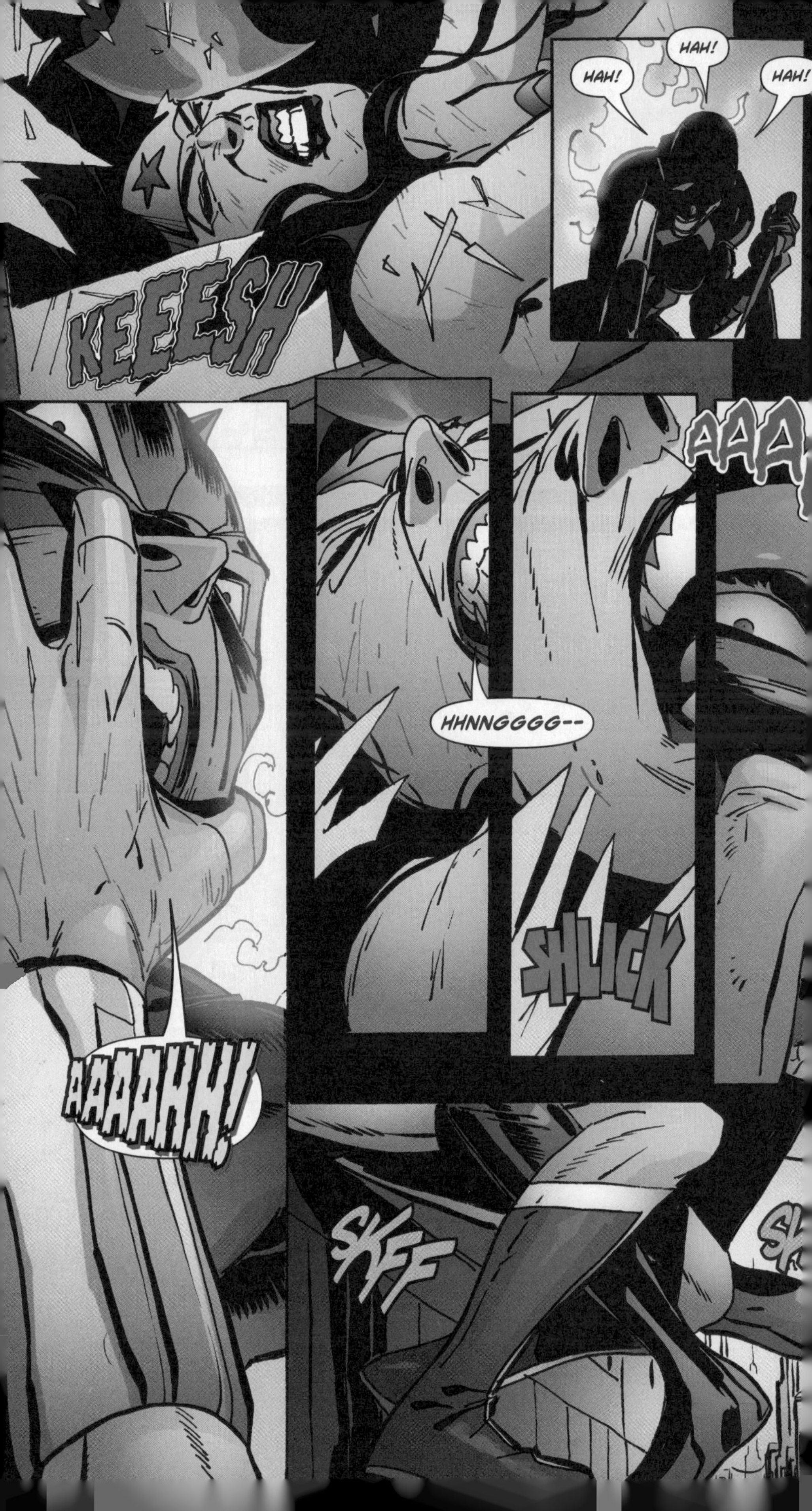
KEEESH
HAH!
HAH!
HAH!
AAAAHH!
HHNNGGGG--
AAA
SHLICK
SKFF

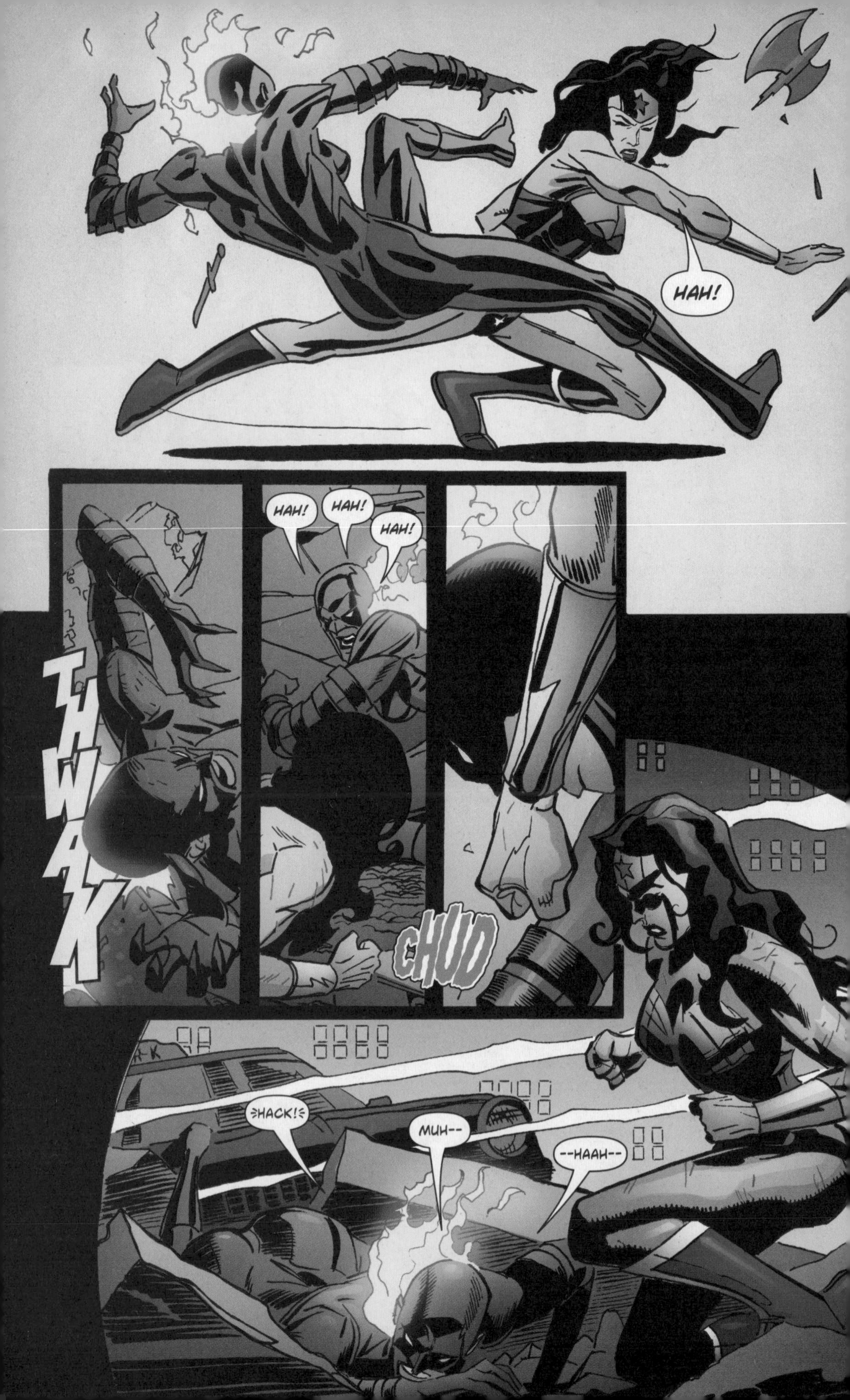
HAH!
THWAK
HAH!
HAH!
HAH!
CHUD
HACK!
MUH--
--HAAH--

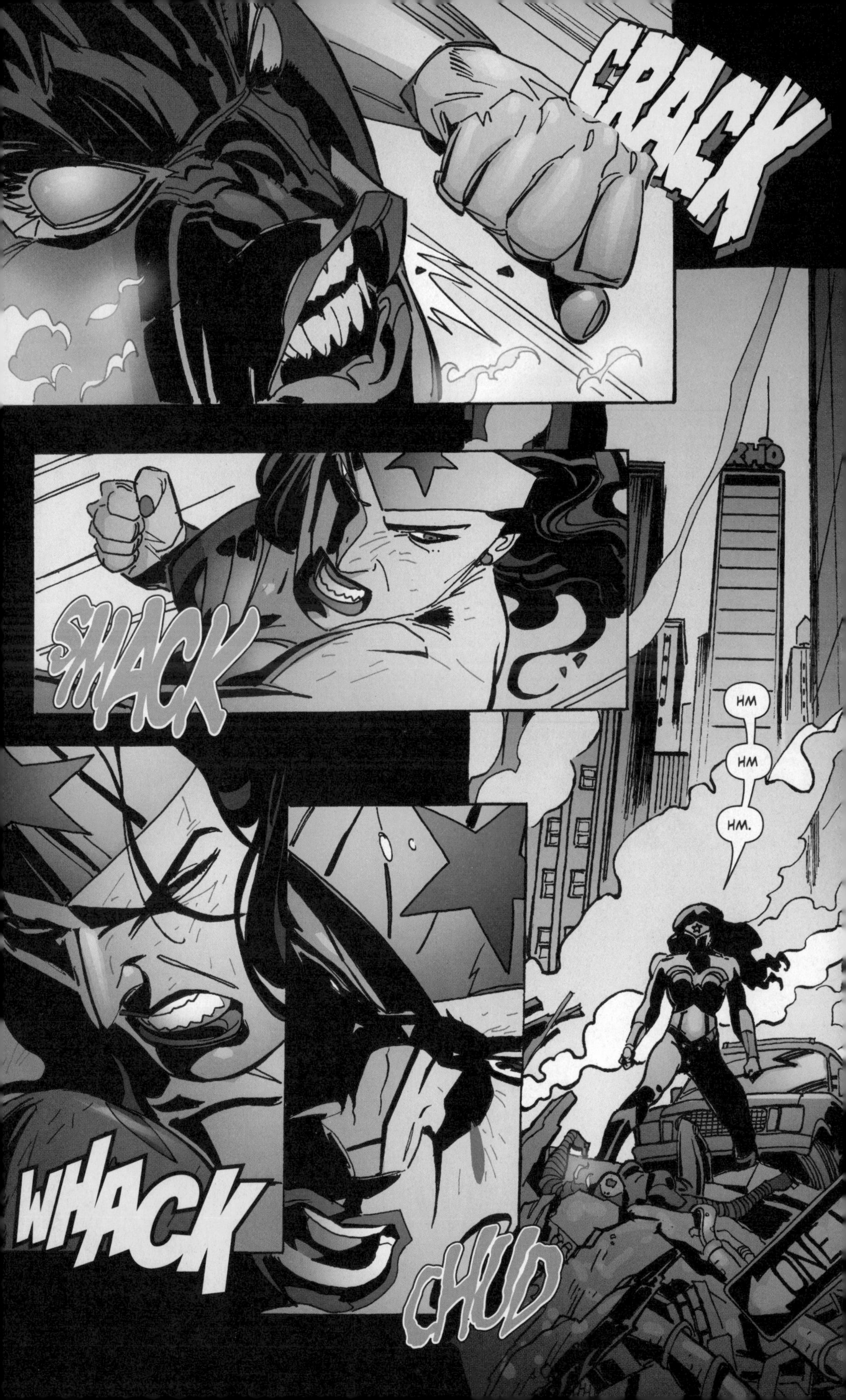
CRACK
SMACK
WHACK
CHUD
HM
HM
HM.

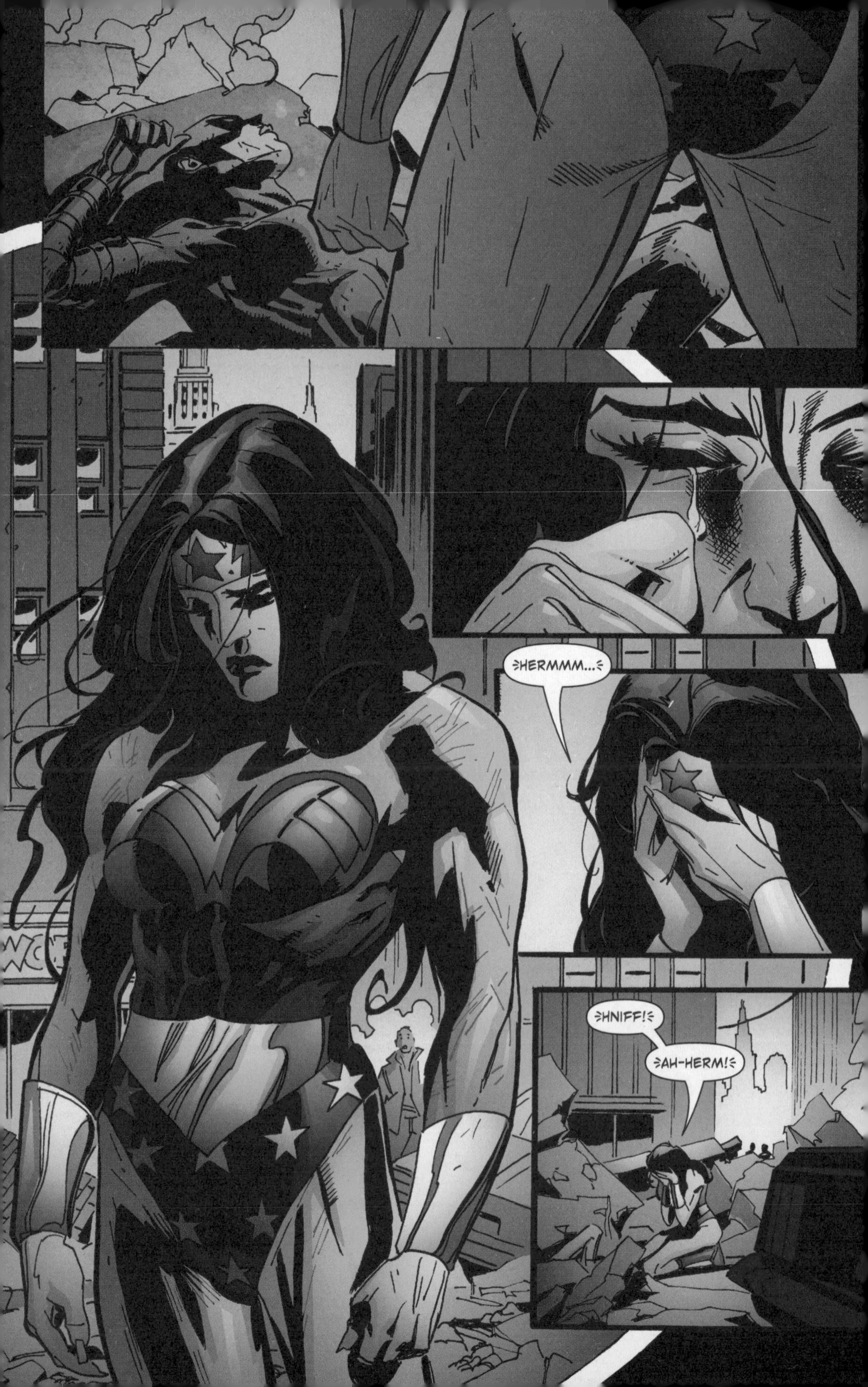
HERMMM...
HNIFF!
AH-HERM!

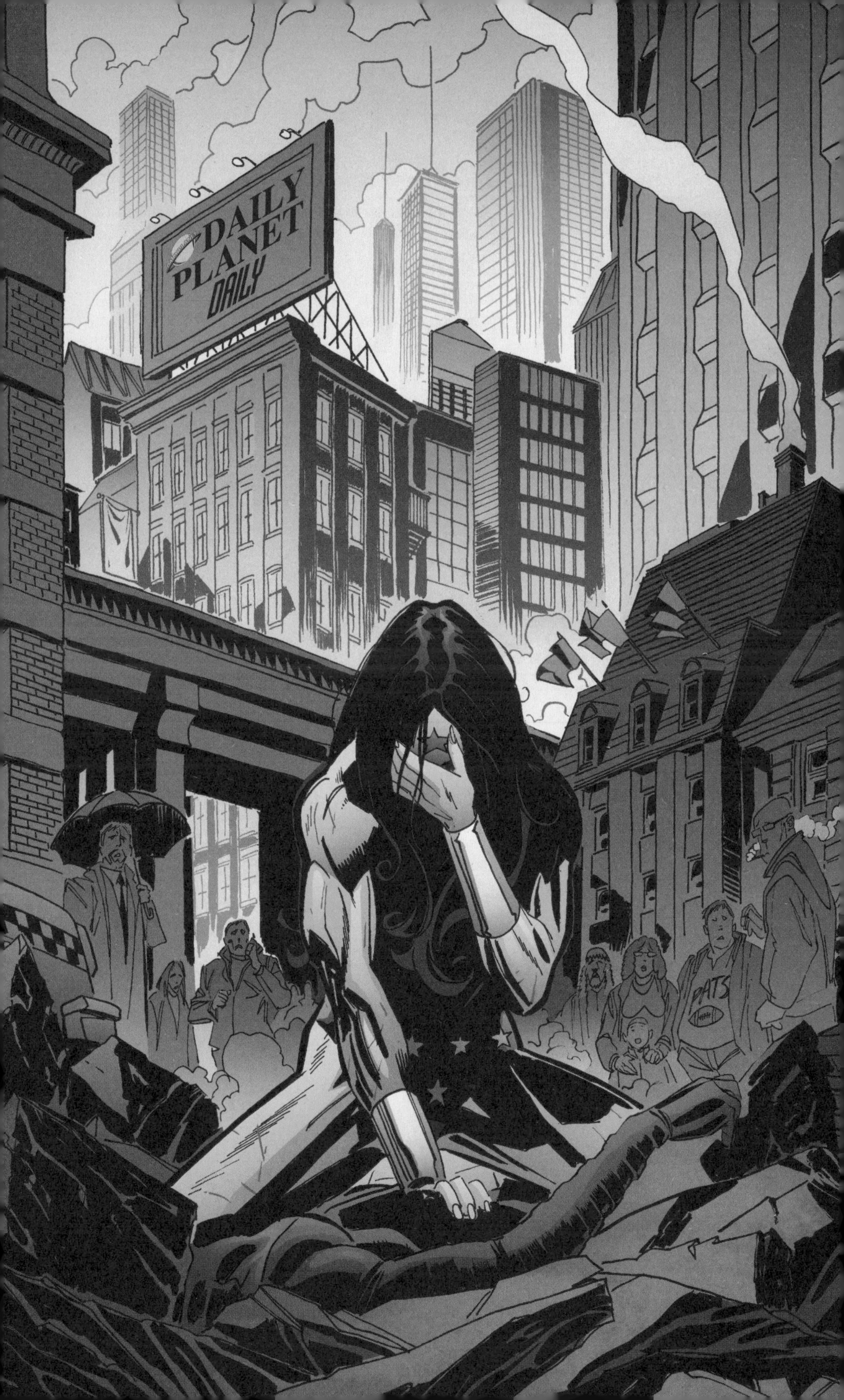
DAILY PLANET
DAILY
PATS

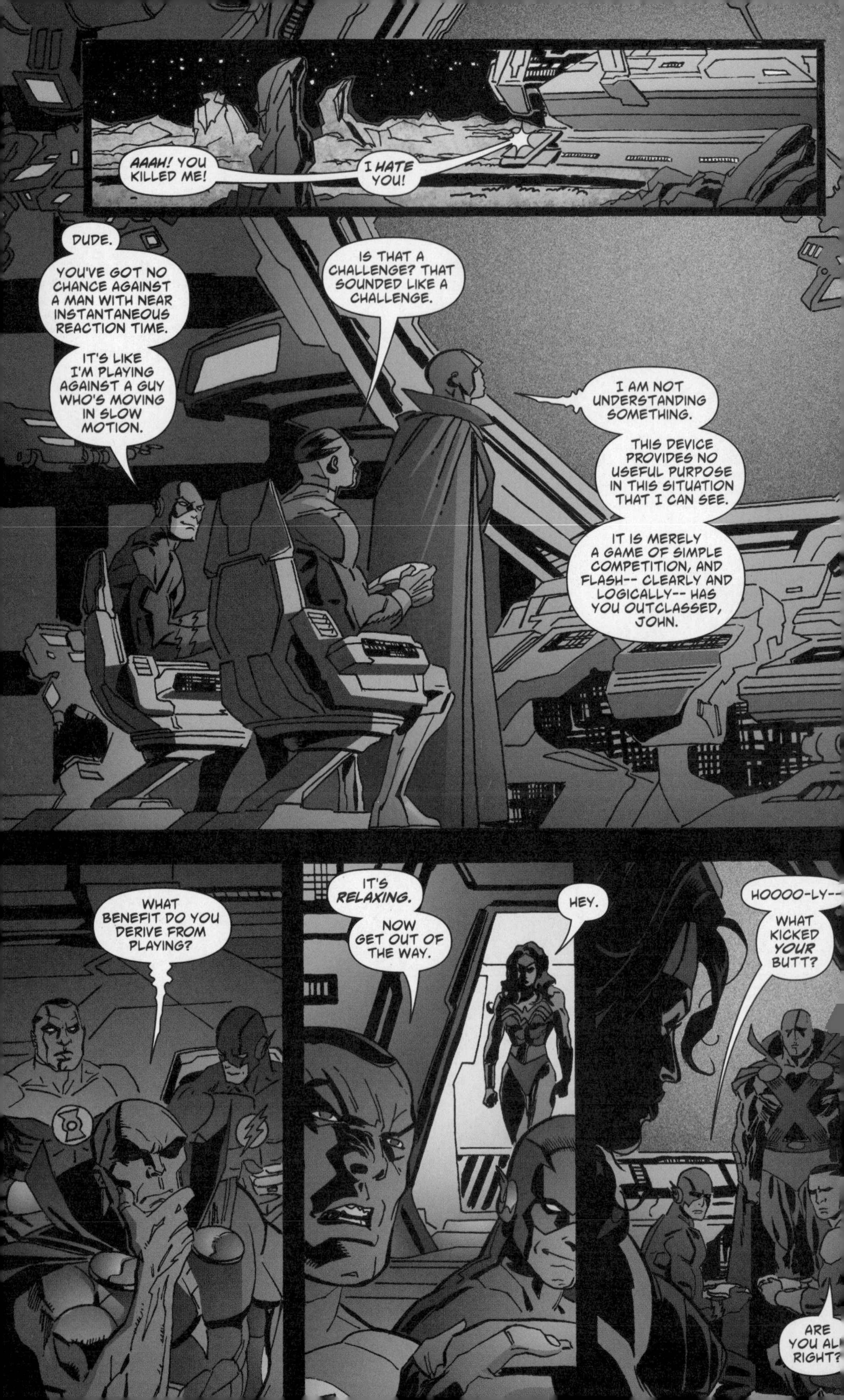

AAAH! YOU KILLED ME!
I HATE YOU!
DUDE.
YOU'VE GOT NO CHANCE AGAINST A MAN WITH NEAR INSTANTANEOUS REACTION TIME.
IT'S LIKE I'M PLAYING AGAINST A GUY WHO'S MOVING IN SLOW MOTION.
IS THAT A CHALLENGE? THAT SOUNDED LIKE A CHALLENGE.
I AM NOT UNDERSTANDING SOMETHING.
THIS DEVICE PROVIDES NO USEFUL PURPOSE IN THIS SITUATION THAT I CAN SEE.
IT IS MERELY A GAME OF SIMPLE COMPETITION, AND FLASH-- CLEARLY AND LOGICALLY-- HAS YOU OUTCLASSED, JOHN.
WHAT BENEFIT DO YOU DERIVE FROM PLAYING?
IT'S RELAXING.
NOW GET OUT OF THE WAY.
HEY.
HOOOO-LY--
WHAT KICKED YOUR BUTT?
ARE YOU AL RIGHT?

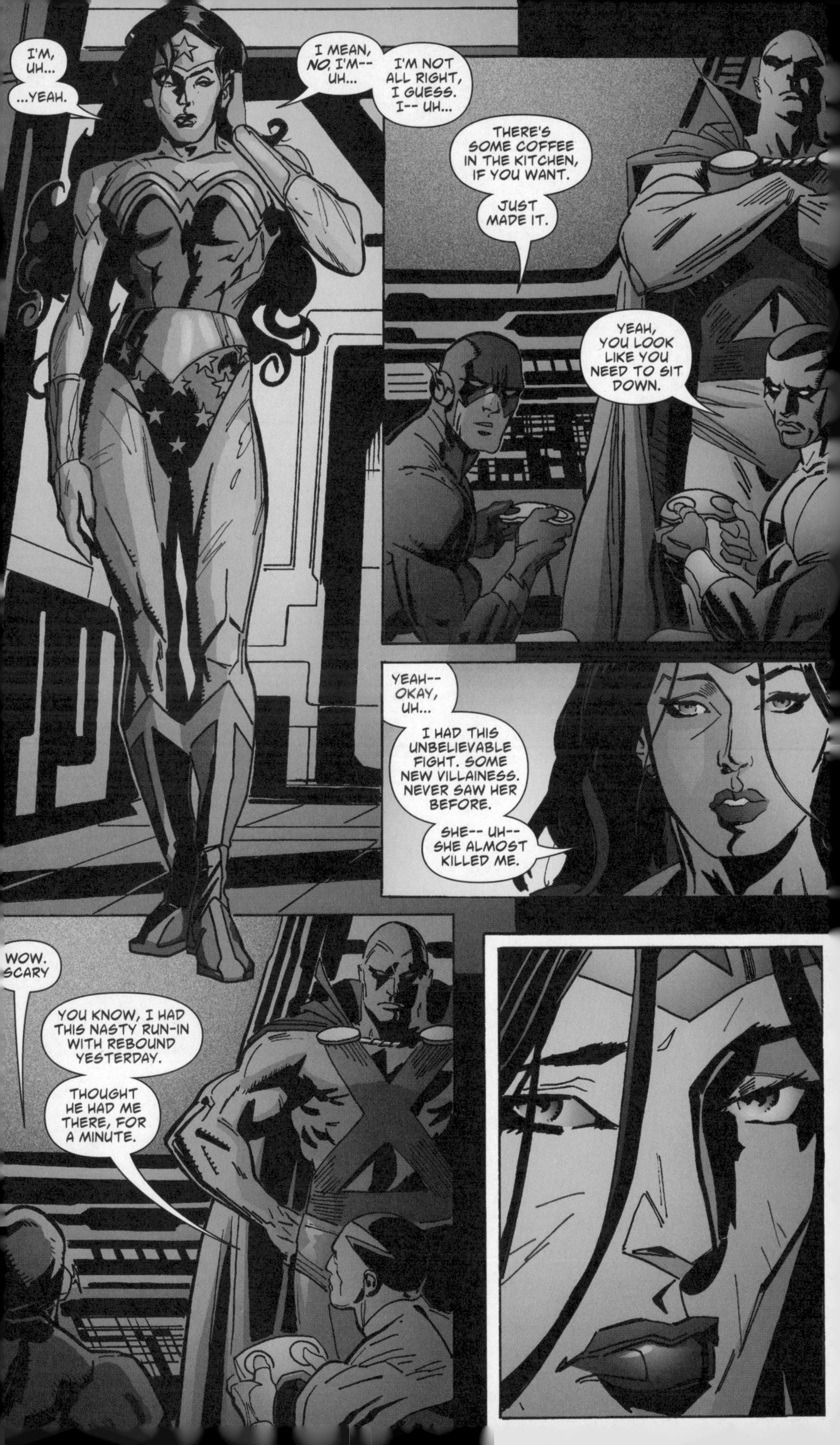
I'M, UH...
...YEAH.
I MEAN, NO, I'M-- UH...
I'M NOT ALL RIGHT, I GUESS. I-- UH...
THERE'S SOME COFFEE IN THE KITCHEN, IF YOU WANT.
JUST MADE IT.
YEAH, YOU LOOK LIKE YOU NEED TO SIT DOWN.
YEAH-- OKAY, UH...
I HAD THIS UNBELIEVABLE FIGHT. SOME NEW VILLAINESS. NEVER SAW HER BEFORE.
SHE-- UH-- SHE ALMOST KILLED ME.
WOW. SCARY
YOU KNOW, I HAD THIS NASTY RUN-IN WITH REBOUND YESTERDAY.
THOUGHT HE HAD ME THERE, FOR A MINUTE.

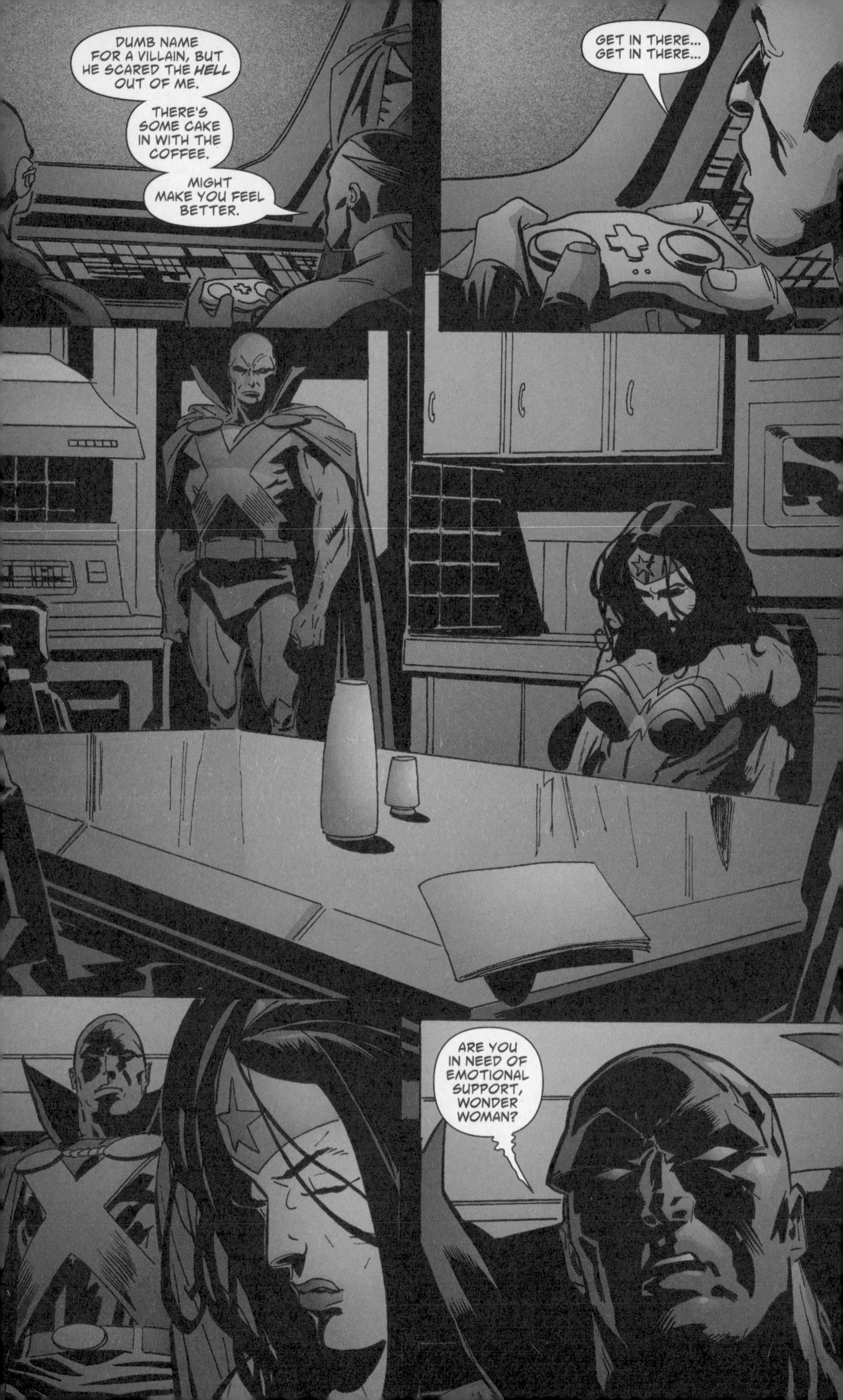
DUMB NAME FOR A VILLAIN, BUT HE SCARED THE HELL OUT OF ME.
THERE'S SOME CAKE IN WITH THE COFFEE.
MIGHT MAKE YOU FEEL BETTER.
GET IN THERE... GET IN THERE...
ARE YOU IN NEED OF EMOTIONAL SUPPORT, WONDER WOMAN?

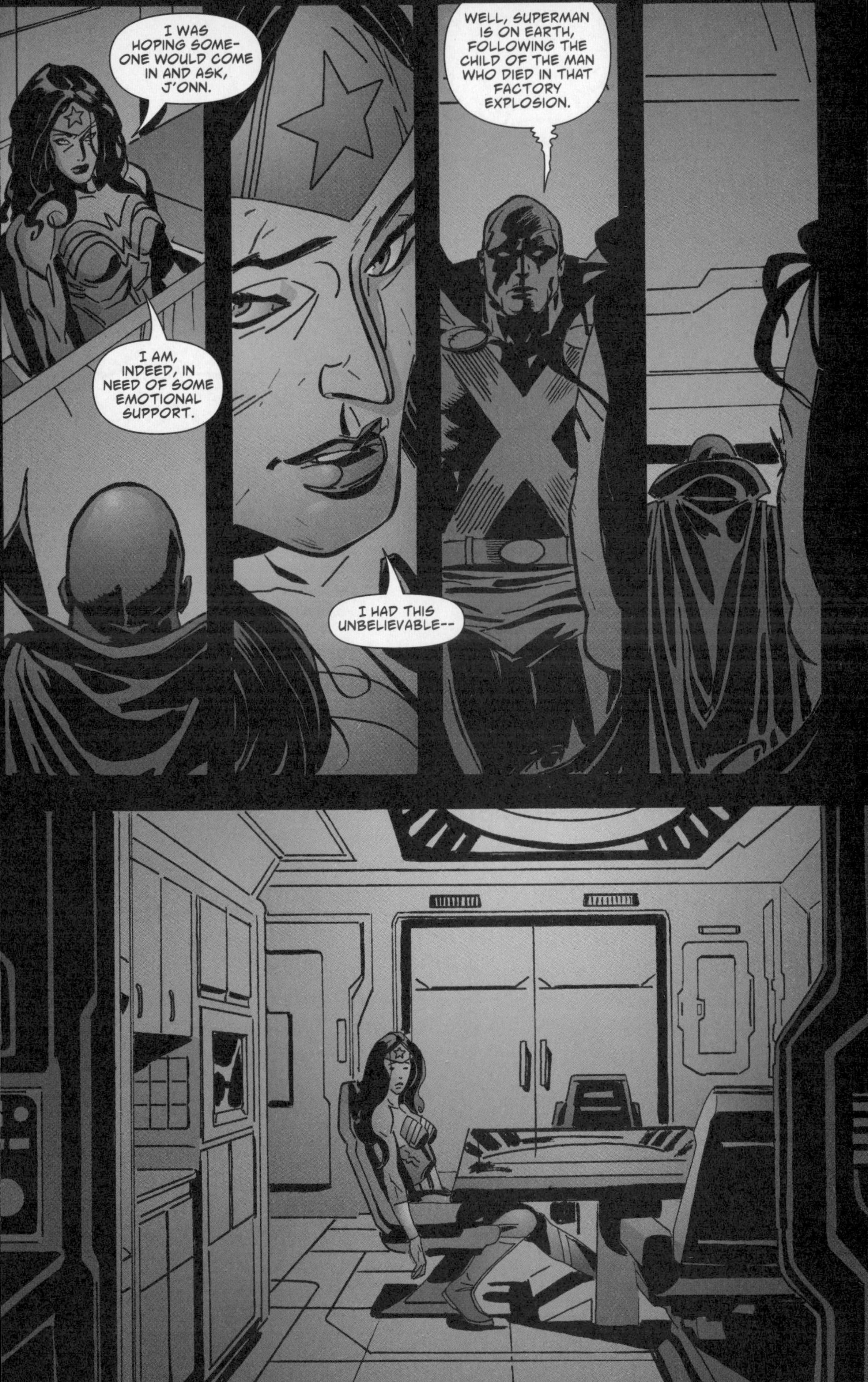
I WAS HOPING SOME-ONE WOULD COME IN AND ASK, J'ONN.
I AM, INDEED, IN NEED OF SOME EMOTIONAL SUPPORT.
I HAD THIS UNBELIEVABLE--
WELL, SUPERMAN IS ON EARTH, FOLLOWING THE CHILD OF THE MAN WHO DIED IN THAT FACTORY EXPLOSION.

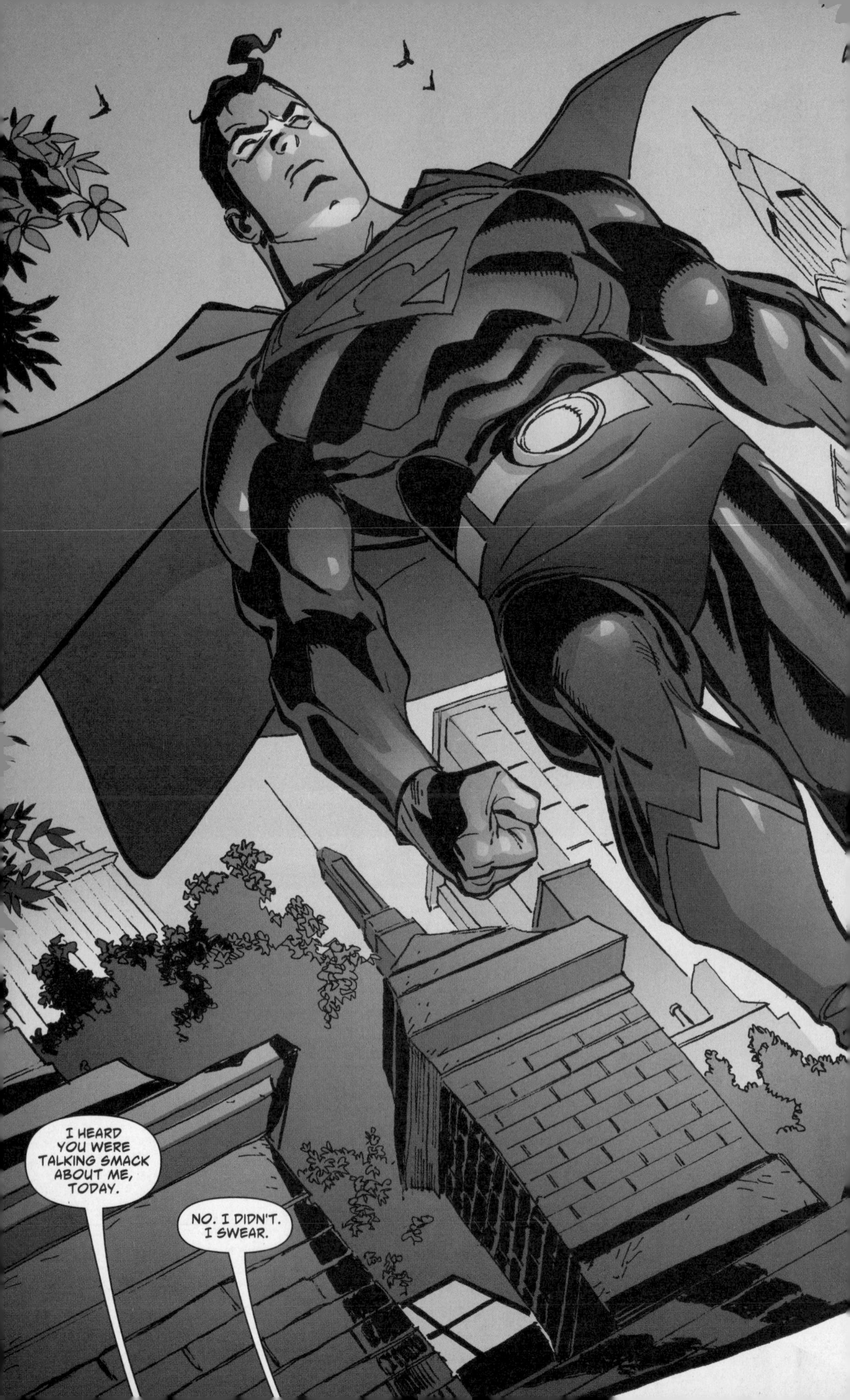
I HEARD YOU WERE TALKING SMACK ABOUT ME, TODAY.
NO. I DIDN'T. I SWEAR.

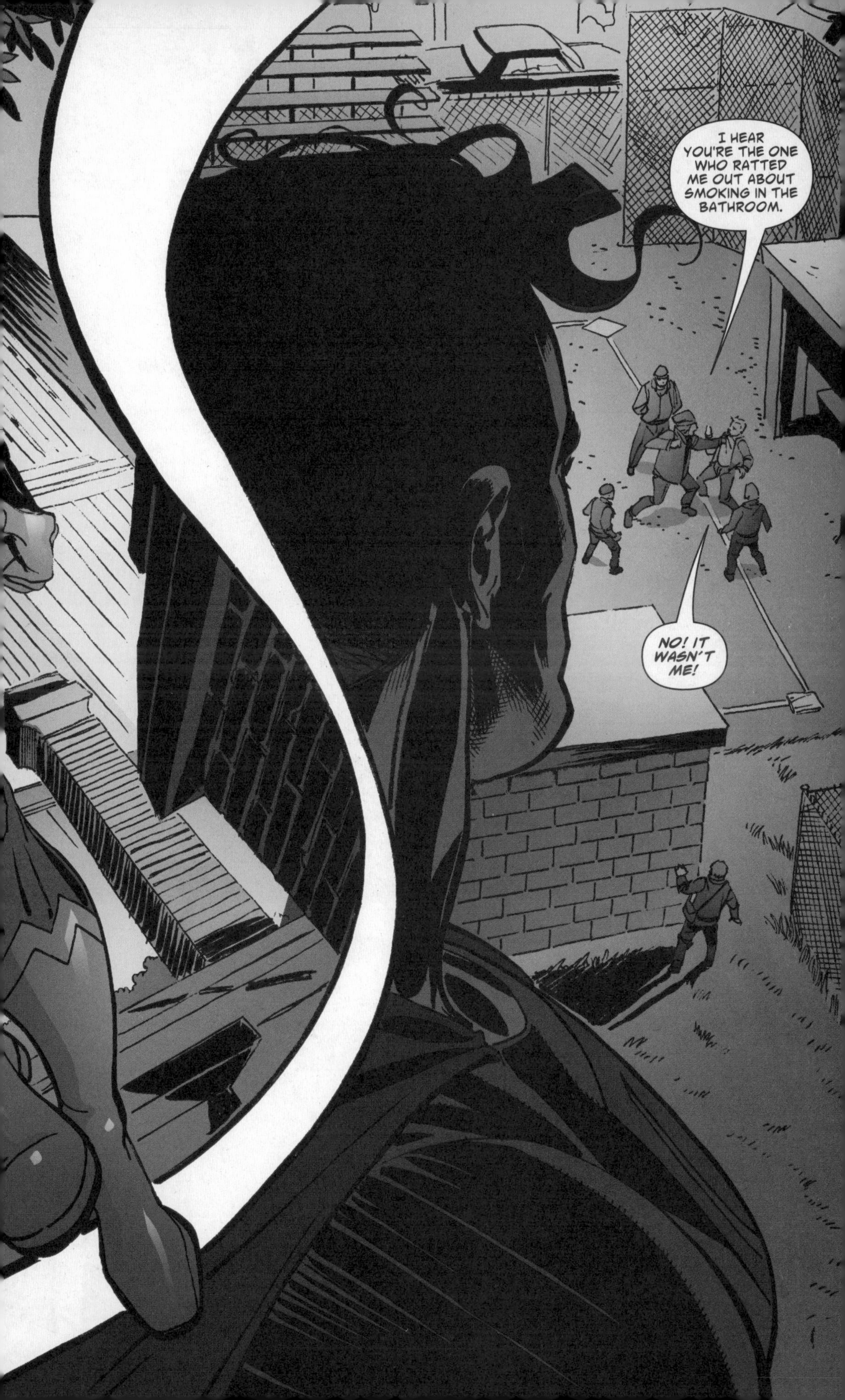
I HEAR YOU'RE THE ONE WHO RATTED ME OUT ABOUT SMOKING IN THE BATHROOM.
NO! IT WASN'T ME!

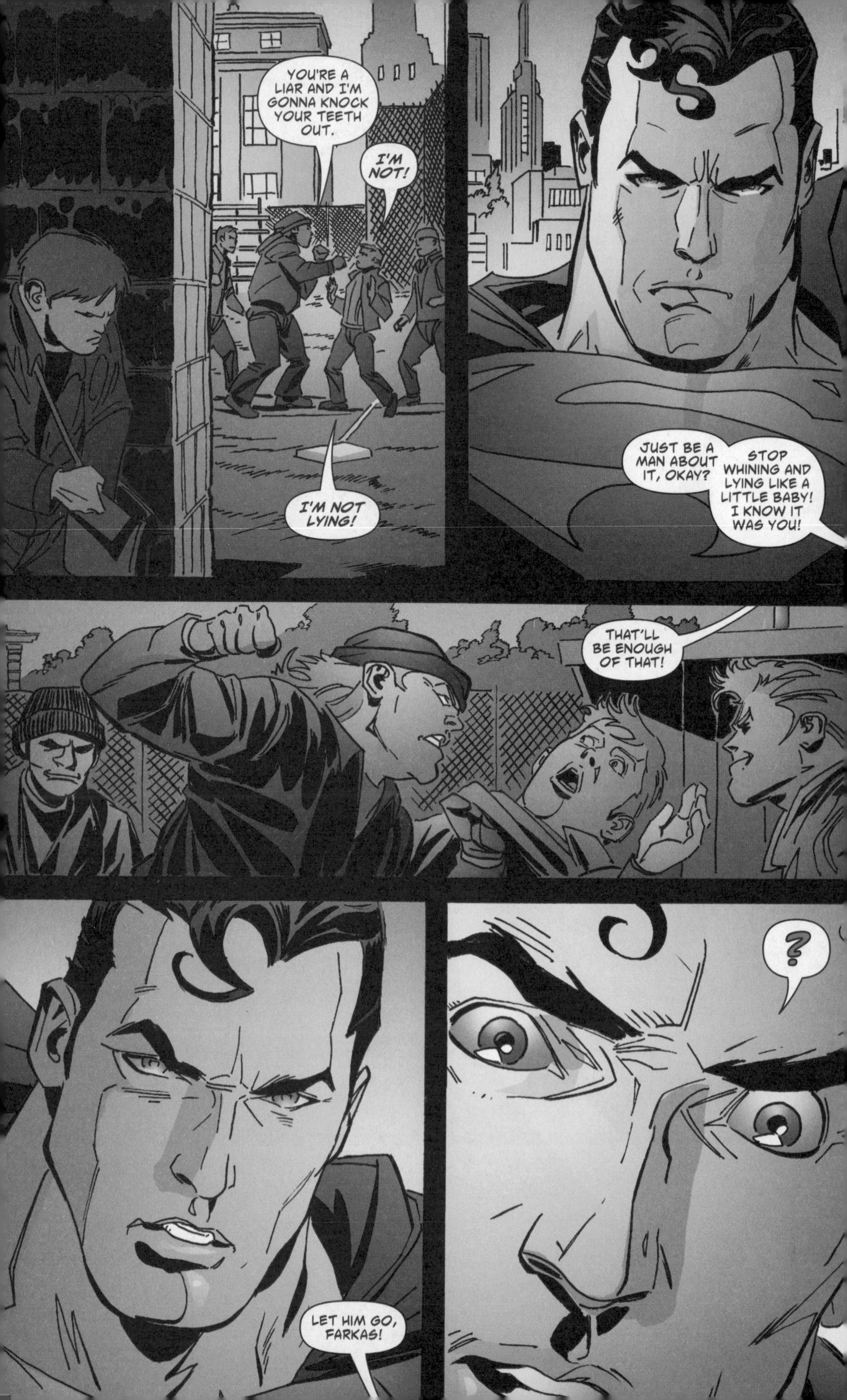
YOU'RE A LIAR AND I'M GONNA KNOCK YOUR TEETH OUT.
I'M NOT!
I'M NOT LYING!
JUST BE A MAN ABOUT IT, OKAY?
STOP WHINING AND LYING LIKE A LITTLE BABY! I KNOW IT WAS YOU!
THAT'LL BE ENOUGH OF THAT!
LET HIM GO, FARKAS!
?

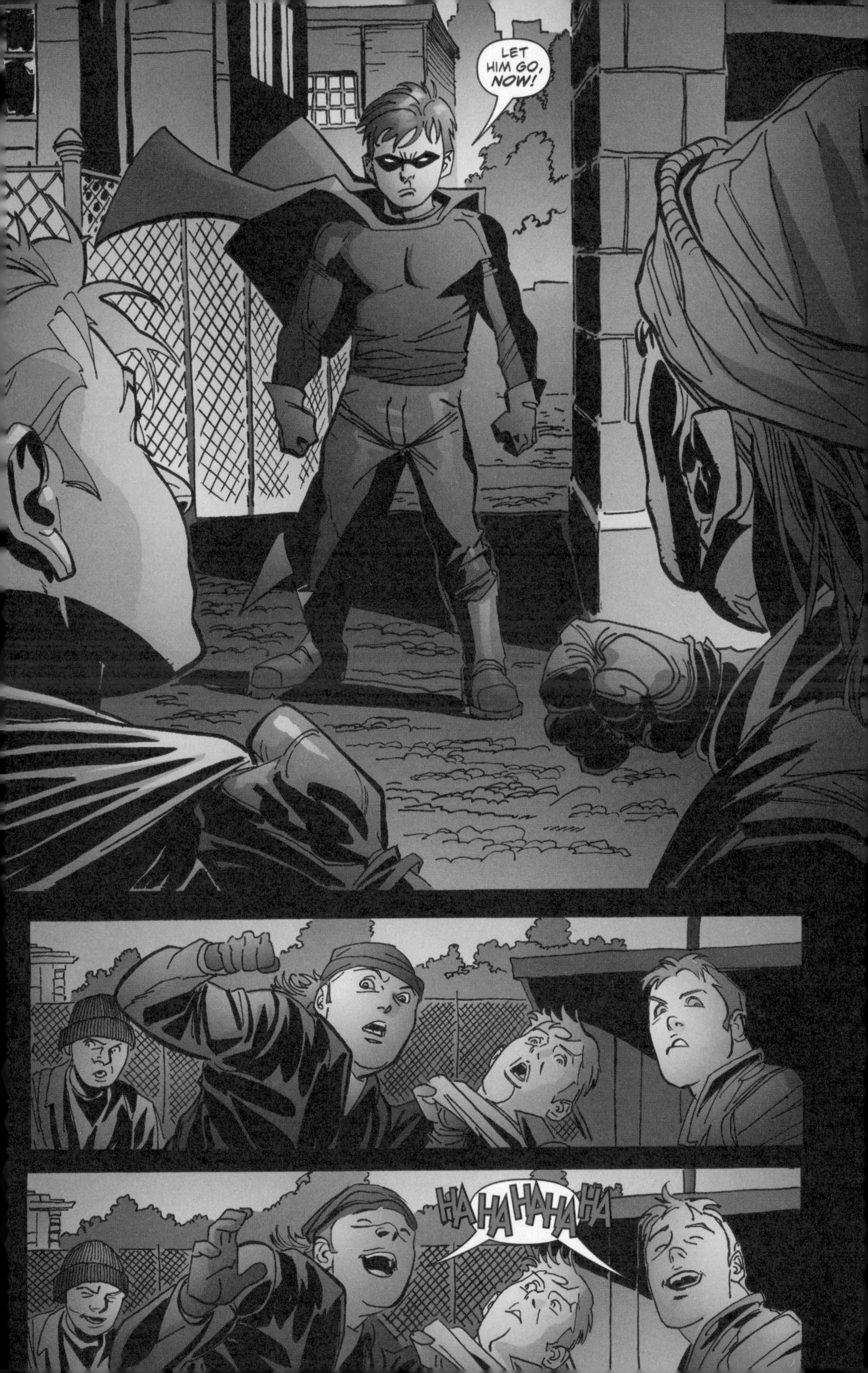

LET HIM GO, NOW!
HA HA HAHAHA HA

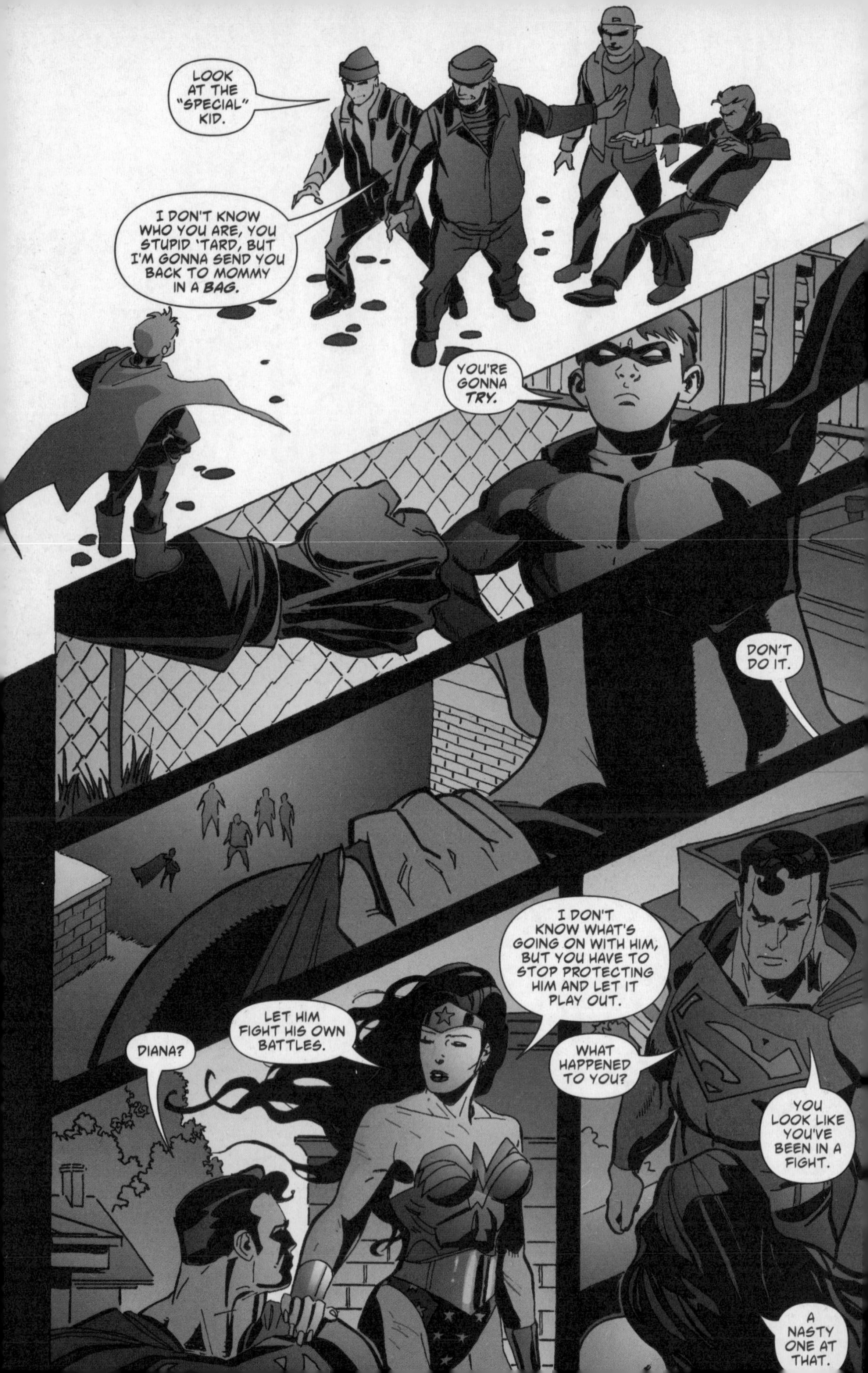
LOOK AT THE "SPECIAL" KID.
I DON'T KNOW WHO YOU ARE, YOU STUPID 'TARD, BUT I'M GONNA SEND YOU BACK TO MOMMY IN A BAG.
YOU'RE GONNA TRY.
DON'T DO IT.
DIANA?
LET HIM FIGHT HIS OWN BATTLES.
I DON'T KNOW WHAT'S GOING ON WITH HIM, BUT YOU HAVE TO STOP PROTECTING HIM AND LET IT PLAY OUT.
WHAT HAPPENED TO YOU?
YOU LOOK LIKE YOU'VE BEEN IN A FIGHT.
A NASTY ONE AT THAT.

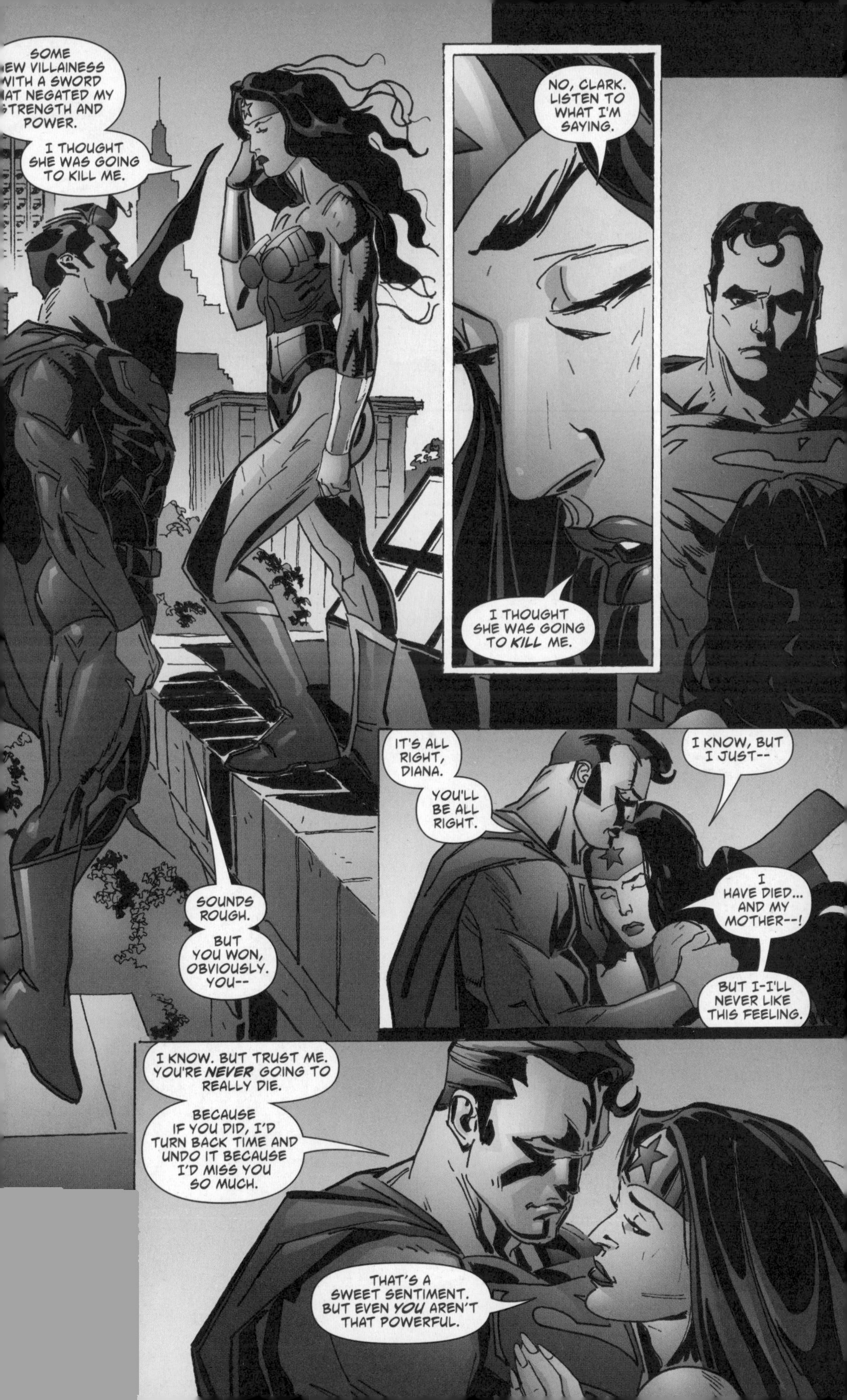
SOME
EW VILLAINESS
WITH A SWORD
AT NEGATED MY
STRENGTH AND
POWER.
I THOUGHT SHE WAS GOING TO KILL ME.
SOUNDS ROUGH.
BUT YOU WON, OBVIOUSLY. YOU--
NO, CLARK. LISTEN TO WHAT I'M SAYING.
I THOUGHT SHE WAS GOING TO *KILL* ME.
IT'S ALL RIGHT, DIANA.
YOU'LL BE ALL RIGHT.
I KNOW, BUT I JUST--
I HAVE DIED... AND MY MOTHER--!
BUT I-I'LL NEVER LIKE THIS FEELING.
I KNOW. BUT TRUST ME. YOU'RE *NEVER* GOING TO REALLY DIE.
BECAUSE IF YOU DID, I'D TURN BACK TIME AND UNDO IT BECAUSE I'D MISS YOU SO MUCH.
THAT'S A SWEET SENTIMENT. BUT EVEN *YOU* AREN'T THAT POWERFUL.

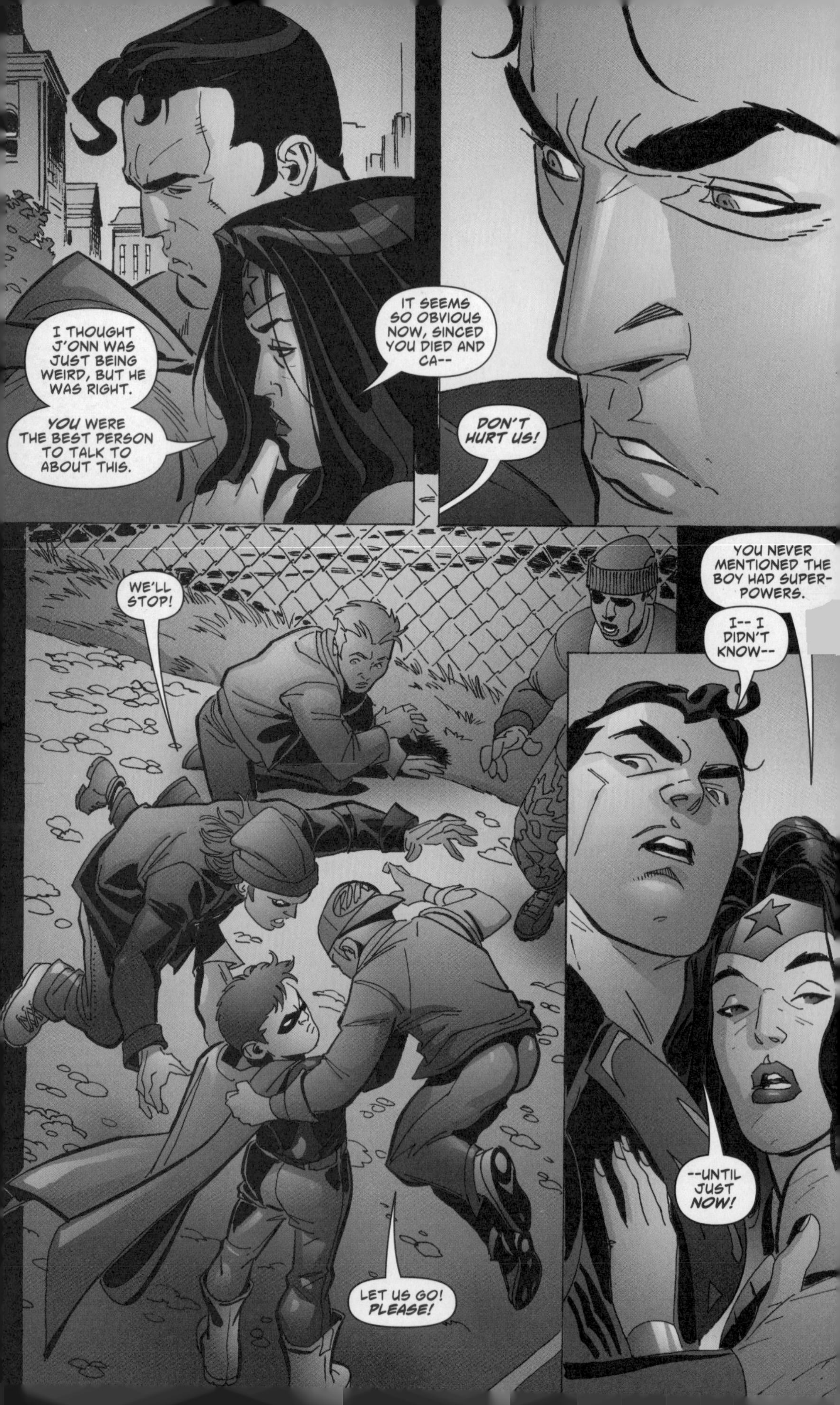
I THOUGHT J'ONN WAS JUST BEING WEIRD, BUT HE WAS RIGHT.
YOU WERE THE BEST PERSON TO TALK TO ABOUT THIS.
IT SEEMS SO OBVIOUS NOW, SINCED YOU DIED AND CA--
DON'T HURT US!
WE'LL STOP!
YOU NEVER MENTIONED THE BOY HAD SUPER-POWERS.
I-- I DIDN'T KNOW--
--UNTIL JUST *NOW!*
LET US GO! *PLEASE!*

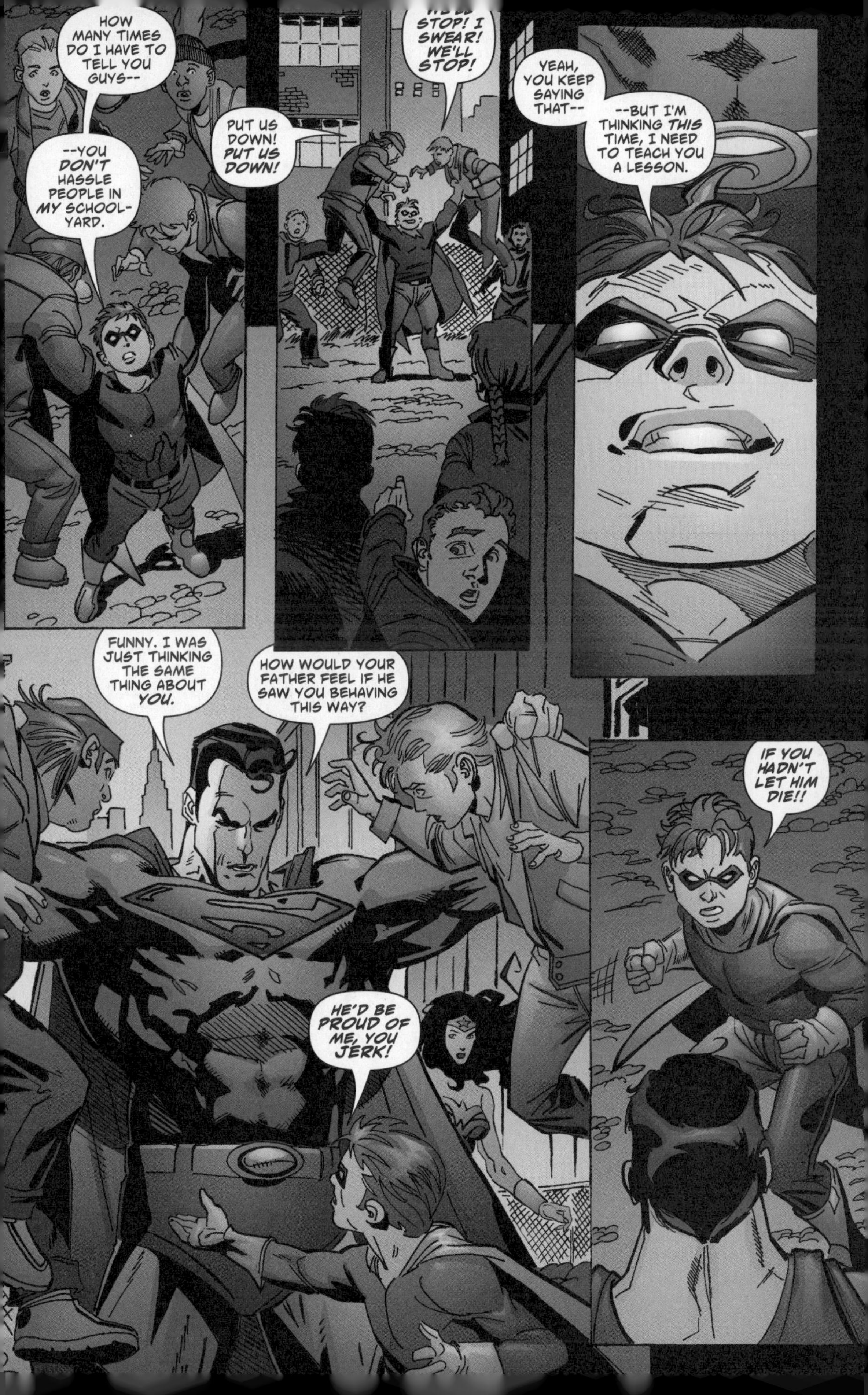
HOW MANY TIMES DO I HAVE TO TELL YOU GUYS--
--YOU DON'T HASSLE PEOPLE IN MY SCHOOL-YARD.
PUT US DOWN! PUT US DOWN!
STOP! I SWEAR! WE'LL STOP!
YEAH, YOU KEEP SAYING THAT--
--BUT I'M THINKING THIS TIME, I NEED TO TEACH YOU A LESSON.
FUNNY. I WAS JUST THINKING THE SAME THING ABOUT YOU.
HOW WOULD YOUR FATHER FEEL IF HE SAW YOU BEHAVING THIS WAY?
HE'D BE PROUD OF ME, YOU JERK!
IF YOU HADN'T LET HIM DIE!!

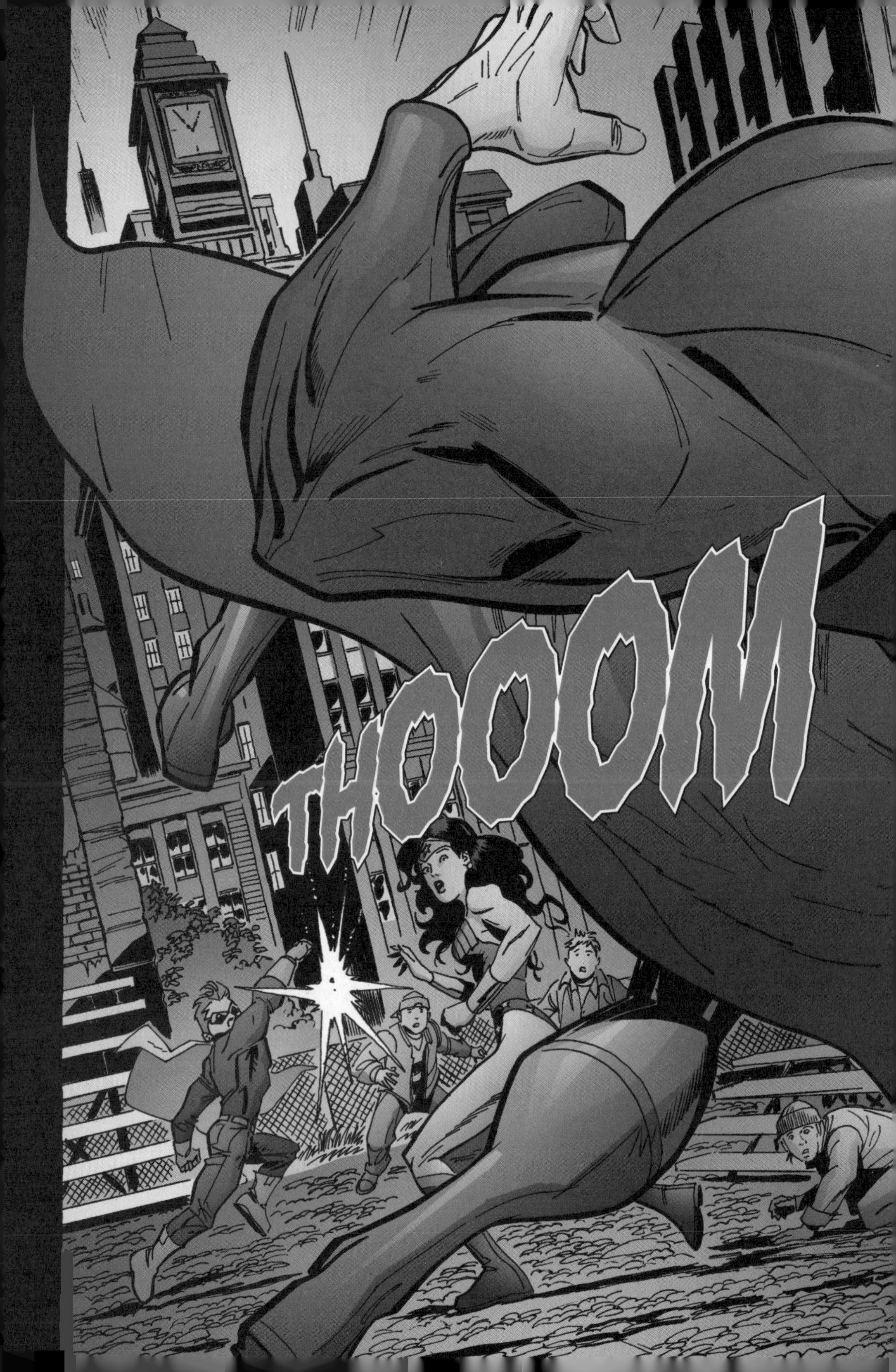
THOOOM

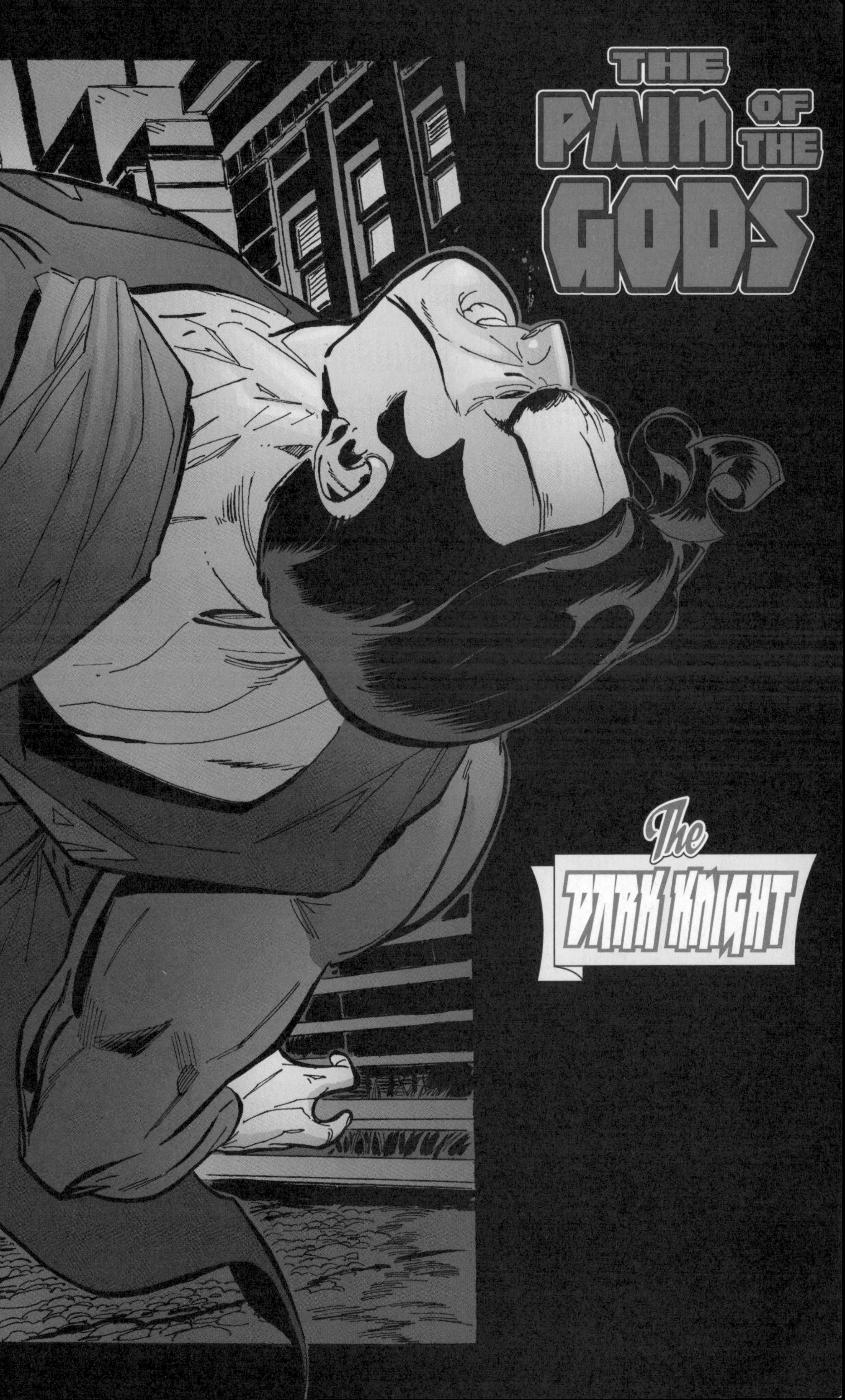
THE PAIN OF THE GODS
The DARK KNIGHT

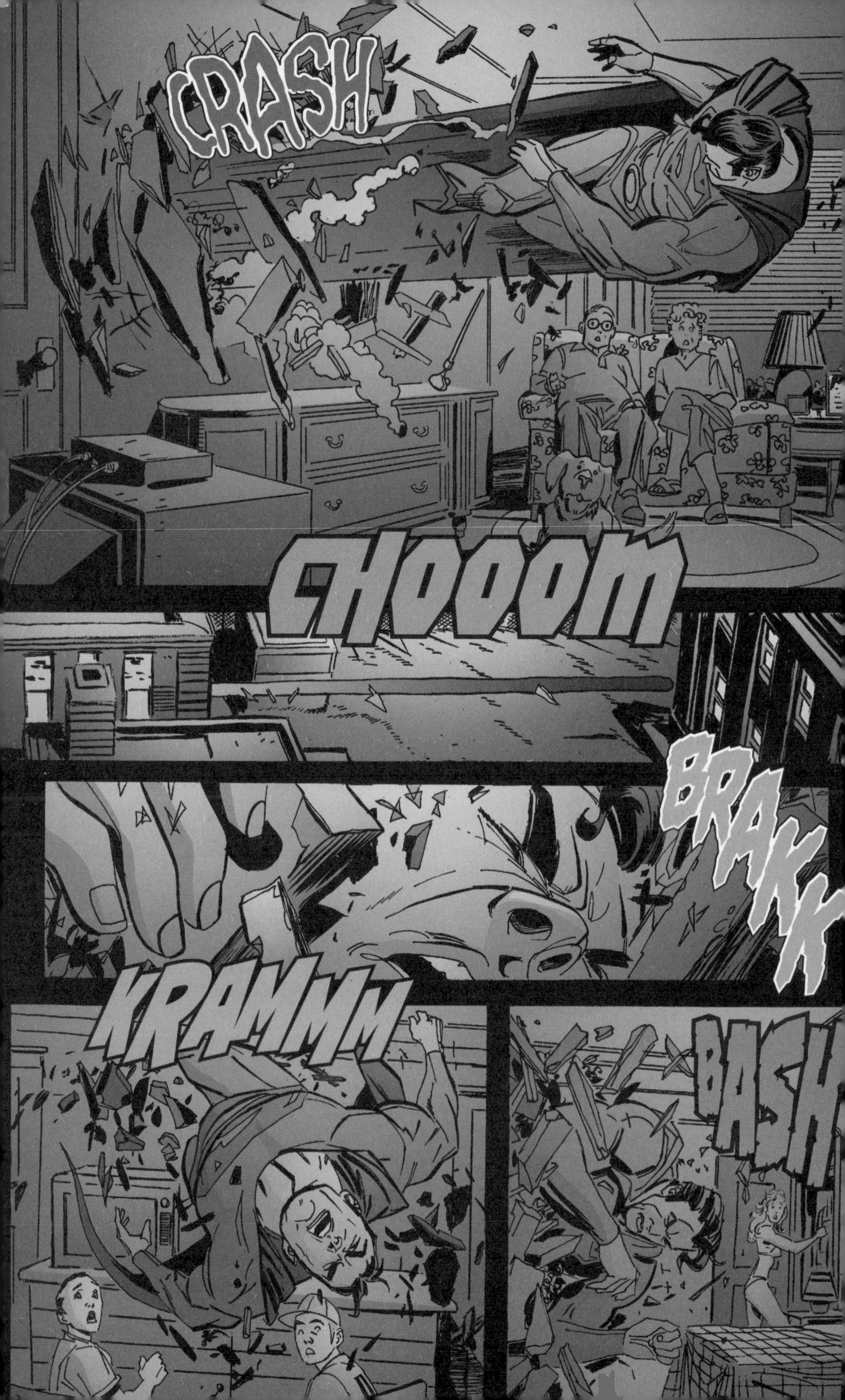
CRASH
CHOOOM
BRAKK
KRAMMM
BASH

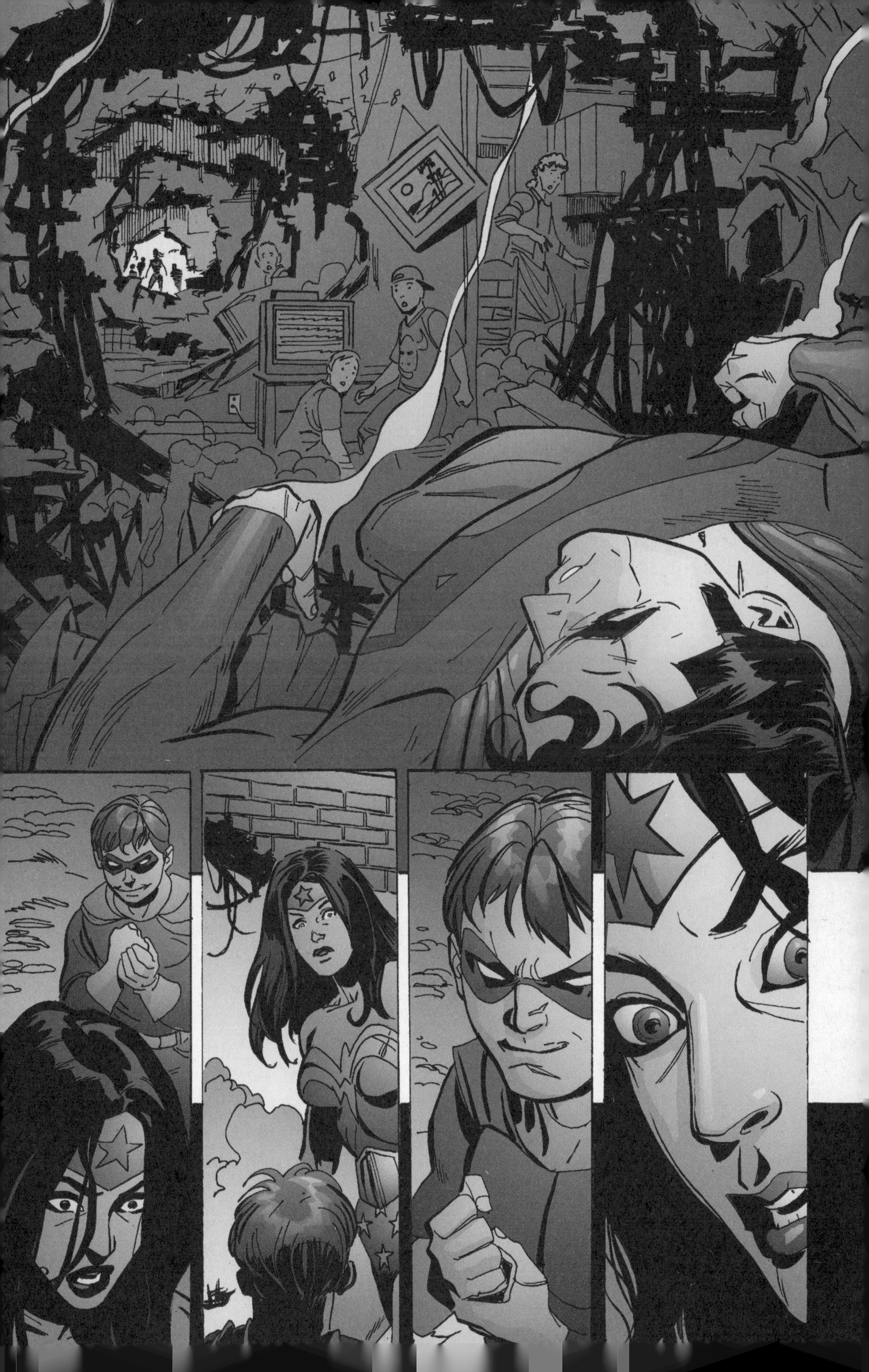

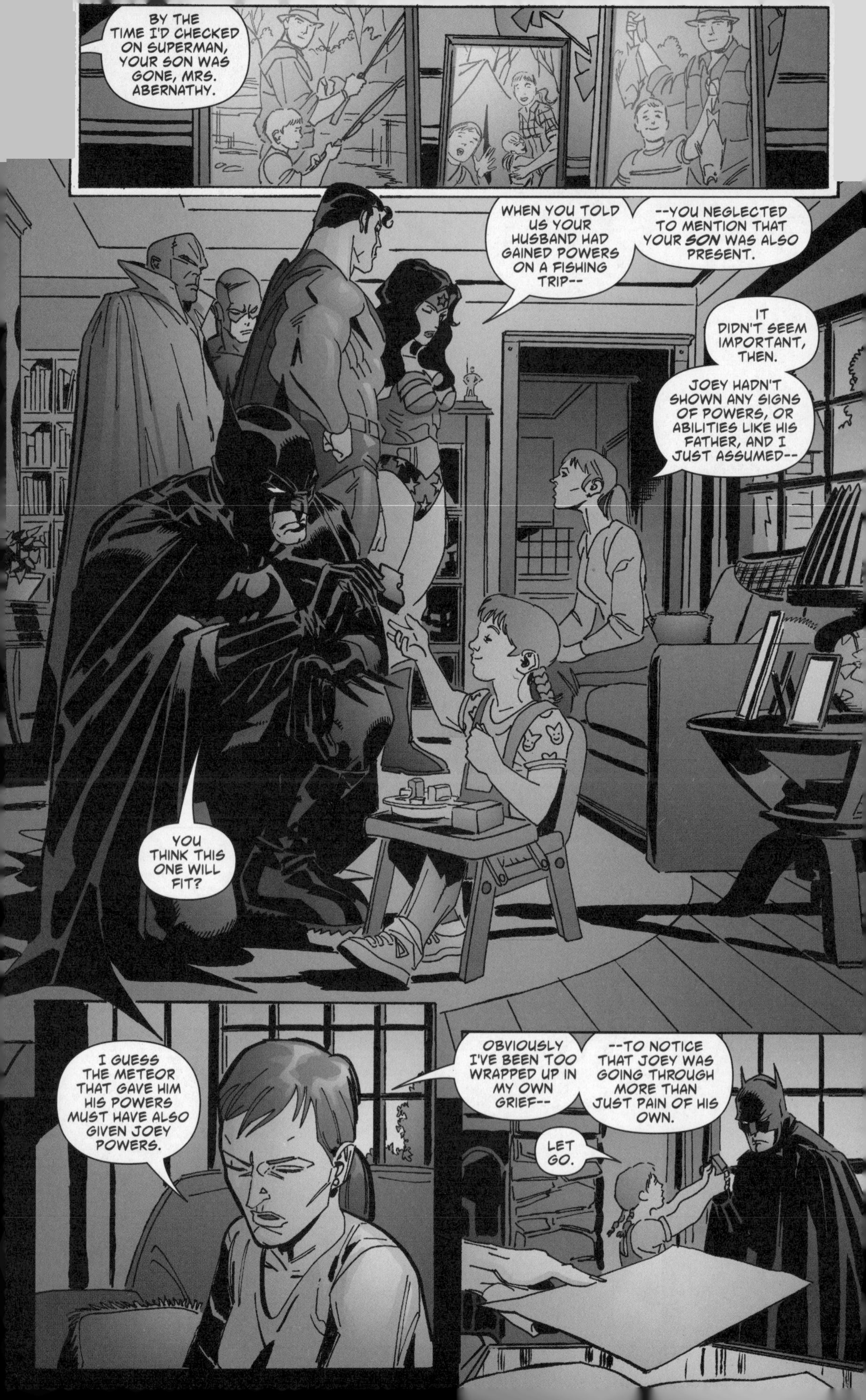
BY THE TIME I'D CHECKED ON SUPERMAN, YOUR SON WAS GONE, MRS. ABERNATHY.
WHEN YOU TOLD US YOUR HUSBAND HAD GAINED POWERS ON A FISHING TRIP--
--YOU NEGLECTED TO MENTION THAT YOUR SON WAS ALSO PRESENT.
IT DIDN'T SEEM IMPORTANT, THEN.
JOEY HADN'T SHOWN ANY SIGNS OF POWERS, OR ABILITIES LIKE HIS FATHER, AND I JUST ASSUMED--
YOU THINK THIS ONE WILL FIT?
I GUESS THE METEOR THAT GAVE HIM HIS POWERS MUST HAVE ALSO GIVEN JOEY POWERS.
OBVIOUSLY I'VE BEEN TOO WRAPPED UP IN MY OWN GRIEF--
--TO NOTICE THAT JOEY WAS GOING THROUGH MORE THAN JUST PAIN OF HIS OWN.
LET GO.

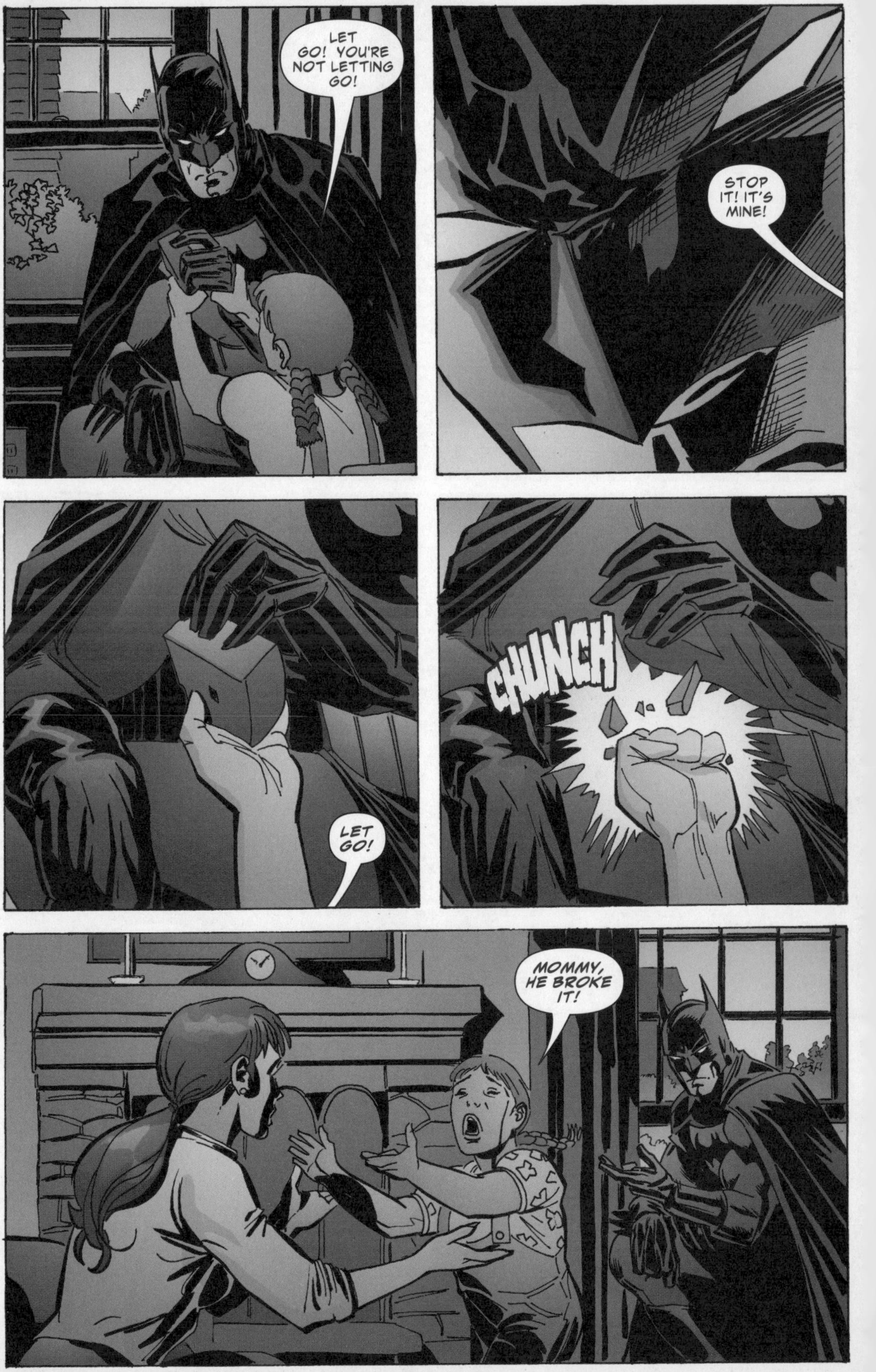
LET GO! YOU'RE NOT LETTING GO!
STOP IT! IT'S MINE!
LET GO!
CHUNCH
MOMMY, HE BROKE IT!

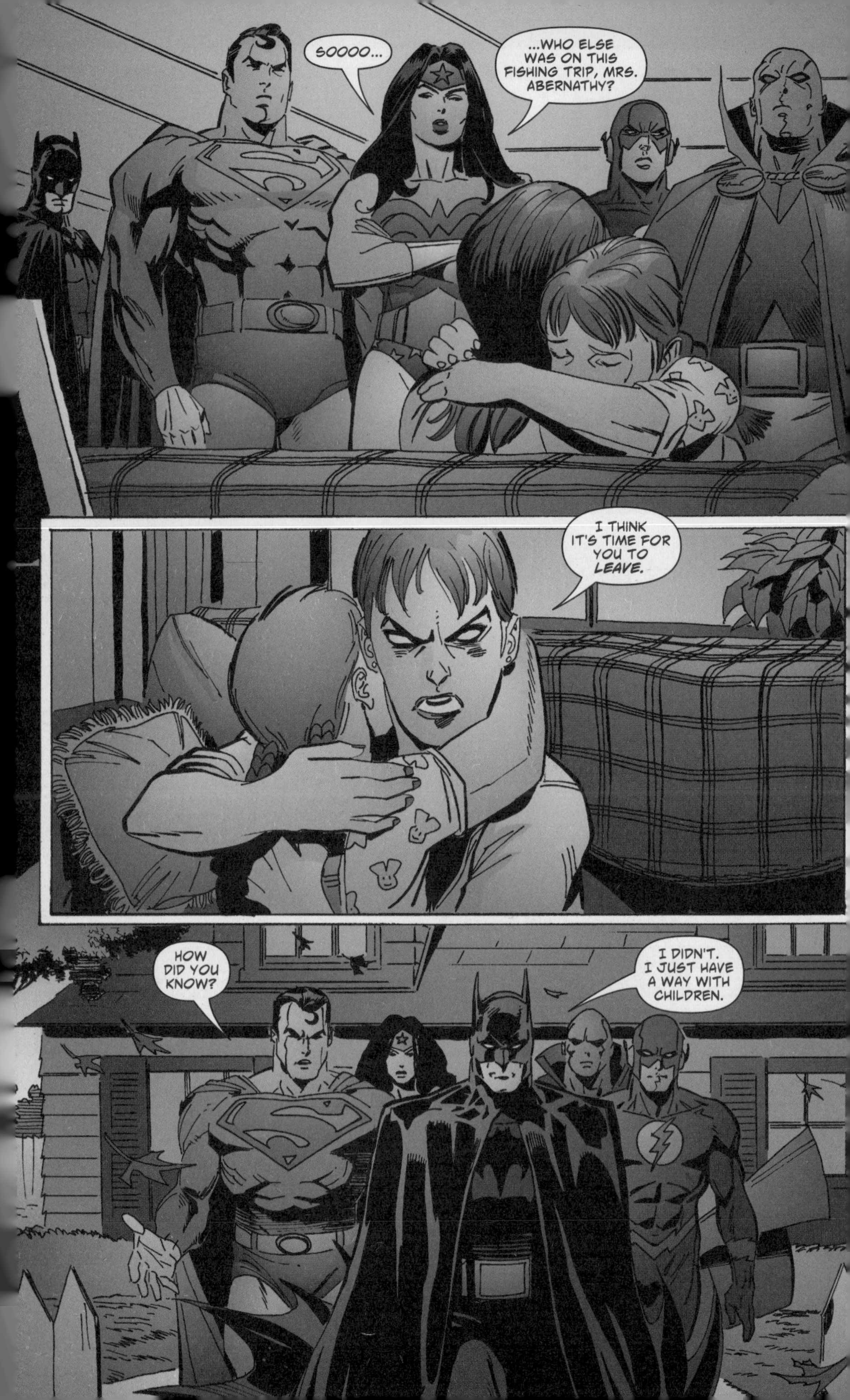
SOOOO...
...WHO ELSE WAS ON THIS FISHING TRIP, MRS. ABERNATHY?
I THINK IT'S TIME FOR YOU TO LEAVE.
HOW DID YOU KNOW?
I DIDN'T. I JUST HAVE A WAY WITH CHILDREN.

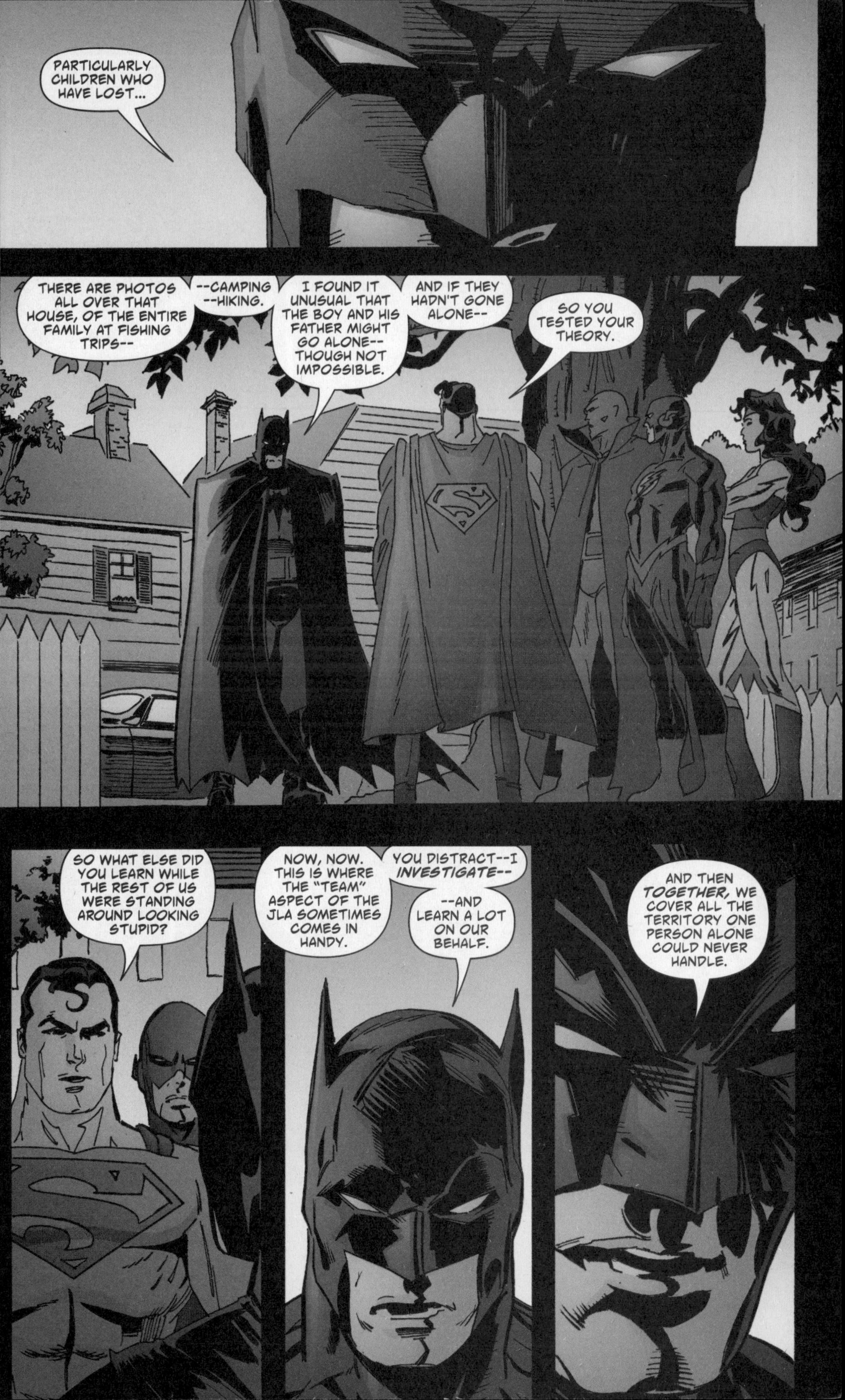
PARTICULARLY CHILDREN WHO HAVE LOST...
THERE ARE PHOTOS ALL OVER THAT HOUSE, OF THE ENTIRE FAMILY AT FISHING TRIPS--
--CAMPING --HIKING.
I FOUND IT UNUSUAL THAT THE BOY AND HIS FATHER MIGHT GO ALONE-- THOUGH NOT IMPOSSIBLE.
AND IF THEY HADN'T GONE ALONE--
SO YOU TESTED YOUR THEORY.
SO WHAT ELSE DID YOU LEARN WHILE THE REST OF US WERE STANDING AROUND LOOKING STUPID?
NOW, NOW. THIS IS WHERE THE "TEAM" ASPECT OF THE JLA SOMETIMES COMES IN HANDY.
YOU DISTRACT--I *INVESTIGATE*--
--AND LEARN A LOT ON OUR BEHALF.
AND THEN *TOGETHER,* WE COVER ALL THE TERRITORY ONE PERSON ALONE COULD NEVER HANDLE.

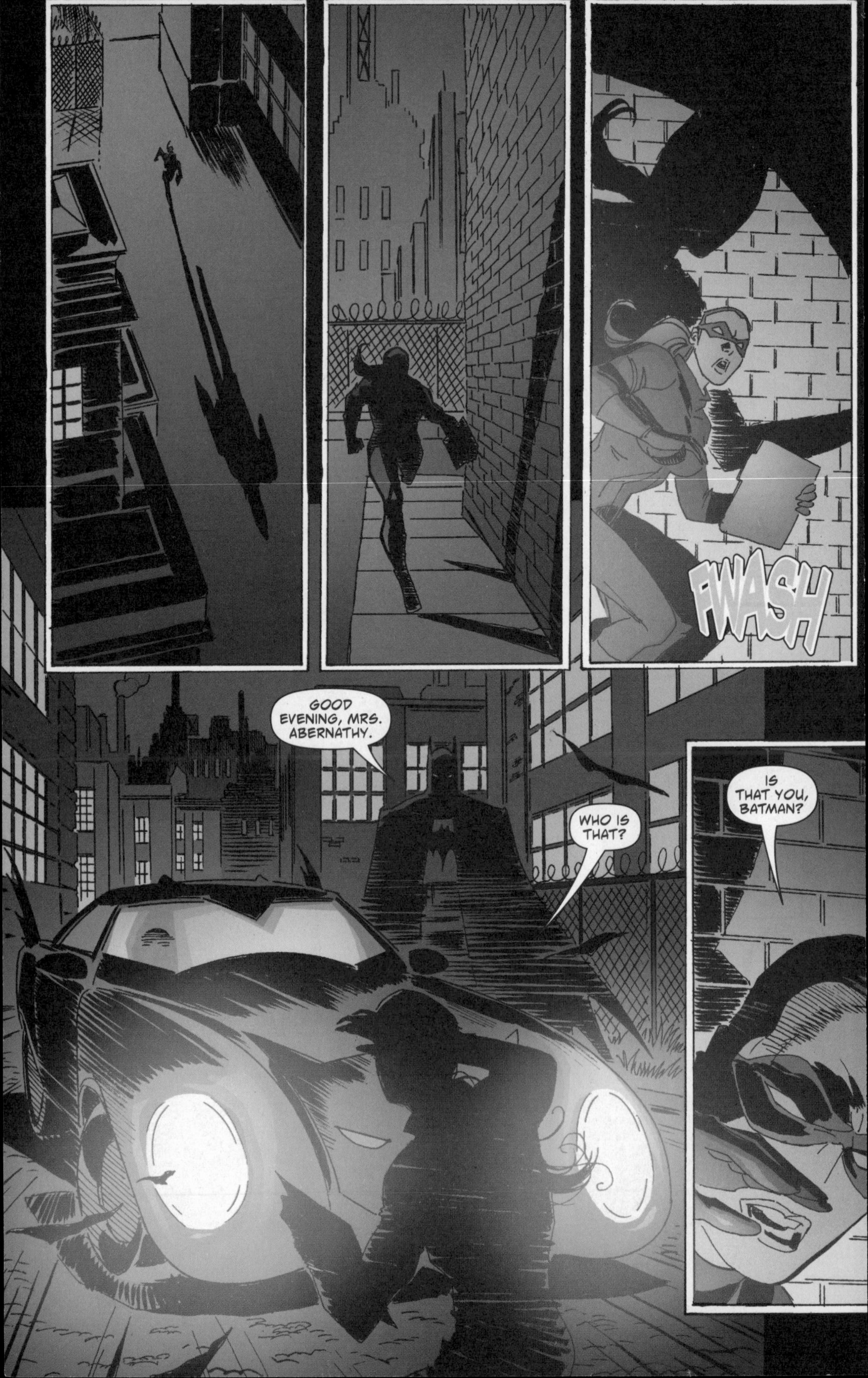
FWASH
GOOD EVENING, MRS. ABERNATHY.
WHO IS THAT?
IS THAT YOU, BATMAN?

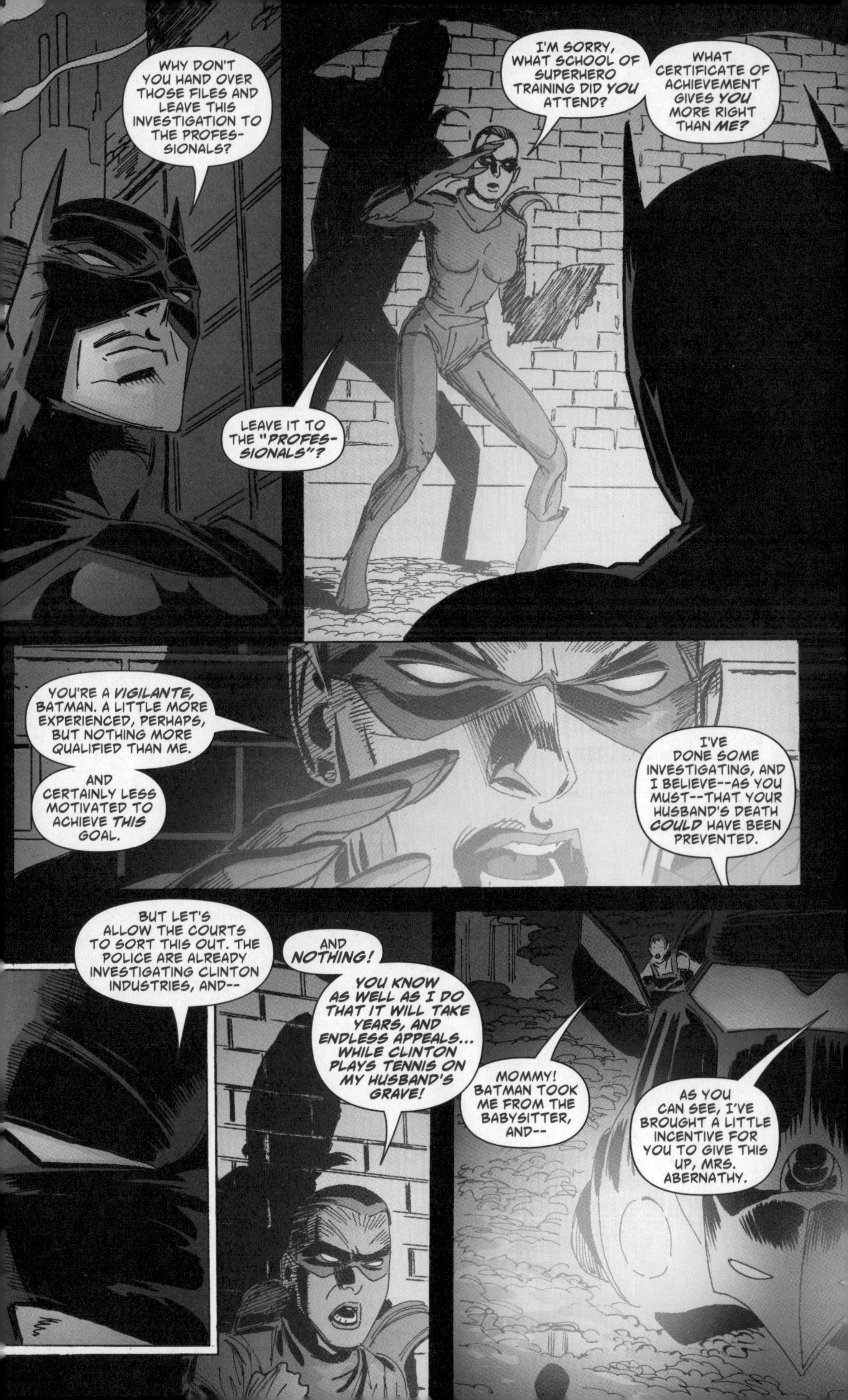
WHY DON'T YOU HAND OVER THOSE FILES AND LEAVE THIS INVESTIGATION TO THE PROFES-SIONALS?
I'M SORRY, WHAT SCHOOL OF SUPERHERO TRAINING DID YOU ATTEND?
WHAT CERTIFICATE OF ACHIEVEMENT GIVES YOU MORE RIGHT THAN ME?
LEAVE IT TO THE "PROFES-SIONALS"?
YOU'RE A VIGILANTE, BATMAN. A LITTLE MORE EXPERIENCED, PERHAPS, BUT NOTHING MORE QUALIFIED THAN ME.
AND CERTAINLY LESS MOTIVATED TO ACHIEVE THIS GOAL.
I'VE DONE SOME INVESTIGATING, AND I BELIEVE--AS YOU MUST--THAT YOUR HUSBAND'S DEATH COULD HAVE BEEN PREVENTED.
BUT LET'S ALLOW THE COURTS TO SORT THIS OUT. THE POLICE ARE ALREADY INVESTIGATING CLINTON INDUSTRIES, AND--
AND NOTHING!
YOU KNOW AS WELL AS I DO THAT IT WILL TAKE YEARS, AND ENDLESS APPEALS... WHILE CLINTON PLAYS TENNIS ON MY HUSBAND'S GRAVE!
MOMMY! BATMAN TOOK ME FROM THE BABYSITTER, AND--
AS YOU CAN SEE, I'VE BROUGHT A LITTLE INCENTIVE FOR YOU TO GIVE THIS UP, MRS. ABERNATHY.

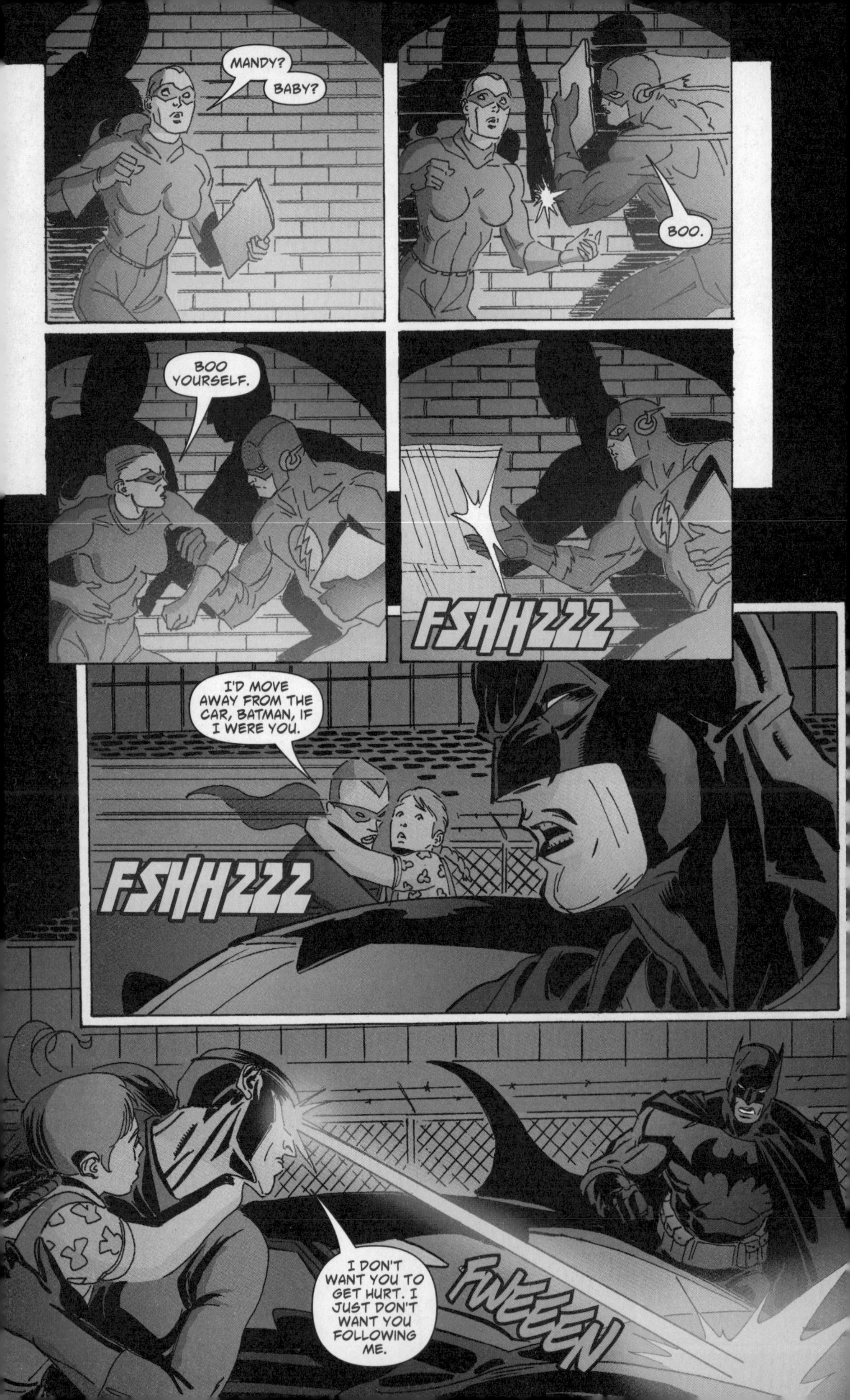
MANDY?
BABY?
BOO.
BOO YOURSELF.
FSHHZZZ
I'D MOVE AWAY FROM THE CAR, BATMAN, IF I WERE YOU.
FSHHZZZ
I DON'T WANT YOU TO GET HURT. I JUST DON'T WANT YOU FOLLOWING ME.
FWEEEN

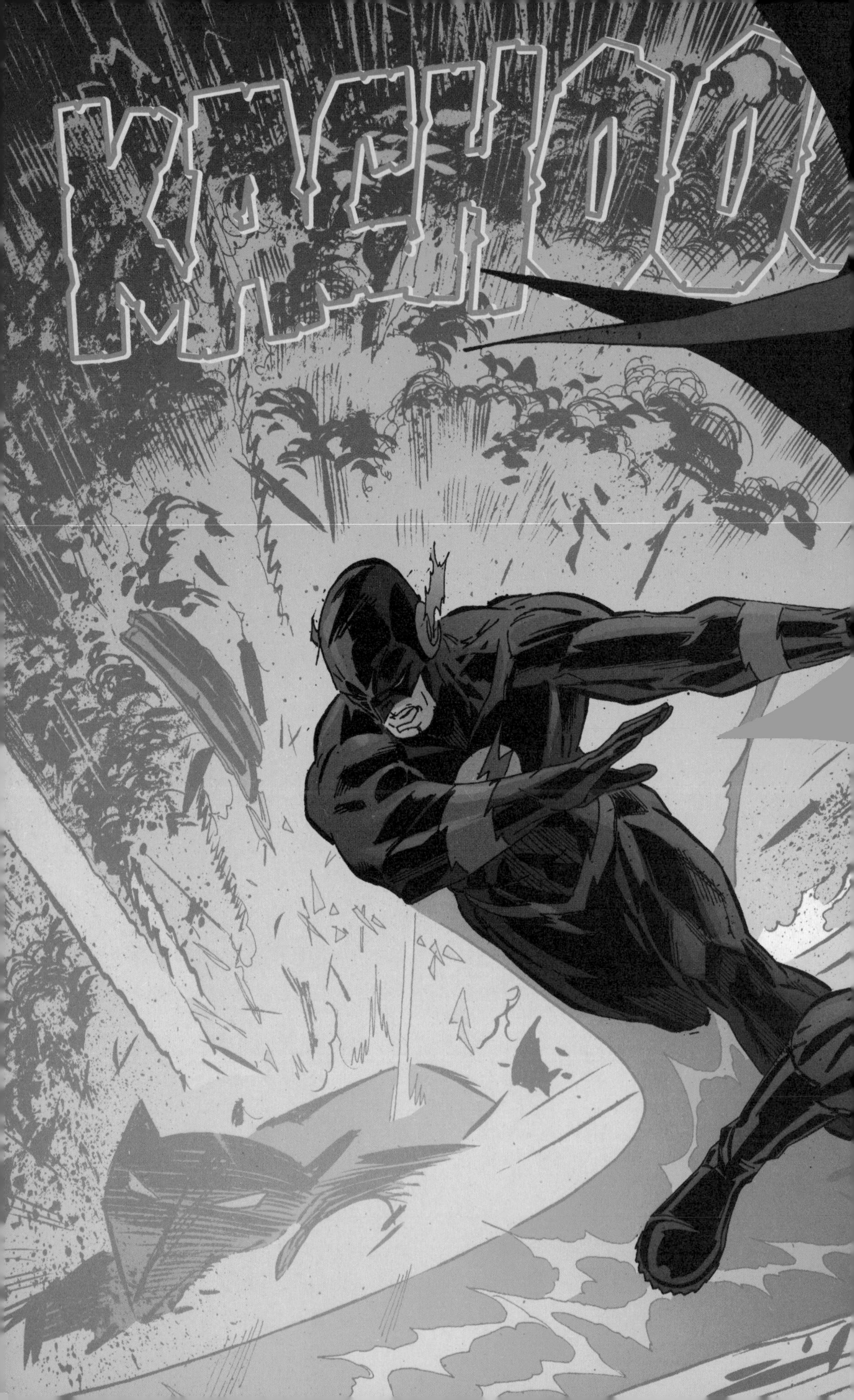
KRAKOO

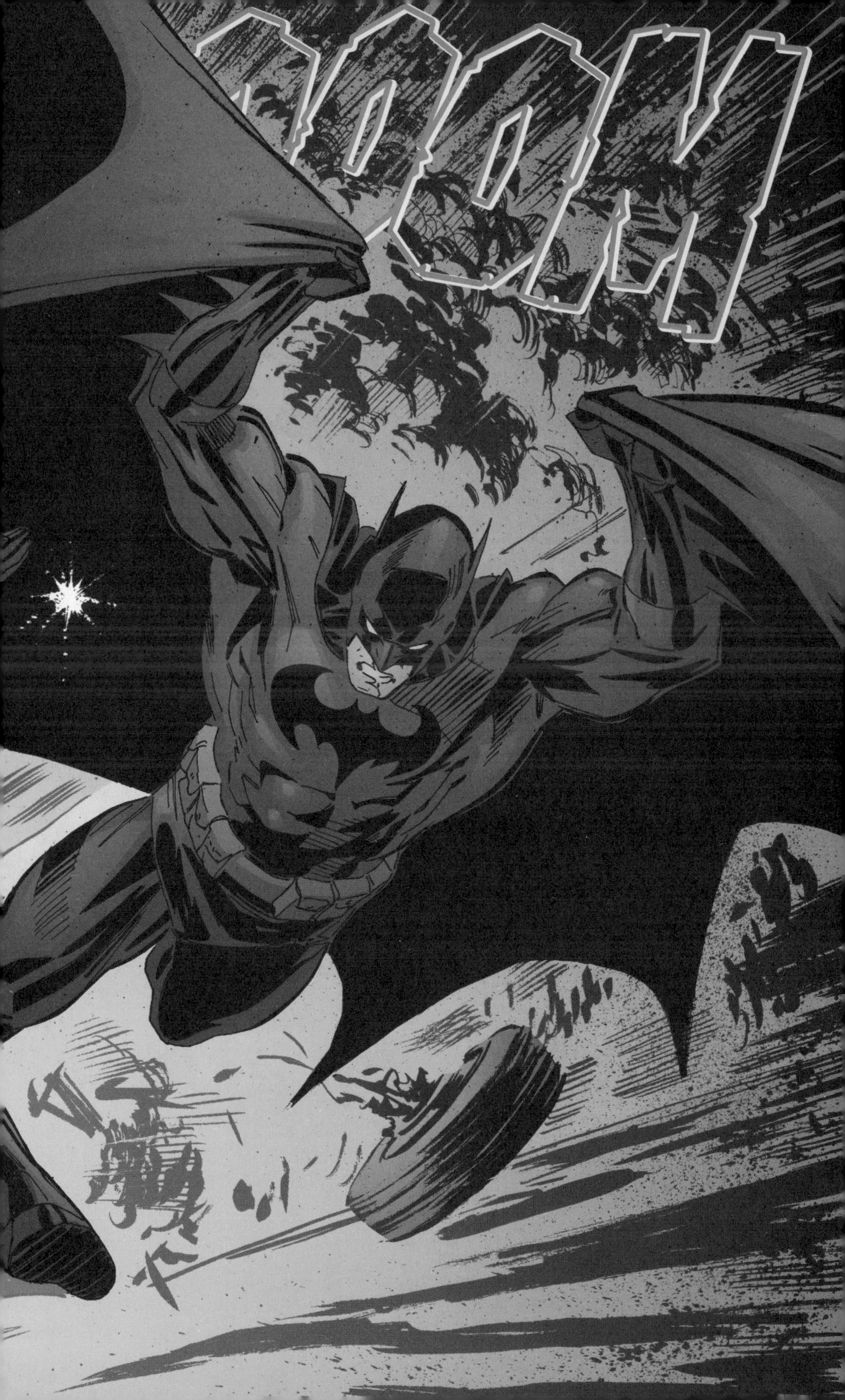
OOM

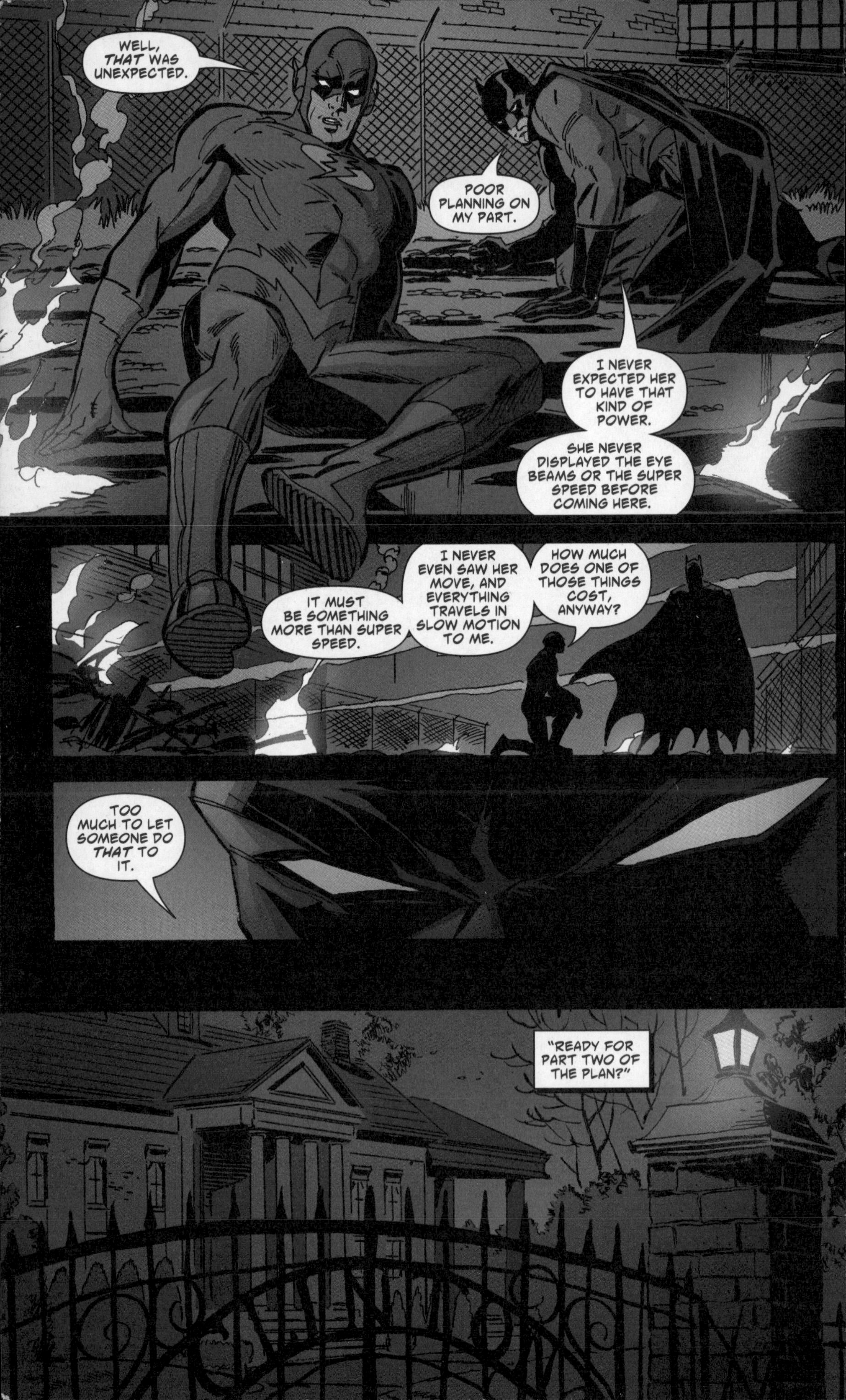
WELL, THAT WAS UNEXPECTED.
POOR PLANNING ON MY PART.
I NEVER EXPECTED HER TO HAVE THAT KIND OF POWER.
SHE NEVER DISPLAYED THE EYE BEAMS OR THE SUPER SPEED BEFORE COMING HERE.
IT MUST BE SOMETHING MORE THAN SUPER SPEED.
I NEVER EVEN SAW HER MOVE, AND EVERYTHING TRAVELS IN SLOW MOTION TO ME.
HOW MUCH DOES ONE OF THOSE THINGS COST, ANYWAY?
TOO MUCH TO LET SOMEONE DO THAT TO IT.
"READY FOR PART TWO OF THE PLAN?"

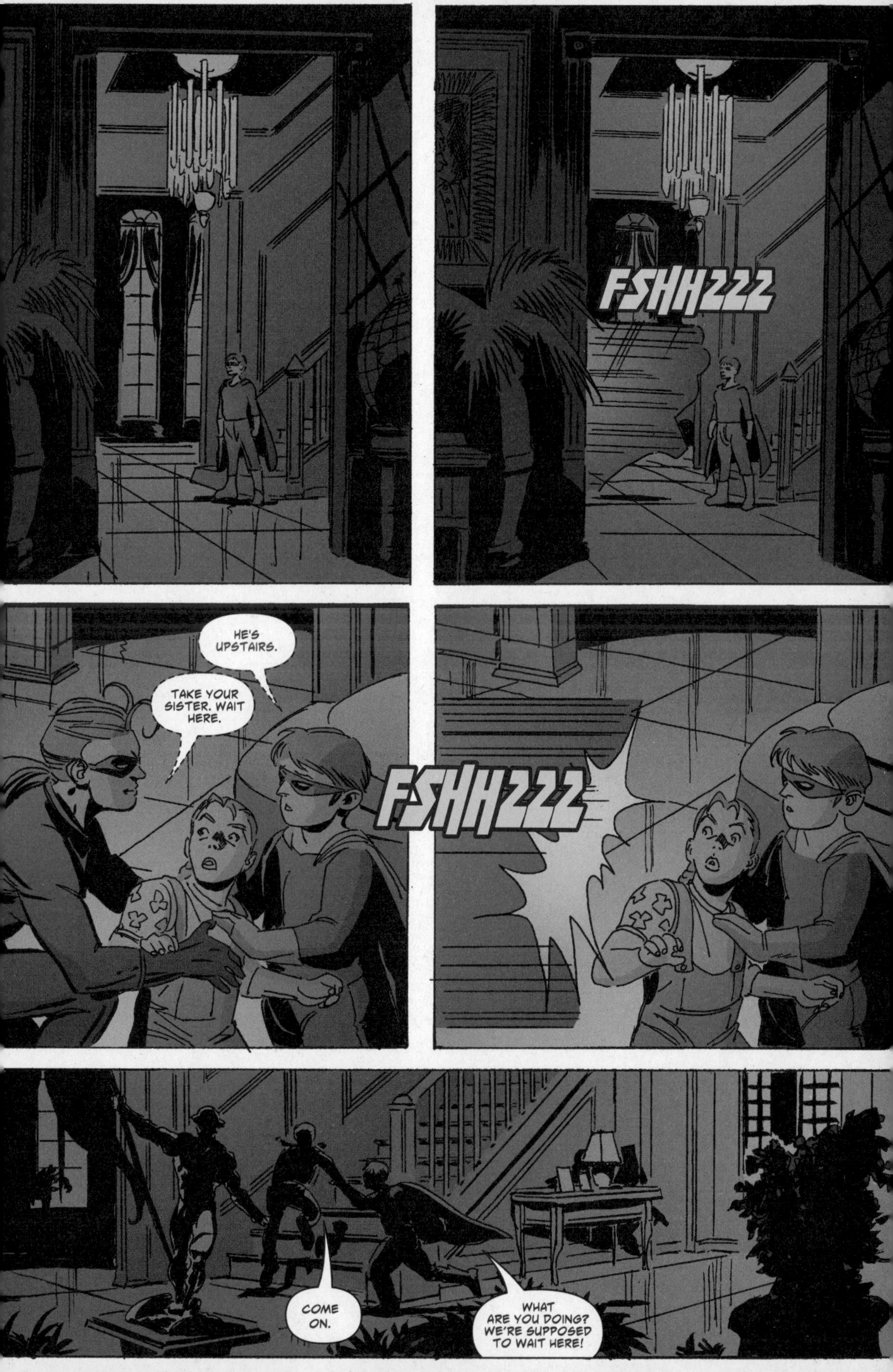
FSHHZZZ
HE'S UPSTAIRS.
TAKE YOUR SISTER. WAIT HERE.
FSHHZZZ
COME ON.
WHAT ARE YOU DOING? WE'RE SUPPOSED TO WAIT HERE!

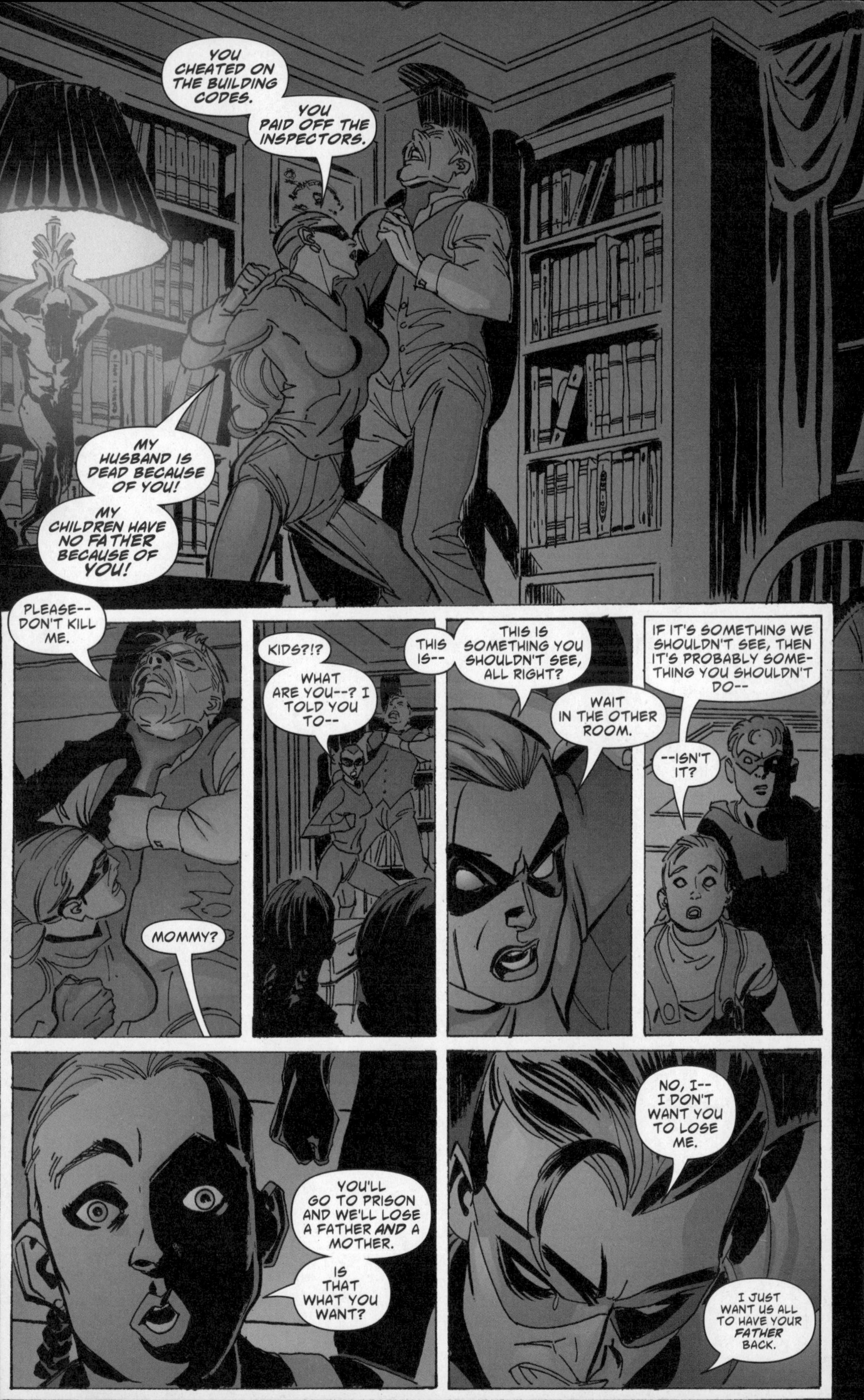

YOU CHEATED ON THE BUILDING CODES.
YOU PAID OFF THE INSPECTORS.
MY HUSBAND IS DEAD BECAUSE OF YOU!
MY CHILDREN HAVE NO FATHER BECAUSE OF YOU!
PLEASE-- DON'T KILL ME.
MOMMY?
KIDS?!?
WHAT ARE YOU--? I TOLD YOU TO--
THIS IS--
THIS IS SOMETHING YOU SHOULDN'T SEE, ALL RIGHT?
WAIT IN THE OTHER ROOM.
IF IT'S SOMETHING WE SHOULDN'T SEE, THEN IT'S PROBABLY SOMETHING YOU SHOULDN'T DO--
--ISN'T IT?
YOU'LL GO TO PRISON AND WE'LL LOSE A FATHER AND A MOTHER.
IS THAT WHAT YOU WANT?
NO, I-- I DON'T WANT YOU TO LOSE ME.
I JUST WANT US ALL TO HAVE YOUR FATHER BACK.

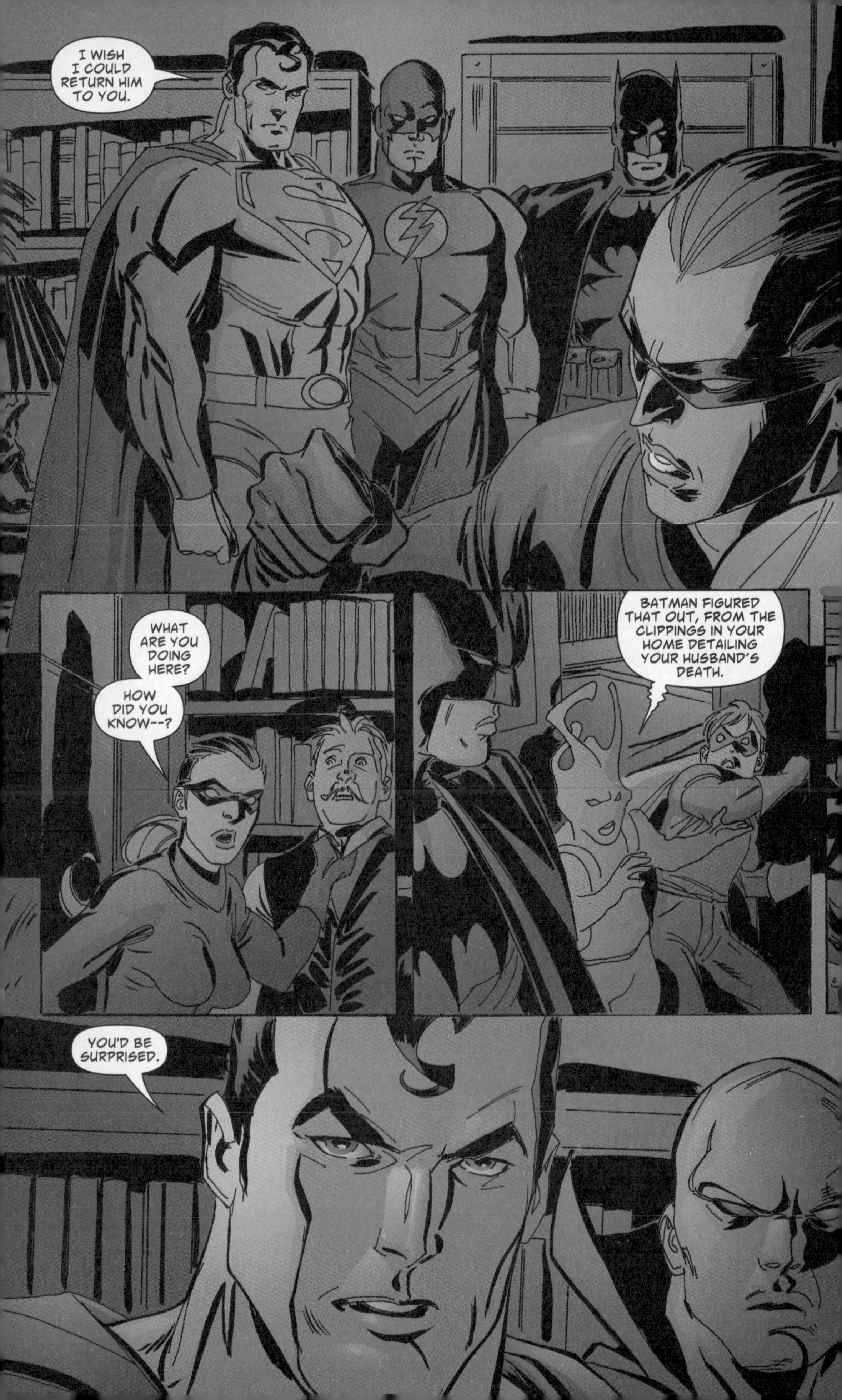

I WISH I COULD RETURN HIM TO YOU.
WHAT ARE YOU DOING HERE?
HOW DID YOU KNOW--?
BATMAN FIGURED THAT OUT, FROM THE CLIPPINGS IN YOUR HOME DETAILING YOUR HUSBAND'S DEATH.
YOU'D BE SURPRISED.

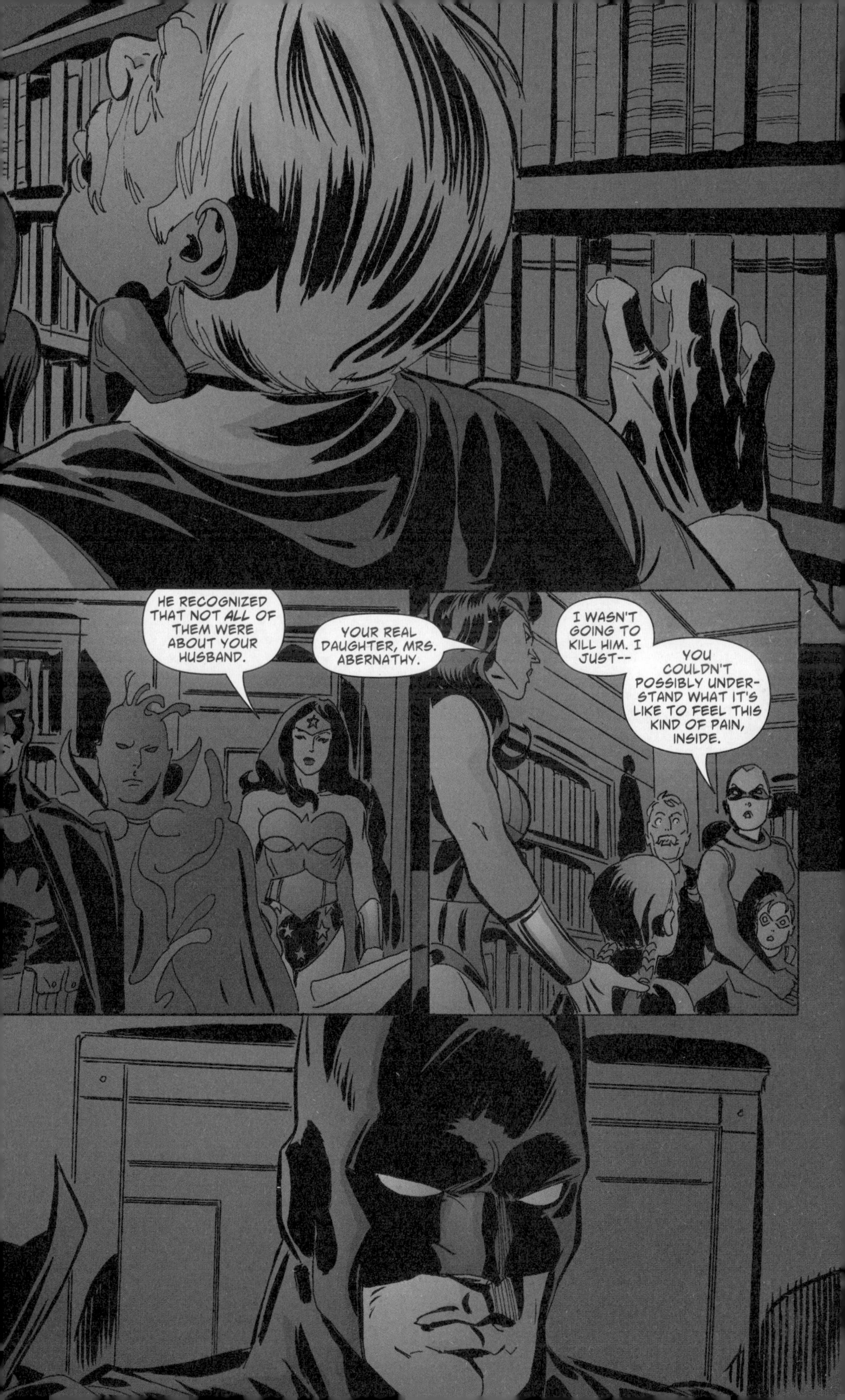
HE RECOGNIZED THAT NOT ALL OF THEM WERE ABOUT YOUR HUSBAND.
YOUR REAL DAUGHTER, MRS. ABERNATHY.
I WASN'T GOING TO KILL HIM. I JUST--
YOU COULDN'T POSSIBLY UNDERSTAND WHAT IT'S LIKE TO FEEL THIS KIND OF PAIN, INSIDE.

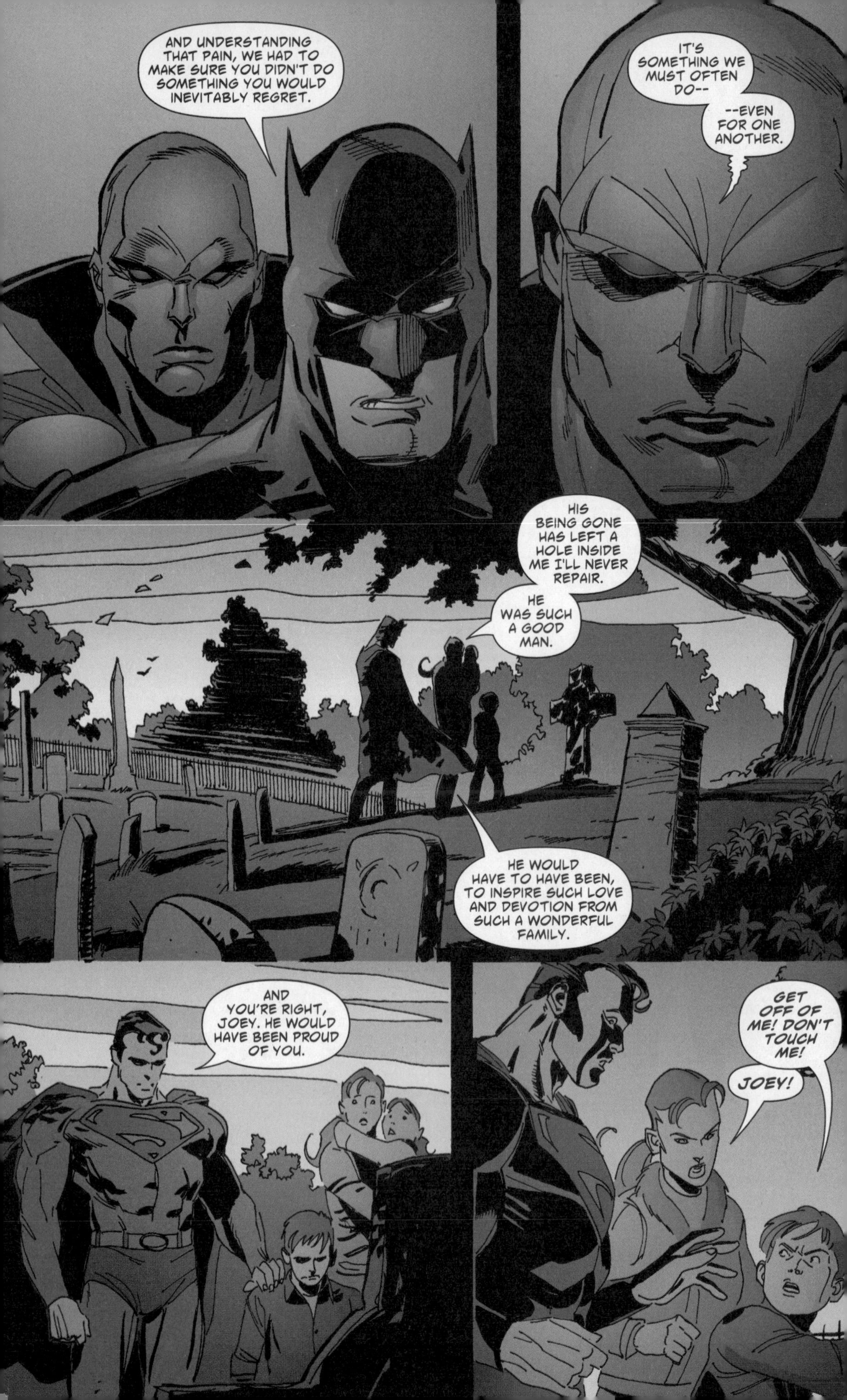
AND UNDERSTANDING THAT PAIN, WE HAD TO MAKE SURE YOU DIDN'T DO SOMETHING YOU WOULD INEVITABLY REGRET.
IT'S SOMETHING WE MUST OFTEN DO--
--EVEN FOR ONE ANOTHER.
HIS BEING GONE HAS LEFT A HOLE INSIDE ME I'LL NEVER REPAIR.
HE WAS SUCH A GOOD MAN.
HE WOULD HAVE TO HAVE BEEN, TO INSPIRE SUCH LOVE AND DEVOTION FROM SUCH A WONDERFUL FAMILY.
AND YOU'RE RIGHT, JOEY. HE WOULD HAVE BEEN PROUD OF YOU.
GET OFF OF ME! DON'T TOUCH ME!
JOEY!

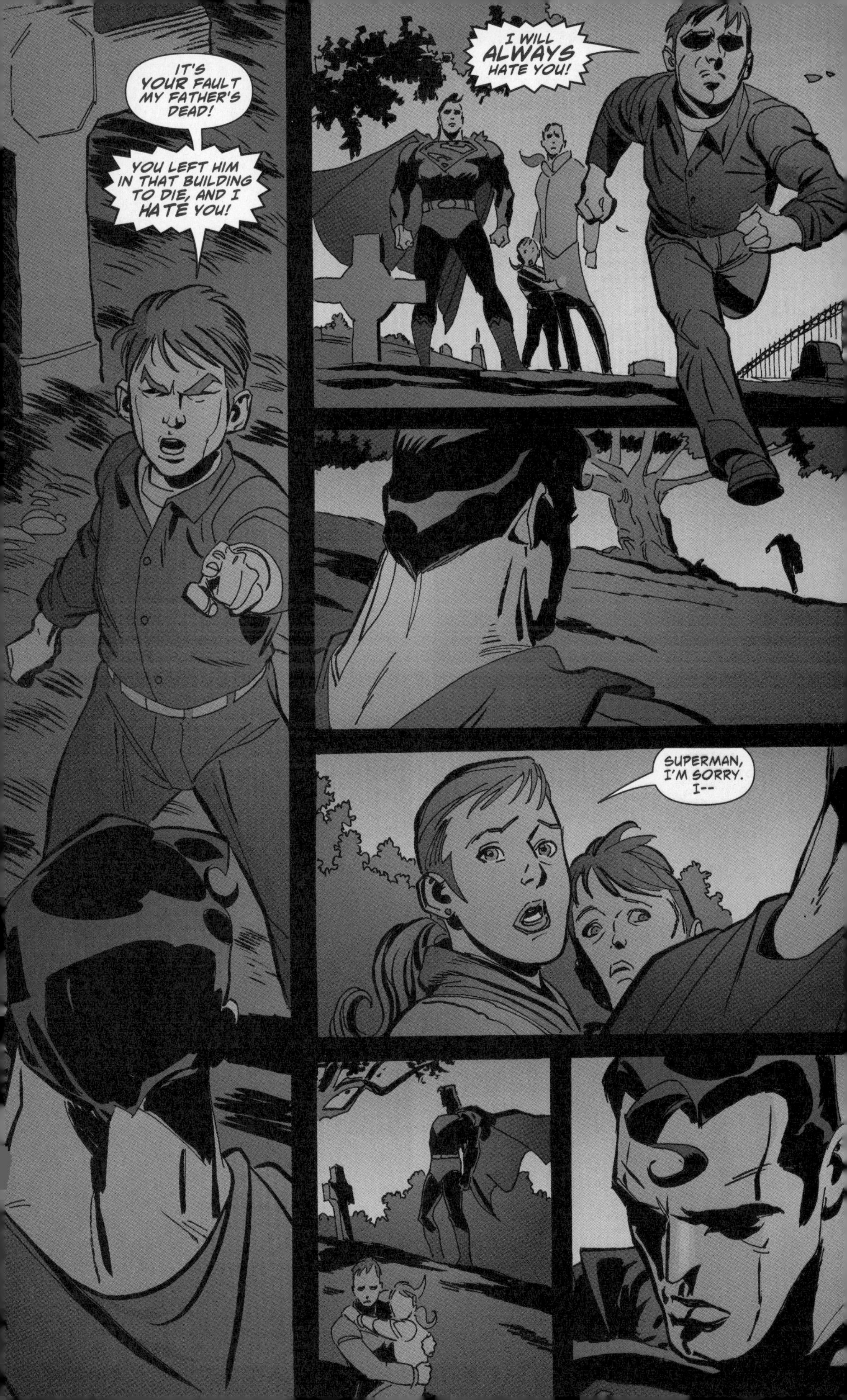
IT'S YOUR FAULT MY FATHER'S DEAD!
YOU LEFT HIM IN THAT BUILDING TO DIE, AND I HATE YOU!
I WILL ALWAYS HATE YOU!
SUPERMAN, I'M SORRY. I--

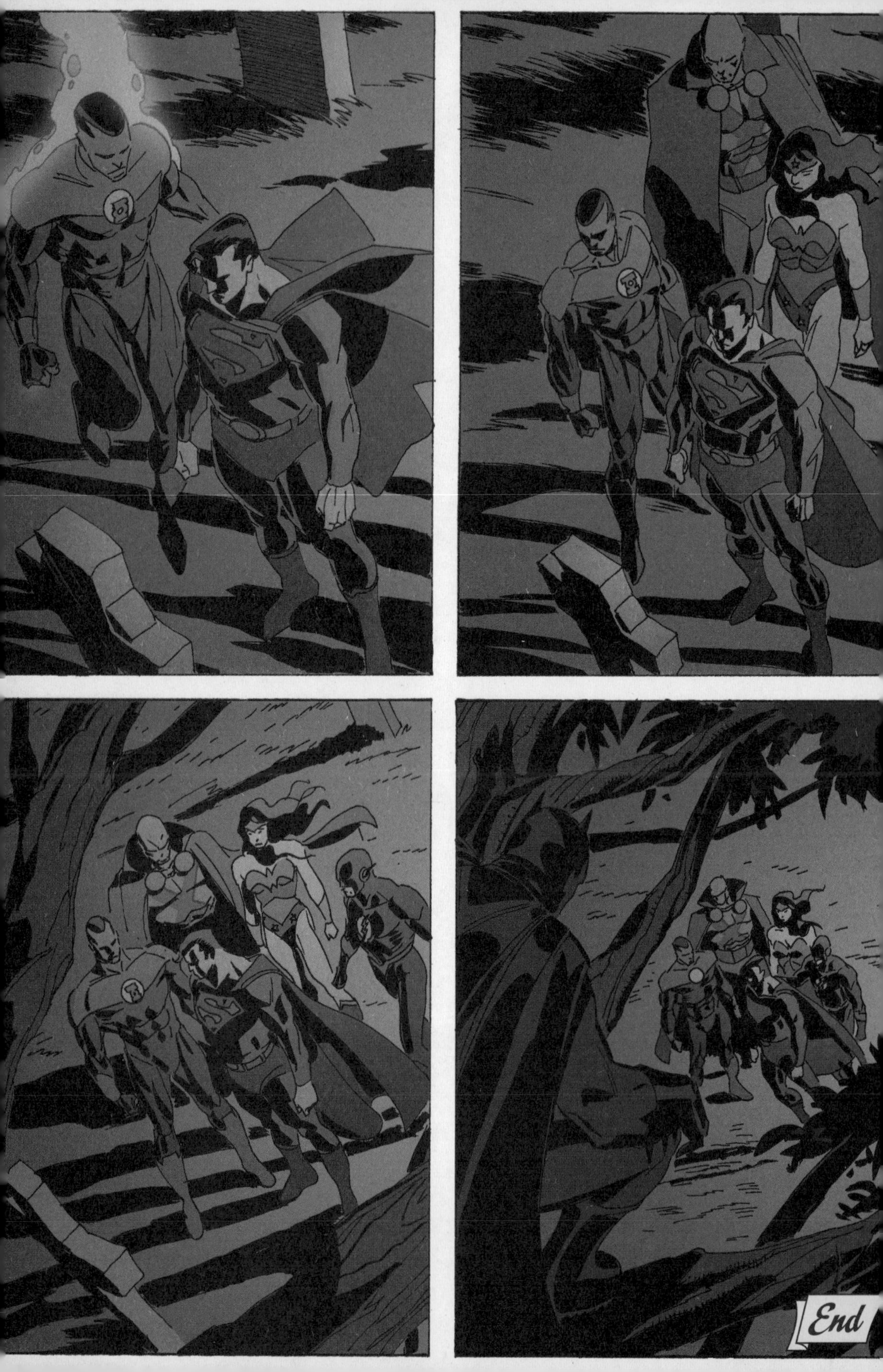
End

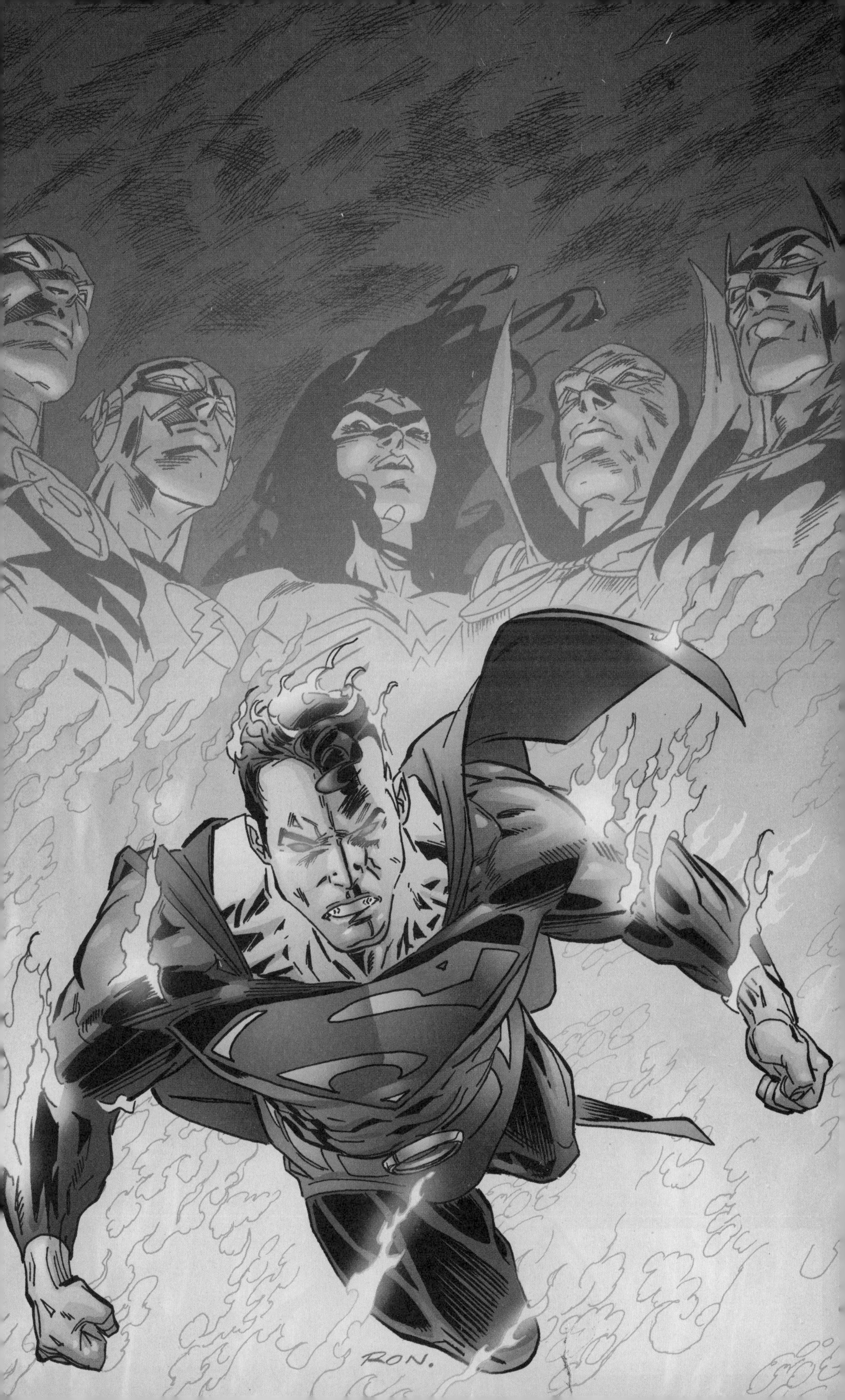
RON.

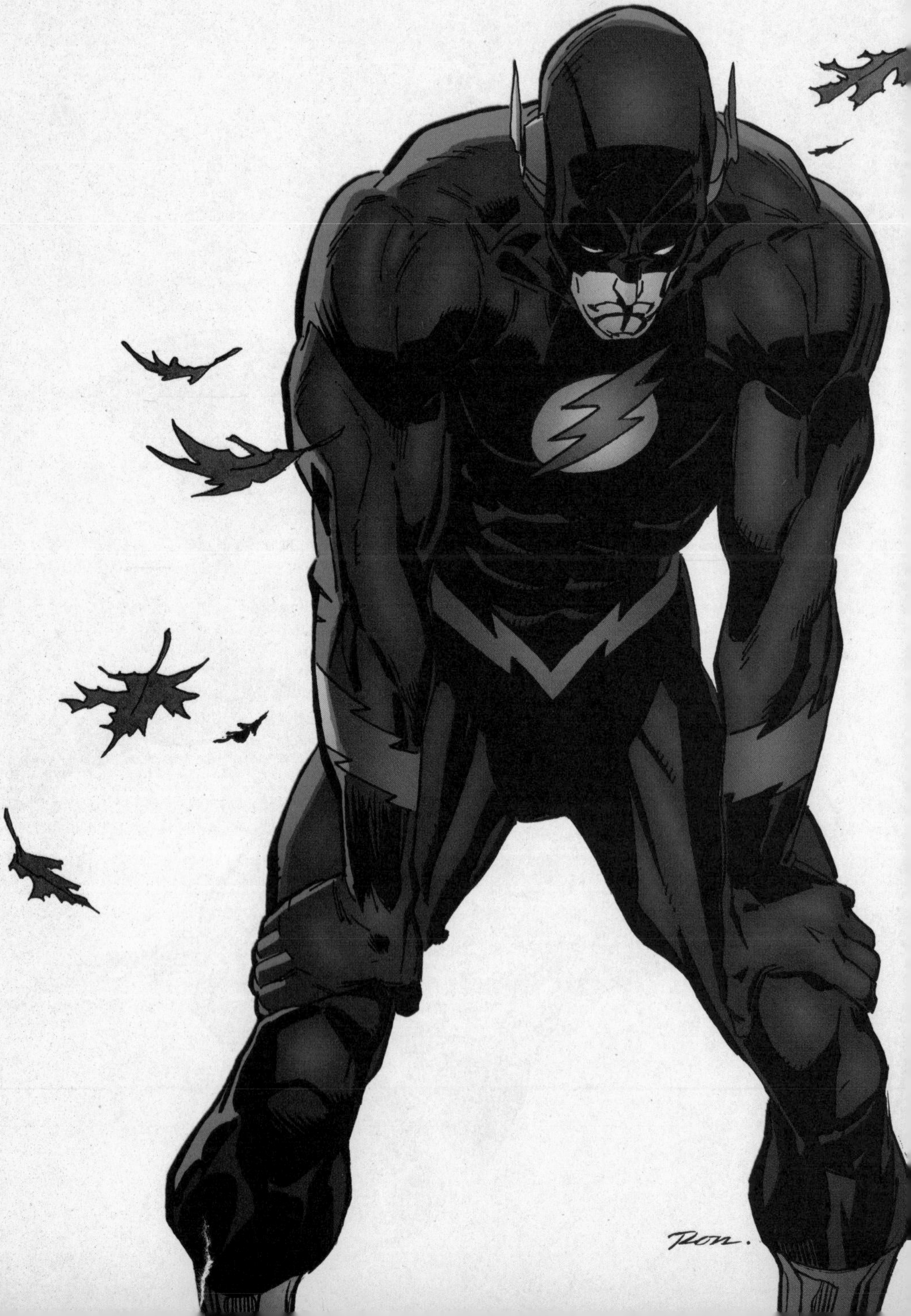
Ron.

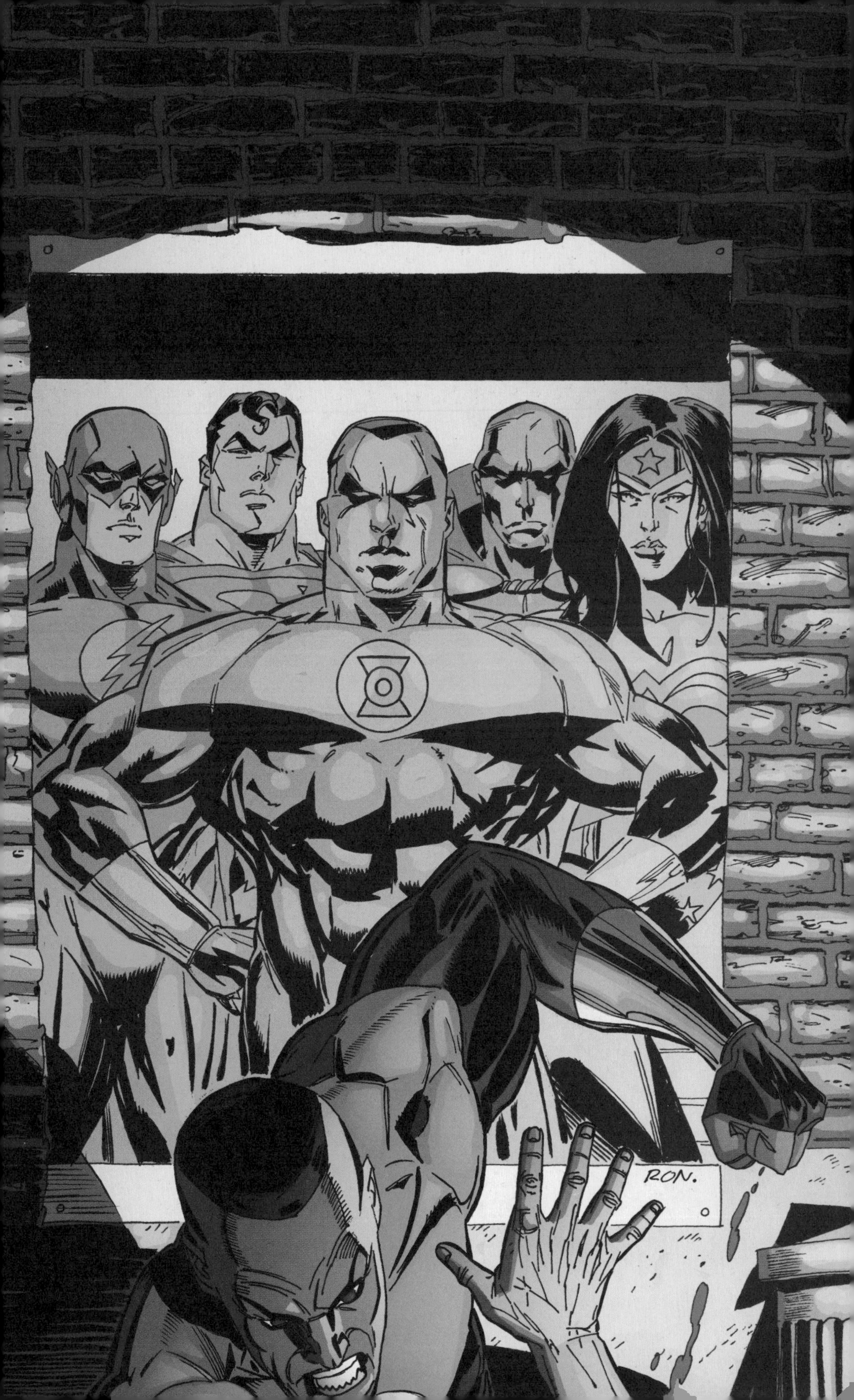
RON.

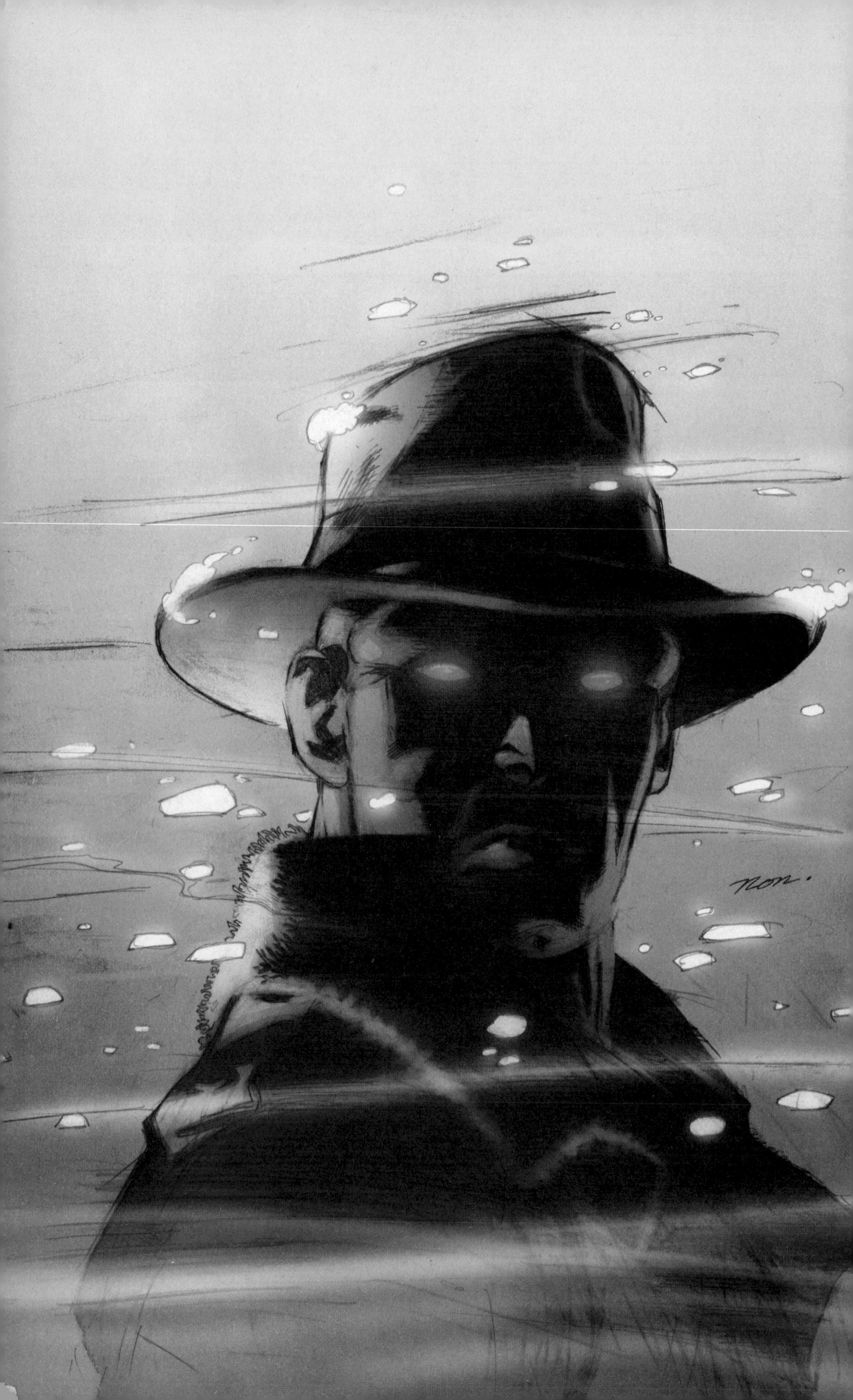

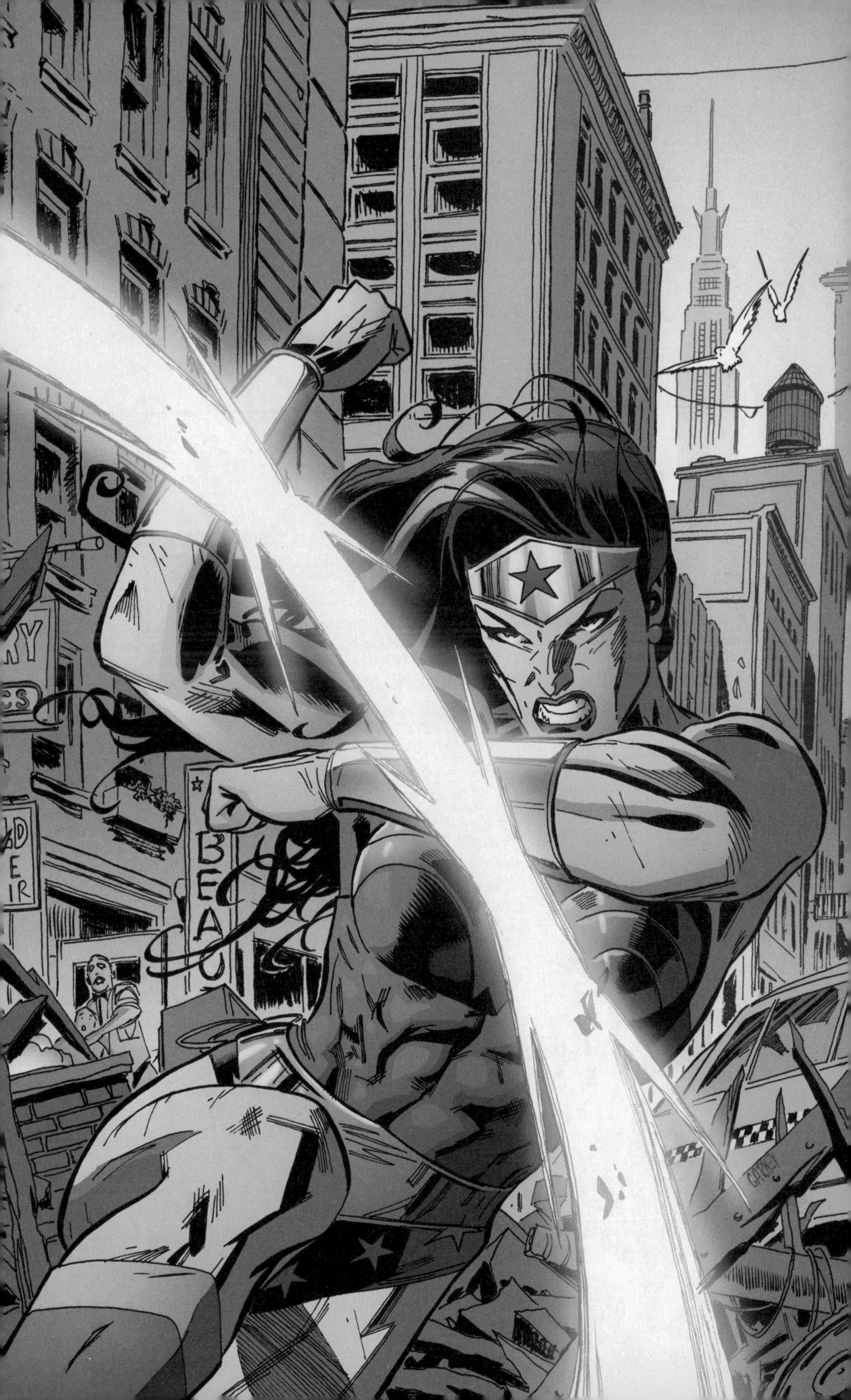
BEAU

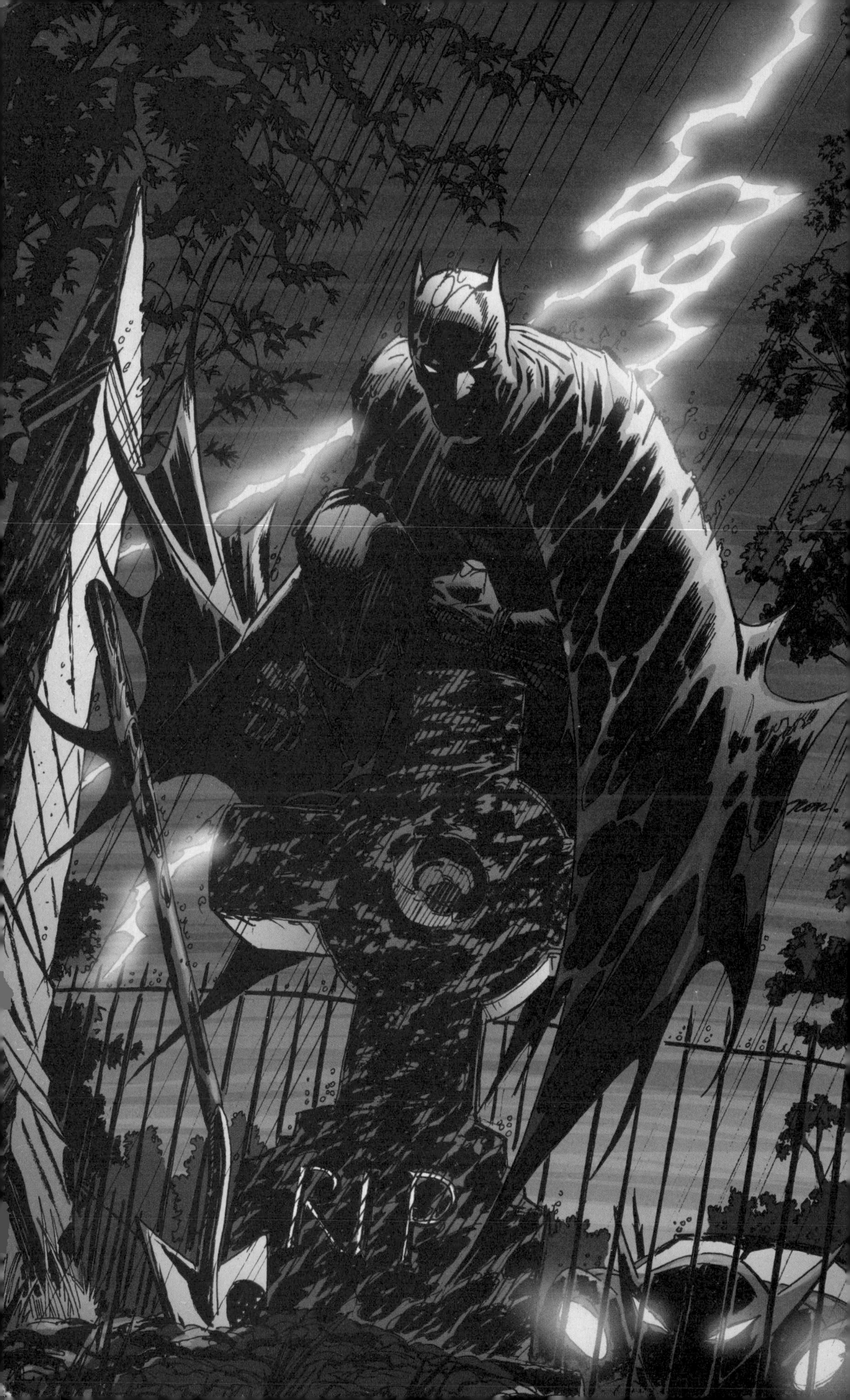
RIP